WITH DISTANCE IN HIS EYES

WITH DISTANCE IN HIS EYES

The Environmental Life and Legacy of
STEWART UDALL

Scott Raymond Einberger

UNIVERSITY OF NEVADA PRESS   *Reno & Las Vegas*

University of Nevada Press | Reno, Nevada 89557 USA
www.unpress.nevada.edu
Copyright © 2018 by University of Nevada Press
All rights reserved
Cover design by Louise OFarrell

LIBRARY OF CONGRESS CATALOGING-IN-PUBLICATION DATA
Names: Einberger, Scott, author.
Title: With distance in his eyes : the environmental life and legacy of Stewart Udall
    / by Scott Raymond Einberger.
Other titles: Environmental life and legacy of Stewart Udall
Description: First edition. | Reno : University of Nevada Press, [2017] | Includes
    bibliographical references and index.
Identifiers: LCCN 2017041049 (print) | LCCN 2017041589 (e-book) |
    ISBN 978-1-943859-62-7 (cloth : alk. paper) | ISBN 978-1-943859-63-4 (e-book)
Subjects: LCSH: Udall, Stewart L. | Cabinet officers—United States—Biography. |
    Conservationists—United States—Biography. | Environmentalists—United
    States—Biography. | Reformers—United States—Biography. | United States—
    Politics and government—20th century.
Classification: LCC E840.8.U34 E46 2017 (print) | LCC E840.8.U34 (e-book) |
    DDC 352.2/93092 [B]—dc23
LC record available at https://lccn.loc.gov/2017041049

The paper used in this book meets the requirements of American National
Standard for Information Sciences—Permanence of Paper for Printed Library
Materials, ANSI/NISO Z39.48-1992 (2002).

FIRST PRINTING

Manufactured in the United States of America

For Grayson Birch Einberger
May you grow up to be a steward of planet Earth

~

In memory of Douglas H. Strong
1935–2015
environmental historian, poet, and author

Contents

Acknowledgments

In addition to the staff of the University of Arizona Special Collections Department and the Library of Congress, who pulled a massive number of boxes and books for me and were always helpful, I am highly grateful to a select set of individuals. First, the staff and contractors of the University of Nevada Press were a delight to work with every step of the way. Specifically, I am grateful for the guidance, editing, and support of Justin Race, Annette Wenda, Virginia Fontana, Sara Hendricksen, Lynne Ferguson Chapman, and the two anonymous scholarly editors who "red-penned" the book.

Prior to his passing in 2015, Douglas H. Strong edited my early text and provided guidance. Strong was an early environmental historian, a San Diego State University professor, and an author whose writing I admire, and it was an honor getting assistance from him. Thank you, also, to my friend and former colleague Barbara D'Emilio for her edits in the book's early phases. Additionally, Michelle Moriarty encouraged me to write the book in the first place, and Sandra Crooms of the University of Pittsburgh Press brought the book to the attention of Justin Race, which made all the difference. To all of these people, in addition to my wife and "better half," Andria Hayes-Birchler, I say thank you.

Finally, it must be noted that historians stand on the shoulders of past historians. My book benefitted from the previous work of every single author and every publication listed in the endnotes and bibliography. Without them, this book would have no basis and would be nonexistent. Of course, the author who looms largest is Stewart Udall himself. From the moment I first learned of him in 2008 and started reading *The Quiet Crisis,* I was hooked. His writings and sayings express my own thoughts and opinions better than even I can. His health was degenerating rapidly in 2009 and he had to politely decline my request to meet him and shake his hand, but his memory, philosophy, and writings must live on.

Abbreviations

AEC	Atomic Energy Commission
AT	Appalachian Trail (Appalachian National Scenic Trail)
BLM	Bureau of Land Management
BOR	Bureau of Outdoor Recreation
CAP	Central Arizona Project
CCC	Civilian Conservation Corps
C&MU	Classification and Multiple Use Act (of the Bureau of Land Management)
DOI	Department of the Interior
DOJ	Department of Justice
FWPCA	Federal Water Pollution Control Administration
GLO	General Land Office
LMRA	Labor-Management Reform Act of 1959
LWCF	Land and Water Conservation Fund
NPS	National Park Service
NWR	National Wildlife Refuge
OIA	Office of International Affairs (of the National Park Service)
ORRRC	Outdoor Recreation Resources Review Commission
PCT	Pacific Crest Trail (Pacific Crest National Scenic Trail)
PSWP	Pacific Southwest Water Plan
USFS	US Forest Service
USFWS	US Fish and Wildlife Service
VIP	Volunteers-in-Parks
YCC	Youth Conservation Corps

WITH DISTANCE IN HIS EYES

Introduction

THE 1960S WAS A DECADE of civil rights debates and ultimate progress that included the rise and consequential racial assassinations of Dr. Martin Luther King Jr., Malcolm X, and many other African Americans. It was a decade of the Beatles and of counterculture, of peace, love, and happiness in the form of sex, drugs, and rock and roll. It was a decade of Vietnam, Cold War, JFK, LBJ, and RFK. In addition to these important events and key figures, the 1960s ushered in the modern environmental movement, a fact that is largely overlooked in many standard history textbooks and classrooms of high schools and colleges across the country.

Indeed, in the 1960s, numerous new national park units, federal wilderness areas, and federal wild and scenic rivers were established and protected via new legislation. The Land and Water Conservation Fund (LWCF), the National Wilderness Preservation System, the National Wild and Scenic Rivers System, the Water Pollution Control Act, and the Endangered Species Preservation Act were all passed by a bipartisan Congress, as were unprecedented expansions to the US National Park System and National Wildlife Refuge (NWR) System.

Many individuals can rightfully claim to have been a part of the 1960s environmental movement. There were grassroots organizations and citizens that wanted to preserve specific pieces of beautiful land or wild animals; progressive politicians, both Republican and Democrat; and farsighted individuals such as Rachel Carson and others. But only one person can claim to have been the US secretary of the interior for eight years during the 1960s, and this individual was a progressive Mormon Democrat from rural Arizona named Stewart Lee Udall. As a JFK and LBJ administration cabinet member and the highest-ranking public official fully dedicated to the causes of natural resource conservation and environmental

3

protection, Udall fully embraced the 1960s environmental movement and in some ways helped create it and steer it along.

With a long-term view of sustainability for humans, natural resources, and public lands, Udall helped establish an unprecedented
number of new national park units, including Guadalupe Mountains National Park in Texas, a superlative natural area home to the
Lone Star State's highest peak; Indiana Dunes National Lakeshore
in Indiana, one of the most biologically diverse units of the National Park System; and many more. He pushed for the protection of
nearly extinct species, such as bald eagles and whooping cranes, by
creating and expanding national wildlife refuges, writing the first
draft of the Endangered Species Preservation Act, and banning pesticide use on public lands administered by the Department of the Interior (DOI). Udall pushed for cleaner water and increased outdoor
recreational opportunities for urban and suburban masses, and he
even warned of human-caused global warming decades before the
term was a regular part of US and world discourse. And then, at
only forty-nine years of age, having completed more than fifteen
years of federal government service, in 1969 private citizen Udall
became even more of an active and outspoken environmentalist.
Udall wasn't perfect through all these years, but he did do a lot of
good. Furthermore, Udall did not operate in a vacuum, as other politicians, federal employees, and individuals were needed to pass
important conservation bills. But Udall was an imperative in this
equation.

Renowned nature photographer Ansel Adams, second US National Park Service (NPS) director Horace Albright, President
Lyndon Baines Johnson, Sierra Club executive director David
Brower, and many others believed that Udall was the best interior
secretary the nation has ever had.[1] Yet somehow, in contemporary
discussions of, as well as courses taught in, modern history, environmental history, climate-change mitigation, energy and oil
issues, energy independence, sustainability, and Cold War history,
Stewart Udall's name is not commonly invoked.

He should be. Because from the early 1960s until just a few years
before his death in 2010, few individuals wrote more eloquently

and passionately about—or fought more ardently for—protecting the environment. "Plans to protect air and water, wilderness and wildlife are in fact plans to protect man," Udall once wrote.[2] He also wrote about, spoke about, and lobbied for improving the plight of inner cities, African Americans, American Indians, and the land itself.

Today, more than ever before, a look back at Stewart Udall's environmental life and legacy can offer us inspiration and guidance, for many of his proposed solutions for the environmental problems of the 1960s and '70s arguably remain solutions for the environmental problems of today. Furthermore, Udall's constant emphasis on considering the needs of future generations when making decisions about natural resource use offers us a lesson in moral leadership. "Stewardship is a survival concept.... It should be welcomed by all who are concerned about the tomorrows of the unborn," the distance-eyed Mormon from Arizona once noted.[3] Finally, his close work with Republicans and others of differing political opinions, social backgrounds, and races offers contemporary politicians and individuals a moral compass—debate and compromise are founding principles of democracy, and everyone would do well to remember this.

Book Overview

The pages that follow represent one of the first "cradle to grave" environmental biographies of Stewart Udall that has ever been written. It should not be the last, though, as Udall is a largely underanalyzed conservation leader who deserves more study and attention. I do hope this publication helps historians, public lands enthusiasts, and others learn more about this fascinating figure. For politicians and policy makers, I hope the three takeaway messages I emphasize in the concluding chapter, as well as the eight reasons I suggest for Udall's success in chapter 3, are thought about deeply.

To date, three other books exist on Udall. One of these, written by longtime Udall friend and work associate L. Boyd Finch, focuses on his accomplishments and work in the arts. The second book, written by Henry Sirgo, a political science professor at McNeese State

University, is beneficial for Udall environmental researchers but is also very specific in focus, as it spotlights his work primarily in the contexts of public policy and political theory. Furthermore, it analyzes only Udall's eight years as interior secretary, not the other eighty-one "environmentally important" years of his life. Finally, with my book already deep into the publication process, like-minded historian Thomas G. Smith released his *Stewart L. Udall: Steward of the Land* in late 2017. Thus, his environmental biography of Udall, which was unknown to me before its publication, was released just a few months before mine. Smith's book is well written and informative. That said, he and I are different people; while both books focus on the environmentalism of Stewart Udall, they are distinct.

Regarding the many journal articles on Udall, most focus on one specific topic during his years as secretary, most commonly reclamation and national parks. By contrast, what I have done with the text that follows is try to broadly yet comprehensively cover the majority of Udall's environmental accomplishments throughout his entire life. Moreover, all of the main environmental topics focused on by Udall during his years as interior secretary are spotlighted in this book.

The book is set up in general chronological order, beginning with "he was born and raised" and ending with Udall's passing away at the solid age of ninety in 2010. As a result, chapter 1 focuses on Udall's upbringing in St. Johns and Tucson, Arizona, as well as his experiences during his Mormon missionary work and over the skies of Europe as a B-24 bomber during World War II. Chapter 2 takes an in-depth look at Representative Stewart Udall. His congressional district included the entire state of Arizona outside the Phoenix metropolitan area, and his experiences in the US House of Representatives in many ways served as a primer for his work as interior secretary.

Chapters 3 to 12 cover the major (though not sole) subject of the book: Udall's years as US secretary of the interior. The chapters spotlighting Udall's work from 1961 to 1969 each focus on a different topic, with each topic roughly spanning the eight years. While many of the topics are interrelated, I believe that arranging the chapters by topic rather than chronology makes it easier for the reader to grasp the material. As such, chapter 3 focuses on Udall's first months in the Department of the Interior as well as his 1963 publication, *The Quiet Crisis*. The context of the time, an overview of DOI, and several reasons for Udall's success are also provided.

Chapters 4 to 5 paint a picture of how Udall helped expand the National Park System. No other interior secretary has ever been as involved in establishing new national park units nor come close to creating as many new parks as Stewart Udall. Chapter 5 also discusses Udall's involvement in establishing the National Trails System as well as in bringing the science of ecology to the forefront of the National Park Service, the government agency comprising the employees who manage the National Park System.

Chapter 6 focuses on Udall's accomplishments in wildlife protection and expansion of the National Wildlife Refuge System, while chapter 7 spotlights his work in reinvigorating and modernizing Bureau of Land Management (BLM) policies and lands. Chapter 8 discusses Udall's involvement in "all things water." Udall pushed for water-pollution mitigation, the establishment of the National Wild and Scenic Rivers System, and dam building. He also went on domestic and international conservation-reclamation trips, becoming the first Kennedy cabinet member to meet with Nikita Khrushchev in the Soviet Union in the process.

Chapter 9 delves into Udall's work overseeing the extractive industries. LBJ made Udall his point man on oil policy, and the interior secretary was also active in the battle against shortsighted corporate strip-mining executives in Appalachia. Chapter 10 focuses on Udall's involvement in the 1964 passage of the National Wilderness Preservation System Act, or Wilderness Act, an unprecedented piece of legislation.

Chapter 11 turns to Udall's efforts in improving the environment of cities. His 1968 book, *1976: Agenda for Tomorrow*, is spotlighted here, as is his work with Lady Bird Johnson, the first lady. Chapter 12 delves into Udall's controversies, failures, and final days at the post. Undoubtedly, Udall's biggest controversy involved his initial support for a dam that would have affected the Colorado River within Grand Canyon National Park and Grand Canyon National Monument. Chapter 13 briefly discusses Udall's final days in office.

Udall was just forty-nine years old in early 1969, but out of work due to the change in presidential administrations, and specifically the turnover in political parties. Chapter 14 looks at his writings and endeavors of the 1970s. Key to these was his outspokenness on the need for energy reform and conservation, especially in light of the Arab oil embargoes of the decade. Many if not all of Udall's suggested solutions to the energy crises of the 1970s remain, I believe, solutions to our energy dependence, global warming, and climate change problems of today.

Chapters 15 to 16 analyze Udall's activities and writings of the 1980s, 1990s, and early 2000s. Specifically, chapter 15 spotlights his long battles in court representing Navajo uranium miners. These 1950s miners were not notified of the dangers of working with uranium and were placed in unventilated mines. Twenty and thirty years later, large numbers of them died from the radiation exposure. Chapter 16 goes over Udall's lobbying for climate-change mitigation and his final writing projects as a historian. During these years, Udall moved from Phoenix to Santa Fe, where he passed away in 2010.

Environmentalist or Conservationist?
A Note on Terminology

Throughout the text, in describing Udall, I use the terms *conservationist* and *environmentalist* interchangeably, in part because Udall embraced both conservation and environmentalism and in part because the 1960s was a transitional and overlapping period between the two terms and their respective movements. In a tiny nutshell, let me explain.

In general, the "American conservation movement" occurred between about 1860 and 1960, peaking with Theodore Roosevelt and again with the other president in the family, Franklin Delano Roosevelt. For much of this time period, conservation referred generally to both the preservation of specific tracts of land—national parks such as Yosemite and Yellowstone, for instance—and the sustainable use and development of natural resources, such as national forests. Gifford Pinchot, a high-society member as well as the influential chief forester of the US Forest Service (USFS) under Theodore Roosevelt, referred to sustainable natural resource development, or conservation, as "the greatest good for the greatest number for the longest time." John Muir, the great naturalist and Yosemite National Park advocate, represented a more preservationist "don't-touch-anything-in-nature-and-just-admire-it-and-let-it-be" stance.

Blurred between the preservationist and sustainable-use lines of conservation during this time period were two additional subgroups, both of which have been traditionally lesser thought of in terms of conservation. The urban parks movement of the mid- and late 1800s is the first subgroup, which featured landscape architect Frederick Law Olmsted and Central Park and also included the establishment of Washington, DC's Rock Creek Park as well as many other city oases. The second subgroup in early conservation was "wildlife protection entities," including both the defenders of wild critters and the National Wildlife Refuge System itself, which informally began in the early 1900s and whose constituency of hunters and fishermen largely believed in recreational use of these lands but also in making sure species of waterfowl and mammals did not go extinct. All of these different entities and causes—national forests, urban parks, and wildlife protection—can be lumped under the term *conservation*.

In the early and mid-1900s, the term *conservation* was expanded to include three other goals, a big one being reclamation, the peculiar word used to describe massive dam building, reservoir construction, and other water-resource development projects. Soil conservation also gained a foothold during this era, especially during the years of the Dust Bowl and Great Depression, when progressives within the FDR administration pushed for major measures to improve soil conditions and decrease erosion both on private farmlands and in the public domain. A third group that developed during this time period was a wilderness faction of preservationists that broke away from the national park supporters, advocating for a more primitive, rugged, natural experience and despising the scenic road, trail, and tourist-facility developments in the national parks.

Finally, as American progress in standards of living, economics, and health expanded dramatically in post–World War II America (in part due to oil), so too did various types of air, water, and land pollution. Think the plastics industry, automobiles, highway development, and the growth of suburbia. Thus, in the 1960s and '70s, the terms *total environment*, *environmental protection*, and *the environmental movement* came to the forefront, referring to the ways, means, and needs of protecting wildlife, land, air, and water from human-induced declines. In many ways, then, conservation and its factions evolved, morphed, and expanded into environmentalism exactly at the time Udall was serving as interior secretary.[4]

~

John Muir, Theodore Roosevelt, Franklin Delano Roosevelt, Aldo Leopold, Rachel Carson, and a few other farsighted Americans are often regarded as the key environmental heroes and staunch supporters of conservation in US history. Stewart Udall must be added to this list, and this book is an attempt to explain why.

Notes

1. Ansel Adams to Lyndon B. Johnson, September 4, 1964, box 190, folder 1; Horace Albright to Johnson, December 8, 1963, box 190, folder 2; and Johnson to Stewart Udall, January 7, 1969, box 207, Stewart Udall Papers, University of Arizona, Special Collections Department.

2. Stewart L. Udall, *1976: Agenda for Tomorrow*, 101.

3. Stewart L. Udall, foreword to *Responsibilities to Future Generations: Environmental Ethics*, edited by Ernest Partridge (Buffalo, NY: Prometheus Books, 1981).

4. The evolution of conservation to environmentalism is briefly but eloquently explained in James Morton Turner, *The Promise of Wilderness: American Environmental Politics Since 1964* (Seattle: University of Washington Press, 2012), 40.

PART ONE

Udall's Formative Years, 1920–1960

1 | Early Years

The land made me a conservationist.

"THE GREAT DEPRESSION didn't affect us in St. Johns because we were already depressed."[1] This is one of the jokes Stewart and his younger brother Morris, himself an environmentalist and US representative from Arizona from 1961 to 1991, quipped when discussing their hometown. In the 1920s and 1930s, St. Johns, Arizona, was a small, remote community of fewer than two thousand inhabitants. Situated on the Colorado Plateau between Petrified Forest National Park and the Fort Apache (American Indian) Reservation, and also just a few miles from the New Mexico border, St. Johns sits at an elevation of more than fifty-six hundred feet. It's an arid land where high desert meets dry grassland meets juniper woodland. During Udall's childhood, the community was composed of approximately two-thirds white Mormon residents and one-third Mexican American Catholics.[2]

Udall's Parents and Grandparents

Arizona was part of Mexico until 1848. Stewart Udall's Mormon ancestors left the Midwest and central United States just after this time to escape religious persecution. "This is the place," said church leader Brigham Young as he looked out over the Salt Lake Valley in present-day Utah. Later, in the early 1880s, Stewart Udall's paternal grandfather, the polygamous David King Udall, was the person tasked by Salt Lake City with leading a group of Mormon pioneers south to St. Johns.

Husband of three and father of fifteen, David spent his time in St. Johns raising his families, leading the St. Johns Stake (or branch) of the Mormon Church, and farming and raising cattle on the land to provide a livelihood. In this last endeavor, David learned the challenges of trying to farm a dry landscape. "It proved to be a land of extremes, with alternating periods of drought and flood, undependable seasons, and devastating spring winds. Washes and gullies grew deeper and deeper from the forces of erosion," he wrote. Facing all of these issues, the grandfather told his family to "be good to the ground. It is holy. It is origin, possession, sustenance, [and] destiny."[3] Stewart Udall would heed these words three quarters of a century later.

One of David King Udall's wives was Eliza Luella Stewart, known as "Ella" to her family and close friends. While both of Stewart Udall's paternal grandparents were devout Mormons, David King was perhaps the more politically and morally conservative, as he fully subscribed to Joseph Smith's belief in plural marriages and kept multiple wives even after the federal government formally outlawed Mormon polygamy in 1882. Because of this, David was indicted and sent to prison in Michigan (in another instance, he was sent to jail for his part in a fraudulent land claim). While it is not fully known how she felt about all of this, Eliza was progressive in that she was a staunch supporter of women's suffrage. She was also an avid reader; lent a helping hand to the poor, including the poor Mexican Americans of the area; and mastered Morse code at fifteen years old. In this last endeavor, she served as an early telegraph operator out of Pipe Springs, Arizona, now Pipe Springs National Monument. In a religion that was historically male-centric and in a family with a big political name, it is perhaps interesting to note how much influence a progressive woman may have had on the Udall family: to date, every descendant of Eliza Luella Stewart Udall who has held political office, including the subject of this book, has been a liberal Democrat. By contrast, each of the six political descendants of Ida Hunt Udall, another of David King Udall's wives, has been a Republican.[4]

Eliza had nine children with David, but as was common in that day and age, some did not survive to adulthood. In fact, Eliza's first-born, named Stewart, died on the day he was born.[5] Stewart Lee Udall was perhaps named in part to honor this deceased baby and in part to honor the three familial last names from which he descended, Stewart, Lee, and Udall.

Another of Eliza and David's children was Levi, Stewart Lee's father. While David became a senator in the Twentieth Territorial Legislature (Arizona was a US territory until 1912) after returning from prison, his son Levi focused on law, working his way up from superior court judge to, eventually, justice of the Arizona Supreme Court. A deeply religious man like his parents, Levi served as the president of the St. Johns Stake. Like his mother, Levi was very progressive in that he was fully supportive of voting rights and full civil rights for American Indians and African Americans before the term *civil rights* was widely used. These values would be passed down to his children.[6]

Levi Udall married Louise Lee in a Salt Lake City Mormon temple in 1914.[7] They had six children, one of whom was Stewart Lee Udall, born on January 31, 1920. Stewart was the third child and first boy in the family. He was followed by Morris in 1922.[8]

Growing Up in Rural Arizona

For Stewart Udall as a boy and then a teenager in St. Johns, Arizona, both in the 1920s and the Great Depression, life was much different from growing up in a small town today. There was little electricity, few automobiles, no televisions, outhouses instead of bathrooms, and little water due to the aridity of the area. "Modern civilization rode a slow horse into St. Johns," Udall remembered.[9]

This lack of modernity actually had benefits, though. Because of scarce resources and the challenges that each family faced, people worked together and the town was self-sufficient in many ways. Most important perhaps for the story line of this book, almost everyone was involved in working and taking care of the soil and land. "Our lives made us natural conservationists," and "I was born

into it," reflected Udall years later when people asked him how he
had become a conservationist. "Our parsimonious land put a pre-
mium on wise stewardship; so naturally, recycling and stretching
was a way of life." For instance, Udall remembered:

> The cow or cows kept by each family produced milk, calves,
> and manure. The milk was skimmed of its cream for butter and
> cheese. The male calves were turned out to pasture and were
> later slaughtered for beefsteak. Manure from the stable was
> gathered and spread onto garden plots before spring plowing.
> And all the kitchen leftovers became a nutritious swill which
> was fed to the pigs, whose offal in turn fertilized the family
> garden. In those days, the only unusable household "waste" I
> can remember were tin cans which were gathered in a gunny-
> sack and taken to the town dump once or twice a year.[10]

In a 1982 article, Udall further recalled that building up soil at
every opportunity was a necessity, as was being careful not to over-
graze livestock. "One of the great things about St. Johns was that
everyone worked in some way directly with the earth. Everybody
grew something," Udall noted. "The farmers cultivated their corn
and alfalfa, tree lovers planted shade trees and nursed struggling
orchards; women grew their favorite flowers.... Each family had an
orchard, a garden, and the domesticated animals (cows, pigs, and
chickens) needed to provide the majority of its food. For the most
part, St. Johns was a self-sufficient farm village."[11]

While work was hard and hours were long on the farm, and
though much of this work fell on Stewart and Morris due to their
father often being away on the judge circuit, the Udall boys found
time to complete other endeavors. They attended public school,
Mormon sermons, and classes; played sports; and went out on foot,
exploring the mesas by the Little Colorado River around St. Johns.
Hiking and sleeping outdoors would become lifelong passions of
Stewart Udall's, and years later he would become probably the first
interior secretary in history with these interests. Udall enjoyed the
sense of freedom that exploring the open lands provided him. He
also had great experiences riding horseback on trips through the

nearby White Mountains. Additional regular activities for Stewart were reading and learning about new subjects. Whether it was about a new philosophy or a new skill, "Stew always was reading something new," recalled Morris.[12]

Udall's love for the land and interest in conservation largely came from growing up on a farm in a dry region and from exploring the countryside on his own two feet. Much of his success over the years also came from his law background, and his father's judgeship seems to have influenced Udall tremendously in this regard. As a child, Udall held mock trials with neighborhood boys in the garage. On one occasion, he held court over a St. Johns boy accused of stealing a dime from his mother. Later, while in college, during his Mormon mission, and while serving as a gunner in World War II, he wrote long letters back and forth with Levi; Stewart was always learning about and trying to understand his father's cases and rulings on issues.[13]

College, Mormon Mission, and World War II

After childhood Udall moved south to Tucson to attend junior college and then the University of Arizona. It was there that he thrived on intellectual stimulation and also served as a star point guard on the varsity basketball team, later being inducted into the University of Arizona Basketball Hall of Fame. However, his college course work was interrupted first by missionary work and then by the major war against Germany, Italy, and Japan.

Udall's two years of Mormon missionary work were completed in New York City. His two main reasons for completing the assignment were to learn more about his religion and to abide by his parents' wishes; Levi and Louise instilled in their son a strong allegiance to the Church of Jesus Christ of Latter-day Saints. While not much is known of Udall's missionary work and experience, it was during this time that he established himself as a writer by serving as editor for official church publications in the northeastern United States. He also met with church leaders—including a Pennsylvania Dutch minister—and relished long discussions with them, and attended church conferences. "I look back on my missionary experience as a fruitful experience. I got a lot out of it, and I came away with warm feelings toward the church," Udall recalled years later.[14]

Udall's experience as a Mormon missionary was actually pushing him in the direction of pacifism and conscientious objection, but after returning to Arizona he got caught up in the war effort.[15] In 1942 he became a member of what newsman Tom Brokaw describes as "the Greatest Generation," fighting against Nazi and fascist brutality not for fame and glory but because he felt it was simply necessary. Twentysomething Udall became a "tech sergeant waist gunner in a B-24 bomber," flying from bases in Italy. He flew approximately sixty-five missions with the Fifteenth Air Force, "which bombed ahead of troops in Italy and also went on important missions into Germany."[16]

Stewart corresponded regularly with his family back home during this time and also with Morris, who was involved in the war effort as well. The brothers wrote long letters to each other that discussed, among other topics, the state of the world, right and wrong, and evil and justice.[17] In addition, the future interior secretary read extensively. "You know, army time is 90 percent wasted waiting, and I spent most of my time in libraries," Udall recalled years later. "I began being a very wide reader in terms of religion and literature and history and so on." He also became a member of the National Association for the Advancement of Colored People while in the air force.[18]

Back in Tucson after World War II, where the climate is hot and the Sonoran Desert supports its signature species, the saguaro cactus, Udall completed his university course work, went on to law school, and met a pretty young lady named Ermalee Webb. After her father, Lee, was killed in a canal accident when she was only five, Ermalee took his first name. Born in 1922 in Phoenix, Ermalee (hereafter referred to as Lee) was raised Mormon like Stewart and had some physical difficulties as a child. Like FDR, she got polio and lost the use of her legs. Fortunately, due to her mother's intuition about rigorously applying hot and cold packs to Lee's legs and also making her scramble around on the carpet to increase blood flow and circulation, Lee regained her mobility.[19]

Another painful event in Lee's young life enabled her to meet Stewart. She shattered her leg in a motor-scooter accident while at the University of Arizona and received regular treatment and reflief from a muscle-relaxing machine at the campus hospital, and the machine's operator was Stewart Udall. The two became very close and married in 1947. They eventually produced six children, four of whom grew up to become a renewable energy advocate, a poet-professor, the current US senator from New Mexico, and an environmental lawyer. Lee herself actively supported American Indian culture and arts throughout her life, and Lee and Stewart were best friends and remained faithfully married for fifty-four years until her death in 2001.[20]

Just before graduating from law school and opening up a law office in Tucson, "the brothers Udall" successfully integrated the student union building and campus cafeteria. As with much of the country at the time, Tucson's public places and restaurants were segregated, and many didn't even permit African Americans entry. Morgan Maxwell, a Tucson African American civil rights activist, remembered that Stewart and Morris, who were popular students, went into the cafeteria with him and forced the manager and staff to serve him. Maxwell became the first black person to be served a meal at the campus cafeteria, and afterward all African Americans entering the facility were served. Stewart and Morris then began using the same tactic to desegregate other Tucson restaurants.[21]

Moving into Politics

At the private law firm of Udall and Udall, the close-knit brothers also promoted civil rights for all Americans. Though there were many more Mexican Americans in the Tucson area than there were African Americans, Stewart helped desegregate Arizona's schools prior to the federal *Brown v. Board of Education* ruling in 1954.[22]

Mormons are known in part for their traditionally large families and extended families, and the Udalls certainly fit this description. In the late 1940s and early 1950s, because there were so many Udall family members practicing law in the state, court cases had to be moved around so that a Udall lawyer wouldn't be sitting in a courtroom facing a Udall judge. Indeed, it was said that there were "oodles of Udalls" in politics in the mid-1900s; one family member joked that there were more Udalls in public service than there were people saying "You all" in Texas. Jokes aside, though, to date, the Udalls have produced more officeholders than any other family in the Southwest. This list includes two mayors of Phoenix, six county attorneys, three county judges, two state supreme court justices, and two US senators, not to mention Stewart and Morris, with their successes in politics. Because of all these officeholders, the Udalls, like the Kennedys (though admittedly less well known) have been referred to as an American political dynasty. The point is that the Udall family name was a big one in the Grand Canyon State, and with the highly respected Levi Udall sitting on Arizona's high court, Stewart said that he stood on his father's shoulders.[23]

Stewart in the late 1940s and early '50s became active in local and state politics and on school boards, once quipping that he led three unsuccessful campaigns in his county for candidates for governor. He did, however, help his father win his election to the Arizona Supreme Court by campaigning for Levi in 1946 by way of writing speeches, conducting radio interviews, and being by his side throughout the process. Young Stewart also became active in the Pima County Democratic Party.[24]

As a result of his background, well-known political family, early successes, and interests, when a conservative Democrat of three terms did not seek reelection in 1954 for Arizona's Second Congressional District, Stewart, after much discussion with family and friends, decided to enter the race. While he wasn't sure he would win the election, Udall did campaign door-to-door and town-to-town in many places, meeting with not just Caucasians but also Latinos and American Indians. He spent $12,000 total on his campaign, compared to the more than $1.5 million the average US representative spends today. Even accounting for inflation, Udall's $12,000 would amount to only $107,000 today.[25]

The election pitted Udall against Henry Zipf, an administrative assistant to Senator Barry Goldwater, a fellow Arizonan known from the 1960s onward as "Mr. Conservative." The campaign between Zipf and Udall occurred at the height of Joseph McCarthy's power. Many conservative politicians used McCarthyism scare tactics against their opponents, and Zipf was not above doing so, too. Because Udall supported copper-mine workers and their unions, Zipf attempted to paint Udall as a communist sympathizer. Udall political confidant Orren Beaty also noted that the Zipf campaign attempted to portray Udall as being "too far out in the civil rights extreme." They got hold of some articles Udall had written when he was at the University of Arizona and criticized him for stating that African Americans were equal to everyone else and should have the same rights.[26]

Regarding the claims about his being a communist, Udall friends, work associates, and family members in high places vouched for his good character. In regards to Udall's progressive civil rights stances, perhaps Zipf overlooked the fact that minorities can play a role in Arizona elections. Indeed, with a good friend of Udall's being the head of the largest Latino organization in the state, and with Alfredo Chavez Marques, this friend's son-in-law, working in Udall's law office, Udall was given a political boost.[27]

After the results came in, Udall received 68,085 votes to Zipf's 41,587. Thus, the young progressive defeated his opponent handily. At age thirty-four, then, Stewart Udall was going to be a US representative; the Arizonan was on his way to the nation's capital.[28]

Notes

1. "Life and Career of Stewart Udall," c-span, August 10, 2002, c-span.org /video/?171932-1/life-career-stewart-udall.

2. Donald W. Carson and James W. Johnson, *Mo: The Life & Times of Morris K. Udall*, 5. When Stewart was growing up, the official title of the park was Petrified Forest National Monument. In the 1950s, it was reclassified as the more prestigious Petrified Forest National Park.

3. Ibid., 5–6.

4. Levi Udall, "Eliza Luella Stewart Udall: A Sketch Written by Her Son Levi," in *Arizona Pioneer Mormons: David Kind Udall, His Life and His Family, 1851–1938*, by David King Udall and Pearl Udall Nelson (Tucson: Arizona Silhouettes, 1959), library.arizona.edu/exhibits/davidkudall/mormon/main.html.

5. Ibid.

6. Carson and Johnson, *Mo*, 8–13.

7. Louisa Lee, Stewart Udall's mother, had an extremely controversial grandfather who was actually executed by firing squad for his role in instigating and carrying out the Mountain Meadows Massacre. John D. Lee was this person's

name. With heavy heart, Stewart Udall writes about Lee and the massacre in *The Forgotten Founders: Rethinking the History of the Old West*, 63–73.

8. Ibid. Stewart and Morris's other siblings included Inez, Eloise, Elma, and David Burr. During her life, Elma Udall worked for the Red Cross in Africa and the Middle East during World War II before turning to a career in covert operations with the Federal Bureau of Investigation, Central Intelligence Agency, and US Department of State. She worked in London, Helsinki, Budapest, Berlin, and elsewhere. David Burr Udall, who was always referred to by his middle name, was a longtime lawyer in Tucson. He was nine years Stewart's junior. Not much is known about Inez or Eloise.

9. Stewart L. Udall, "Human Values and Hometown Snapshots: Early Days in St. Johns."

10. Ibid. Udall also discusses how growing up in St. Johns made him a conservationist in "Life and Career of Stewart Udall."

11. Ibid.

12. Wayne Amos, "Inside Interior's Udall: A Long Affair with the Out-of-Doors"; L. Boyd Finch, *Legacies of Camelot: Stewart and Lee Udall, American Culture, and the Arts*, 9; James M. Bailey, "The Udall Brothers Go to Washington: The Formative Years of Arizona's Sibling Politicians," *Journal of Arizona History* 41, no. 4 (2000): 432, jstor.org/stable/41696608?seq=20#page_scan_tab_contents.

13. Orien Fifer Jr., "Stewart Udall Leader as Boy," *Arizona Republic*, February 19, 1962.

14. Marc Bohn, "Remembering Stewart Udall," *Times and Seasons* (blog), March 22, 2010, timesandseasons.org/index.php/2010/03/remembering-stewart -udall/. See also "Mormon Missionary Correspondences," box 225, folder 4, Udall Papers.

15. Stewart Udall, interview in *Candid Conversations with Inactive Mormons*, by James W. Ure, 69.

16. "Wildcat Basketball Stars Once Topped Clouds with Air Forces," *Arizona Daily Star*, January 15, 1946, box 248, Udall Papers.

17. Carson and Johnson, *Mo*, 27.

18. Udall, interview in *Candid Conversations*, 69, 71.

19. Finch, *Legacies of Camelot*, 12.

20. Ibid., 14, 154.

21. Morgan Maxwell Jr., "My Old Main Story," University of Arizona, saveold main.org/my-old-main-story-morgan-maxwell-jr.

22. "Stewart L. Udall: Career Chronology," Udall Papers, library.arizona.edu /exhibits/sludall/career.htm. See also Carson and Johnson, *Mo*.

23. Barbara Laverne Blythe Leunes, "The Conservation Philosophy of Stewart L. Udall, 1961–1968," 24; Elma Stewart and David Burr Udall, interview transcript, "The Udall Family," *Arizona Stories*, azpbs.org; Keith Schneider and Cornelia Dean, "Stewart L. Udall, Conservationist in Kennedy and Johnson Cabinets, Dies at 90," *New York Times*, March 22, 2010.

24. Stewart Udall, transcript of interview, in *Establishment of Environmentalism on the U.S. Political Agenda in the Second Half of the Twentieth Century: The Brothers Udall*, by Henry B. Sirgo, 178.

25. Stewart Udall, Spanish-language election flyer, Udall Papers, azmemory .azlibrary.gov/cdm/ref/collection/uoaslu/id/24.

26. Transcript, Orren Beaty Jr. oral history interview I, by William W. Moss, October 10, 1969, JFK Library, archive2.jfklibrary.org/JFKOH/Beaty,%20orren /JFKOH-OB-01/JFKOH-OB-01-TR.pdf.

27. Ibid.

28. Transcript, Stewart L. Udall oral history interview I, by Joe B. Frantz, April 18, 1969, LBJ Library, lbjlibrary.net/assets/documents/archives/oral _histories/udall/UDALL01.PDF; Udall, transcript of interview, in *Establishment of Environmentalism*, 178; Jay Costa, "What's the Cost of a Seat in Congress?," MapLight, maplight.org/content/73190; "Udall: Career Chronology."

2 | Congressman

I gravitated to Kennedy.

IN THE 1950S, Arizona had more national park units, more acres of American Indian reservations, and a larger percentage of the state as public lands (federally managed lands) than any other state, and practically all of these public lands were included in the congressional district that Udall represented. In fact, with the exception of Phoenix and Maricopa County, Arizona's Second Congressional District included the entire state.[1] This meant that Udall represented the inhabitants of Tucson, St. Johns, and picturesque Sedona as well as Hopi and Navajo peoples. He represented farmers and ranchers, timber harvesters and university professors. His congressional district included ample federal lands and projects managed by the National Park Service, Bureau of Land Management, US Fish and Wildlife Service (USFWS), Bureau of Reclamation, and Bureau of Indian Affairs, all of which fall under the US Department of the Interior umbrella. He also oversaw tens of thousands of acres managed by the US Forest Service, an agency within the US Department of Agriculture. For all these reasons, Udall's six years in Congress representing Arizona, especially his work as a member of the House Interior and Insular Affairs Committee (now known as the House Committee on Natural Resources), served as a primer for his eight years as secretary of the interior. It gave him some of the necessary knowledge and experiences to become an exceptional interior secretary.[2]

Young Man Goes to Washington

While Udall was prone to working hard and took personal responsibility for a significant part of his congressional office duties, it was also important for the junior representative to have a good staff as well as a staff representative of his constituency. Thus walking the talk in terms of civil rights, Udall brought with him from his Arizona law office his Mexican American assistant. Working through tribal councils, Udall also recruited Tilly Bowman, an educated and hardworking Navajo woman. Rounding out his core staff was Orren Beaty, an Arizona political journalist who, less than a year after Udall went to Washington, joined the office staff and remained with Udall through not only his six years in Congress but also his eight years as a cabinet member.[3]

After recruiting his small team, as a freshman congressman Udall had much to learn and study. Fortunately, John Rhodes (R-AZ), the senior congressman from the Grand Canyon State, spent ample time showing Udall the ropes. "Rhodes broke trails for me," Udall remembered. In his first few months on Capitol Hill, Udall also came to admire the strong work ethics and mentorships of Bill Dawson, Republican of Utah, and Democrats Lee Metcalf of Montana, Claire Engle and James Roosevelt of California, Edith Green of Oregon, and Gracie Pfost of Idaho.[4]

It should also be noted that Representative Wayne Aspinall of Colorado was helpful to Udall upon his arrival in Congress. With Udall being twenty-four years younger than Aspinall, the young Arizonan was in some ways Aspinall's protégé. A firm believer in reclamation, multiple use of public lands, and the notion that conservation and national park legislation should come through the legislative branch and not the executive, Aspinall served as the powerful chairman—some would say dictator—of the House Interior and Insular Affairs Committee from 1959 to 1973. Udall and Aspinall generally had a good relationship throughout each other's political careers, though they came to be at opposite ends of the environmental politics spectrum more and more as time went by. Somewhat ironically, the 1950s through the '70s was an era when numerous

Rockefeller Republicans—the term used commonly back then for moderate or even liberal Republicans—helped pass key environmental legislation, yet Aspinall was arguably the opposite of a liberal Republican; he was a conservative Democrat.[5]

Besides being mentored by the above-mentioned politicians, rookie Udall had to spend ample time learning other congressmen's names. This was "one of the most formidable tasks a freshman must tackle," he said. "After three months I found that I knew almost three-fourths of my 435 colleagues 'on sight,' though I'm lucky if more than half of them can identify me."[6]

Another thing Udall had to do in beginning his tenure in the US House of Representatives was to receive his committee assignments. After asking to be placed on it due to the large public land presence in his state, Udall was put on the House Interior and Insular Affairs Committee and all five of its subcommittees. He was also put on the Education and Labor Committee, which would later put him in contact with Senator John F. Kennedy (D-MA).[7]

After these initial learning curves and logistics, Udall, in his first year in Congress and continuing thereafter, found time to champion increased natural resource protection and recreation in the national forests as well as water-pollution mitigation and dam building. Outside of nature and the environment, the junior congressman from Arizona pushed for improvements in the fields of education and labor and was a strong supporter of civil rights during his three terms in office. Nevertheless, historian Ian Robert Stacey claimed that Udall "did little to distinguish himself" during his congressional years. It's up to the reader to decide whether Stacey's statement was true.[8]

Pushing for Increased Protection and Recreation in the National Forests

When Udall was born in 1920, the country's system of national forests had already been around for several years. Established first as forest reserves in the 1890s and then formalized and expanded into official national forests by President Theodore Roosevelt and Gifford Pinchot, the chief forester, the national forests were designated first and foremost for sustainable timber harvesting, with

Stewart Udall, ca. 1960. Courtesy of the White House.

watershed protection, grazing, and mining as important secondary interests. The US Forest Service was the governmental agency comprising the individuals who oversaw the tens of thousands of acres of national forests, and Pinchot told his USFS staff that the country's natural resources needed to be conserved "for the greatest good for the greatest number for the longest time." Thus, there was to be no large-scale clear-cutting of trees in headwater areas of watersheds, as, thanks to previous studies and writings by George Perkins Marsh and others, it was known that the practice would lead to increased runoff, soil erosion, and flooding downstream.[9]

While USFS management of timber-cutting operations ensured ample board feet for generations, there was no such thing as sustainable mining, as mineral extraction policy on public lands was based on an increasingly antiquated law established back in 1872. In addition, with a booming mid-twentieth-century US economy enabling more citizens increased time for leisure and recreation, some believed that national forest lands needed to offer additional formalized forms of outdoor recreation to meet the demand. Enter a freshman US representative named Stewart Udall in 1955.

Udall learned to love scenic views and stewardship of the land while growing up in rural northeastern Arizona. Regarding this land and scenic-view preservation, one area that Representative

Udall took a specific interest in was the highly picturesque Oak Creek Canyon, a natural corridor within the Sedona region of his native state, where a mountain stream flows through towering red-rock formations. The canyon was mostly managed as part of the Coconino National Forest, and Udall learned of some of the problematic commercial and residential practices taking place in the forest domain early in his congressional years.

Specifically, he learned that due to the outdated General Mining Act of 1872, which still served as the preeminent law affecting mining policy on public lands, anyone could file a mining claim in a national forest. While some prospectors did file claims and conducted mineral exploration legitimately, the vast majority of land claims, learned Udall, were filed by non-miners, people seeking to harvest timber, graze cattle, build summer-home sites, or create personal fishing or hunting grounds for themselves, all under the guise of mining activity. They filed these activities as mining claims because mining fees were minimal; other natural resource user fees and extractive fees cost much more.[10]

Udall fundamentally believed that these false mining claims were an abuse of the law, and before more of them could be finalized and approved, the young representative worked to make sure that many more cabins, hunting camps, and timber harvests in the Oak Creek Canyon did not accrue and mar the area's beauty. Senator Carl Hayden (D-AZ) and Udall teamed up and pushed through a bill that protected the canyon area from further encroachment by false mining claims.[11]

In terms of the bigger picture of such claims, Udall introduced a bill, with several other members of the House Interior and Insular Affairs Committee, to outlaw, dispose of, and reclaim all false mining claims on federal lands throughout the country, as the issue was widespread and not solely in the Sedona area. The bill passed and went into effect.[12]

One final note deserves mentioning on the topic of mining and Udall, and this involves his stance on the protection of certain Indian lands. A relatively large tract of land just west of Tucson, the Tohono O'odham Indian Reservation (in Udall's time known as the Papago Indian Reservation), was being encroached upon by small-scale

Caucasian miners trying to strike it rich in Indian country. Udall sponsored legislation to keep the white miners out, thus protecting Native American interests and preventing the Indians from getting taken advantage of, as had been the case so many times throughout US history.[13]

With regard to recreation on public lands, a booming national economy in the mid-twentieth century led to an increase in the amount of free time for millions of citizens. Udall believed that people could and should enjoy more outdoor time when they were not at work or school, and, having a love for hiking and exploring the landscapes in general, he pushed for the Forest Service to place a much greater emphasis on outdoor recreation. As such, less than a month after entering Congress, the rookie representative proposed that some of the Forest Service's lumber and grazing-fee revenues be used for a special recreation fund to develop and maintain additional picnic areas, trails, and fishing lakes. While this specific bill did not pass, Udall would keep the idea in his back pocket, and a few years later, as interior secretary, he would push through a more comprehensive and far-reaching land-conservation and outdoor-recreation bill known as the Land and Water Conservation Fund. In addition, Udall voted in favor of the Forest Service's Multiple Use Sustained Yield Act of 1960, an important piece of legislation that recognized recreation as one of five official purposes of the national forests.[14]

It should also be noted that Congressman Udall voted in favor of the 1958 act establishing the National Outdoor Recreation Resources Review Commission (ORRRC). The bipartisan act called for a broad-scale study to be conducted on the country's outdoor-recreation policies, problems, and opportunities. The ORRRC released its final report soon after Udall became interior secretary, which proved fortuitous as he fully endorsed the report's recommendations and saw much of it through to fruition.[15] (The ORRRC is discussed in more depth toward the end of the next chapter.)

Udall supported additional outdoor-recreation and landscape-protection legislation as a US representative. He voted for the bill establishing the Virgin Islands National Park in the US Virgin Islands and was the primary force behind the establishment of the

Tucson Mountain District of Saguaro National Park. Udall lobbied for this unit of the park as a congressman, but it gained National Park System status during his early interior secretary years. (More on Udall's involvement in the Saguaro National Park expansion is related in chapter 4.) Finally, Udall was a congressional supporter of the Wilderness Act, an important piece of legislation that sought to preserve unspoiled areas of the public domain in their primitive state forever. The act ultimately became law in 1964, due at least in part to Udall's lobbying for it as interior secretary.[16] (See chapter 10 for more information.)

Pushing for Reclamation Projects and Water-Pollution Mitigation

Water-pollution control, effective management of water resources, and reclamation projects were other focuses of Udall during his six years in Congress, from 1955 to early 1961. Reclamation, the odd term that for well over a century has really meant the "claiming" of arid or other land for farming, reservoirs, and energy purposes, was not a new policy for the western United States.

In brief, large-scale federal reclamation projects began with the Reclamation Act of 1902. Also known as the Newlands Reclamation Act, due to Representative Francis Newlands of Nevada's strong push for the bill, the act called for a percentage of government funds accrued from the sale of public lands to be used for dam and irrigation projects throughout the western United States. As a result, dams and associated reservoirs were constructed on numerous rivers, most notably in Montana, New Mexico, Washington, and Colorado. Continuing this tradition, the Franklin Delano Roosevelt era ushered in record-breaking reclamation projects on rivers such as the Tennessee, Columbia, and Colorado.[17]

In the 1950s, as in the 1930s, most western states' politicians, whether in the US Senate or House of Representatives, were major supporters and endorsers of federal reclamation projects. A major reason for the emphasis on reclamation was the fact that much of the West is arid, yet human population and agriculture were expanding at the time. Expanding cities needed additional electricity

and water, as did crop fields. Furthermore, massive dams and related water-storage infrastructure projects were seen as major
feats of engineering, and thus promoted US pride, nationalism, and
muscle on the world stage.

Representative Stewart Udall lobbied for reclamation projects.
"As a congressman in the 1960s I was pro-dam. I voted for the upper
Colorado project that flooded Glen Canyon," Udall noted candidly
in a 1980s interview. "I instinctively identified my values more with
the Sierra Club than with dam-building, except that I was from Arizona, and so you had to be for water. You couldn't go to Congress and
be against dams."[18]

Indeed, Udall pushed for the Navajo Dam in northwestern New
Mexico and for reclamation projects in southeastern Arizona along
the San Pedro River in order to increase the supply of drinking
water for the growing city of Tucson. Udall also supported and voted
in favor of the 1956 Colorado River Storage Project, the bill that authorized Glen Canyon Dam and other projects along the Colorado.
Udall not only pushed for this dam but also, working with Arizona's
congressional delegation, got the dam-construction community,
Page, to be built in Arizona rather than Utah, enabling more unemployed and low-income constituents, most notably Navajo Indians,
to gain a paycheck by working on the project. Udall believed that
the dam's backwater would provide water to parched Navajo lands,
enabling hundreds of impoverished American Indians to become
successful farmers.[19]

Due to its destruction of native fish passageways as well as river
ecosystems, dam building would become more and more controversial throughout the 1950s and '60s. During this time, one of the most
outspoken opponents of dam building, particularly dam building in
national park units, was David Brower, the now almost legendary
executive director of the Sierra Club. As a congressman, Udall was
very much a dam advocate, but in part due to Brower's correspondence and meetings with the crew-cut Mormon once he became interior secretary, in the early 1960s Udall began to see the need for
a balance—some rivers needed to be dammed to support the country's population, and agricultural expansion, but others needed to

be preserved in their natural state. (This topic is discussed in more depth in chapter 8.)

Outside of reclamation but still on the topic of water, specifically water pollution–control efforts, Udall supported a bill in the late 1950s that would have substantially increased federal funding for the development of additional sewage-treatment plants. Massive amounts of sewage were flushed directly into lakes and rivers across the country during this period, and the amount was growing due to the increasing density of cities and suburbs, as well as antiquated sewer systems. Treatment plants were seen as a remedy to water pollution because they remove the vast majority of environmentally dangerous, unhealthy pollutants before discharging the treated water into waterways. When President Eisenhower vetoed the sewage treatment–plant expansion bill because he believed the private sector should be in charge of pollution control rather than the federal government, Udall was one of the people who voted to override the veto. Udall criticized the president's approach to water-pollution mitigation as "shortsighted" and "penny-wise."[20]

To improve the government's efficiency and management of water-pollution mitigation, reclamation, and planning for future water shortages, Udall lobbied for bringing all federal bureaus that were responsible for water management into one umbrella agency. "Our goal should be maximum use and maximum conservation of our full water potential," the US representative claimed, and in order to reach this goal Udall introduced a bill to establish the Federal Water Conservation and Planning Service. The future interior secretary believed that major water research needed to be initiated in order to ensure against future water shortages; specific studies needed to be conducted on the mapping of underground aquifers. Udall's water bureau did not come to fruition, however.[21]

Pushing for Education and Civil Rights

Growing up in arid Arizona, and with his interest in the outdoors, Udall felt most at home with conservation and reclamation politics and projects. He had more of a learning curve as a congressman outside of these realms. Udall overcame this largely through spending significant time reading about political subjects. As Orren Beaty remembered, Udall "grew in the job. He read constantly. There was a constant flow of books and periodicals between the Library of Congress and the Legislative Reference Service and our office." Udall read "issue books, political books...[b]iographies of people who had been active in politics and in government...[c]urrent matters involving inflation, economics, NATO [North Atlantic Treaty Organization].... He read anything that had to do with the role of Congress."[22]

To help him remember what he learned and also to help explain things to his voter base, Udall began writing newsletters to his constituents and to newspapers back home. He took a tremendous amount of time writing, editing, and then rewriting, and the future interior secretary became, in Beaty's opinion, really the first politician from the Grand Canyon State to write articulately about politics. Some of Udall's work was published nationally in the *New York Times Magazine* and *New Republic*.[23]

Outside of Udall's congressional work involving land conservation, recreation, water-pollution mitigation, reclamation, learning, and writing, the US representative wrote ample bills supporting improvements in education. For instance, to help bring the majority of young American Indians out of poverty, Udall cosponsored a bill, with congressmen from other states that had significant populations of American Indians, for the creation of the Indian Scholarship Fund. The fund called for a percentage of government revenues received from offshore oil leases to be given to American Indians to help them through primary and secondary school as well as through university. Udall also pushed for the building of more schools, specifically community colleges.[24] While the future interior secretary ultimately supported the Federal Aid Highway Act of 1956—the bill that authorized payments for and construction of the massive Interstate Highway System—he emphasized the fact that, in his mind, improving the nation's educational system was much more important an endeavor. "If we are forced to place priorities and choose this year between a national highway program and a national classroom construction program, I shall cast my lot with the schools," Udall told his fellow members on the Committee on Education and Labor.[25]

Udall's other major emphasis was civil rights. "In my opinion the paramount domestic problem before our country today is an orderly solution of our school desegregation problem—and the extension of full rights for all our citizens," he said. "These problems must be solved in a peaceful way, and in a manner which will bring credit to our traditions as a democratic country.... The goal of equal treatment for all in the United States is no longer beyond reach." Along this front, Udall pushed for federal government funding efforts in support of school desegregation after the 1954 Supreme Court ruling in *Brown v. Board of Education.*[26]

In another push for civil rights, Udall, representing constituents twenty-seven hundred miles away in rural Arizona, was ironically the congressman most involved in the drive for District of Columbia home rule in the 1950s. Living in the first US city of five hundred thousand residents or more to have a majority African American population, DC residents were taxed but given no representation at the local, state, or national level at the time. Residents did not have a mayor or city council to elect, they did not have a US senator or congressman to elect, and they couldn't vote in presidential elections.

To address these undemocratic anomalies, Udall worked hard to orchestrate a floor vote for a bill that would have given DC residents representation just like residents of all other large US cities. Because the chairman of the congressional committee focusing on District of Columbia affairs did not support the bill, Udall was forced to push the bill to the floor by way of a discharge petition, that is, by getting enough signatures in support of the bill to bring it out of committee and onto the floor without the approval of the powerful chairman. The magic number of signatures needed was 219, and for weeks the *Washington Post* reported almost daily on how many signatures had accrued. Unfortunately, despite Udall's best efforts, he came up just 4 signatures short. Yet the *Post* appreciated Udall's efforts in the battle:

As District residents view the wreckage of their hopes for home rule during the present session of Congress, there is a continued afterglow amid the gloom. This represents the admiration, respect, and appreciation that many voteless Washingtonians have acquired for Rep. Stewart L. Udall (D-Ariz.) who led the fight to discharge the House District Committee from further consideration of the bottled-up home rule bill. The hard fighting legislator from Tucson might well be designated public servant of the year in the District.

Few persons who watched the struggle to move the home rule bill onto the floor of the House realize the volume of work that was entailed in getting 215 congressional signatures on a discharge petition. Mr. Udall took charge of this task, not because his constituents have any special interest in it, but because he believes in the principle of local self-government. Month after month he continued the toilsome process of adding signatures, sometimes under the most disheartening circumstances. He stimulated many congressmen into activity on the issue; he encouraged local home rule groups; with some expert help he surveyed the entire membership of the House and brought the discharge petition within a few names of the required 219 when the time limitation ran out last week....

Of course, many others contributed to the almost successful home rule drive in the House. To all of them the District owes a hearty vote of thanks. It was Stewart Udall, however, who led the fight and exerted the strongest pull for the restoration of local suffrage. The gratitude of the community is nonetheless real because it has no official voice with which to speak.[27]

In part because Udall spurred more interest in the issue, in 1961 DC residents were given the right to vote in presidential elections. But it wasn't until the District of Columbia Home Rule Act of 1973 that residents were allowed to elect their own mayor and city council. And to this day, DC residents have minimal representation in the US Senate and House of Representatives (they have no senator and a single representative who is not allowed to vote); thus, every DC license plate bears the motto "Taxation without representation."

The Presidential Election of 1960

Congressman Stewart Udall was a progressive politician who championed conservation, civil rights, democratic principles, and education. He also championed the rights of workers, resulting in his work on and support for the Labor-Management Reform Act (LMRA) of 1959. A controversial, exhausting bill to work on due to a lack of significant support from the Eisenhower administration as well as foot-dragging from labor-union leaders, the bill was designed, according to then US senator John F. Kennedy of Massachusetts, to help "the labor movement clean its own house and remove the stigma of racketeering for all time to come." In brief, the LMRA significantly scaled back corruption and undemocratic principles within labor unions by requiring union managers to make their financial reports public, thus increasing accountability and transparency for the federal government as well as for union members. The bill also made union elections more democratic.[28]

While the bill was an important one, more significant to Udall personally was that it brought him into direct contact with JFK. "I gravitated to Kennedy when I worked with him on the Labor Reform Bill, because I saw then qualities that I didn't realize that he had—a strength and toughness because this was a mean issue and it could have destroyed him," Udall recalled in 1969. "He also surrounded himself with extremely able people. This was another thing that appealed to me."[29]

Udall identified with JFK due to the fact that he was a political outsider because he was Catholic, much as Udall was an outsider because he was Mormon. Indeed, in one of his last public interviews, not long before his death in 2010, Udall noted that JFK's Catholicism was as revolutionary in the 1960 election as President Barack Obama being African American was in the presidential election of 2008.[30]

Udall won reelection in his Arizona congressional district relatively easily in 1956 and 1958. In addition to campaigning for his own seat in 1960, Udall, in the Democratic primary, endorsed Kennedy and campaigned for him in his home state. The primary pitted JFK against House majority leader and Texas native Lyndon Baines Johnson. While neither of the candidates courted Udall for his vote, Udall courted Arizona to swing for Kennedy. "I was one of the few Congressmen that really stuck my neck out [for Kennedy].... I went over to his office and I told him I was going to go home and go to work for him," Udall remembered. "My idea at that time was that I would line up my Congressional district, get friends of mine that I knew were supporters of his to start working to get on the delegation, to go to the Convention in Los Angeles. I made no public announcement, I just went home and I worked all fall."[31]

Udall's push for Kennedy orchestrated an upset in the Democratic primary. The Johnson campaign, certain that Arizona would vote in their favor, was mightily surprised when the Grand Canyon State voted for Kennedy. JFK went on to beat LBJ in the primary, and he then beat Republican candidate Richard Nixon in the presidential election (though he lost to Nixon in Arizona). As a result, Kennedy became the youngest president-elect in US history.

Meanwhile, Udall, having won a fourth term as US representative but seeing the margin of votes between himself and his opponent cut in half, began, in his own words, "licking my wounds." His prospects improved, however, when in early December he received a phone call from Robert F. Kennedy. On behalf of his brother, RFK asked Udall if he was interested in serving as the secretary of the interior.[32]

From Kennedy's point of view, he was not a conservationist or outdoorsman like Udall, and he needed an interior secretary he could trust to make the right decisions on these issues. JFK had respect for Udall and saw many of the qualities in Udall that Udall saw in him. It also helped that Udall was from Arizona, as the position of secretary of the interior is traditionally given to a politician from the western United States, because this is the area where the majority of public lands are located. Furthermore, Kennedy surely appreciated Udall's working on behalf of the JFK campaign.[33]

From Udall's perspective, serving as interior secretary seemed like an exciting challenge, and the ambitious Arizonan perhaps dreamed of spreading the gospels of natural resource protection and sustainable use, as well as outdoor recreation, from sea to shining sea. For these reasons and more, Udall responded to the question from the Kennedy brothers with a resounding yes.

A quick meeting with JFK in his Georgetown row house and a public announcement then confirmed it: Stewart Lee Udall, at age forty, was going to be serving as US secretary of the interior. He was JFK's first cabinet selection and would become the first cabinet member ever from the state of Arizona. He would also be JFK's only cabinet member with prior experience in Congress. What would Udall do as interior secretary, and how would the 1960s turn out?[34]

Notes

1. Transcript, Stewart L. Udall oral history interview I, by Joe B. Frantz, April 18, 1969, LBJ Library, lbjlibrary.net/assets/documents/archives/oral_histories /udall/UDALL01.PDF.

2. Only a handful of other interior secretaries have served previously on the House Interior and Insular Affairs Committee or its counterpart, the US Senate Committee on Energy and Natural Resources. This short list includes Ryan Zinke, the interior secretary at the time of this book's publication; Dirk Kempthorne, George W. Bush's second interior secretary; Manuel Lujan, George H. W. Bush's interior secretary; and Rogers C. B. Morton, Nixon's second interior secretary.

3. Transcript, Orren Beaty Jr. oral history interview I, by William W. Moss, October 10, 1969, JFK Library, archive2.jfklibrary.org/JFKOH/Beaty,%20orren /JFKOH-OB-01/JFKOH-OB-01-TR.pdf.

4. US House of Representatives, Office of Stewart Udall, press release, "Observations at Mid-Season," April 28, 1955, box 3, folder 3, Udall Papers. James Roosevelt was actually the oldest son of Franklin and Eleanor Roosevelt. Gracie Pfost was the first female to ever be elected to Congress from the state of Idaho; Edith Green was the second from Oregon.

5. For more on Aspinall and his politics, see Carol Edmonds, *Wayne Aspinall: Mr. Chairman* (Lakewood, CO: Great American, 1980); Stephen C. Sturgeon, *The Politics of Western Water: The Congressional Career of Wayne Aspinall*; and Steven C. Schulte, *Wayne Aspinall and the Shaping of the American West*.

6. Newsletter to constituents, Udall Papers.

7. Udall, letters to Jere Cooper, chairman of US House of Representatives Ways and Means Committee, box 3, folder 1, Udall Papers.

8. Ian Robert Stacey, "The Last Conservationist: Floyd Dominy and Federal Reclamation Policy in the American West" (PhD diss., University of Montana, 2013), 205, scholarworks.umt.edu/cgi/viewcontent.cgi?article=2055&context=etd.

9. For good overview histories of the US Forest Service, see James G. Lewis, *The Forest Service and the Greatest Good: A Centennial History* (Durham, NC: Forest History Society, 2005); US Forest Service, *The Greatest Good* (documentary film, 2007); Douglas H. Strong, *Dreamers and Defenders: American Conservationists*, 61–84 (for George Perkins Marsh, see 27–38); and Kenneth Brower, *American Legacy: Our National Forests.*

10. US House of Representatives, Udall, press releases, February 17, May 19, 1955, box 3, folder 3, Udall Papers. This and many other problematic aspects of the General Mining Act of 1872 have been analyzed in numerous works. See Robert C. Anderson, "Federal Mineral Policy: The General Mining Law of 1872," *Natural Resources Journal* 16 (1976): 601; Carol Ann Woody et al., "The Mining Law of 1872: Change Is Overdue," *Fisheries* 35, no. 7 (2010); and Gordon Morris Bakken, *The Mining Law of 1872: Past, Politics, and Prospects* (Albuquerque: University of New Mexico Press, 2008).

11. US House of Representatives, Udall, Report to Constituents, August 22, 1955, box 3, folder 3, Udall Papers.

12. Multiple Surface Use Mining Act of 1955, Pub. L. No. 167, Stat. 367, July 23, 1955, ntc.blm.gov/krc/uploads/238/MultiSurfaceUseAct1955.pdf; US House of Representatives, Udall, press releases, February 17, May 19, 1955.

13. Transcript, Beaty oral history interview I.

14. Multiple Use Sustained Yield Act of 1960, Pub. L. No. 86-517, June 12, 1960, fs.fed.us/emc/nfma/includes/musya60.pdf.

15. National Outdoor Recreation Resources Review Commission Act, Pub. L. No. 85-470, June 28, 1958, gpo.gov/statute-72-pg238.pdf.

16. John C. Miles, *Wilderness in National Parks: Playground or Preserve?* (Seattle: University of Washington Press, 2009), 152–53. According to Tom Turner in *David Brower: The Making of the Environmental Movement* (Berkeley: University of California Press, 2015), 62, Udall was a supporter of wilderness legislation even before serving in Congress. Turner states that Udall attended a wilderness conference as early as 1949.

17. National Park Service, "Bureau of Reclamation Historic Dams, Irrigation Projects, and Power Plants," nps.gov/nr/travel/ReclamationDamsIrrigation ProjectsAndPowerplants/Water_In_The_West.html. See also David P. Billington, Donald C. Jackson, and Martin V. Melosi, *The History of Large Federal Dams: Planning, Design, and Construction* (Washington, DC: US Bureau of Reclamation, 2005).

18. Udall, interview with Tim Palmer, in *Endangered Rivers and the Conservation Movement* (New York: Rowman & Littlefield, 2004), 160.

19. US House of Representatives, Udall, Report to Constituents, August 15, 1956, box 3, folder 4, Udall Papers; Udall, news release, March 24, 1955, box 3, folder 3, Udall Papers.

20. US House of Representatives, Udall, "Arizona's Stake in Unpolluted Water," Congressional Report, March 10, 1960, box 44, folder 5, Udall Papers.

21. US House of Representatives, Udall, press release, February 3, 1956, box 3, folder 4, Udall Papers.

22. Transcript, Beaty oral history interview I.

23. Ibid.

24. US House of Representatives, Udall, press release, February 17, 1955.

25. US House of Representatives, Udall, "Statement on Bills to Provide Federal Assistance for Construction of Public Schools," House Committee on Education and Labor, March 9, 1955, box 3, folder 3, Udall Papers. Beginning in the 1960s, Udall would regret voting for the Interstate Highway System because of the automobile pollution: "I voted in favor of the damn thing," he once lamented.

26. US House of Representatives, Udall, "Congressional Report: Chances for New Civil Rights Bill," May 17, 1955, box 3, folder 4, Udall Papers.

27. "Salute to Stewart Udall," *Washington Post*, June 24, 1960, washingtonpost.com/wp-adv/archives/copyright.htm.

28. US Senate, John F. Kennedy, news release, "The Congress and Labor Reform Bill: Excerpts from the Remarks of Senator John F. Kennedy," 1960, JFK Library, jfklibrary.org/Asset-Viewer/Archives/JFKCAMP1960-1030-031.aspx.

29. Transcript, Udall oral history interview I.

30. "Life and Career of Stewart Udall," C-SPAN, August 10, 2002, c-span.org/video/?171932-1/life-career-stewart-udall.

31. Transcript, Udall oral history interview I.

32. Ibid.

33. Ibid. See also Robert Dallek, *An Unfinished Life: John F. Kennedy, 1917–1963* (New York: Little, Brown, 2003), 319–20; Thomas C. Reeves, *A Question of Character: A Life of John F. Kennedy* (New York: Free Press, 1991), 227; and Jacqueline Kennedy, *Historic Conversations on Life with John F. Kennedy: Interviews with Arthur M. Schlesinger, Jr., 1964* (New York: Hyperion, 2011), 121. According to Schulte, *Aspinall and the Shaping of the American West*, 90–100, Representative Wayne Aspinall (D-CO), chairman of the House Interior and Insular Affairs Committee, thought that he was Kennedy's front-runner for interior secretary. As such, Aspinall was rubbed the wrong way when Udall was chosen by Kennedy. Schulte also discusses Udall and Aspinall's unique relationship in the 1960s as friends and rivals who worked together to achieve their respective legislative goals.

34. Stewart Udall left his congressional seat to take the position of interior secretary. When a special election was held for his former seat, Stewart's brother Morris Udall won. Morris would go on to win fifteen straight elections for his congressional district, holding his seat until his retirement in 1991. Morris's election in 1961 marked the first time in history that two family members from the western United States served in federal office at the same time.

PART TWO

Udall as US Secretary of the Interior, 1961–1969

3 | First Days at the Interior Department

This administration has an opportunity to make a record in conservation that would equal or excel that of Theodore Roosevelt.

AS A CONGRESSMAN, Stewart and his wife, Lee, had fallen in love with the national capital practically right after arriving there. Enjoying its cultural offerings, arts, monuments, and scenery, they bought a house in McLean, Virginia, in the mid-1950s and transferred the family from Arizona. The Udall family home was located in a secluded, heavily forested backstreet near the Potomac River. Inside, they decorated the house lavishly in American Indian art, making it appear much different from the normal home at the time. Because of this unique decor, the *Washington Post* quipped in the 1960s that "the Udall home is a Museum of Indian Art."[1]

Due to Stewart's career as well as the Udalls' interest in the arts—Lee was the primary art connoisseur, while Stewart himself wrote poetry from time to time—the married couple became good friends with aging poet Robert Frost, hosting him for dinner in their McLean home on several occasions. The Udalls were initially drawn to Frost in the late 1950s during the famous poet's tenure as poetry consultant for the Library of Congress. When very few dignitaries and politicians visited him in his new role, the poet was perhaps annoyed and offended. Frost complained about being bored during a press conference, claiming that not a single member of Congress had come to see him. When the Udalls read this, Stewart decided to reach out to the poet and invite him over for dinner. To the surprise

Udall became friends with the poet Robert Frost, the duo
seen here in Dumbarton Oaks Park in Washington, DC.
Courtesy of the National Park Service.

of both Lee and Stewart, Frost accepted the invitation, and out of
this and many more dinner parties the relationship grew.[2]

One thing that came from the relationship between the politician and the poet was the tradition of having a poet conduct a
reading during presidential inaugurations. A few weeks before
President-Elect Kennedy's swearing-in ceremony, Udall proposed
to his boss that Frost read a poem during the inauguration. JFK was
largely seen as an energetic and educated leader, and what better
way to promote this than by having a famous poet-sage do a reading? Kennedy loved the idea, and it was arranged using Udall as

intermediary; Frost read "The Gift Outright" during the inauguration ceremony on a cold January day. Many presidents have since
had poets recite at their inaugurations.[3]

After the ceremony, while Kennedy and his beautiful wife, Jacqueline, were moving into the White House, Stewart Udall found
himself moving into his new workplace, the secretary of the interi-
or's office in the Department of the Interior building, just two blocks
away from the Oval Office.

Overview of the Department of the Interior

In the 1960s, perhaps no federal government department was as
diverse as the Department of the Interior. Upon assuming the role
of interior secretary in January 1961, Udall found himself immediately in charge of fifty-five thousand employees scattered among
approximately two dozen separate agencies and offices.[4] In order
for the reader to most easily make sense of these bureaus, the DOI's
various agencies, though overlapping in many regards, can loosely
be classified into four categories based on the primary natural resources they manage. These categories are public lands, energy and
minerals, water resources, and "other."

The US Fish and Wildlife Service, National Park Service, and
Bureau of Land Management were—and still are—the three Department of the Interior agencies most associated with public lands.
Each of the respective agencies oversees vast expanses of the nation's estate. The Fish and Wildlife Service, referred to colloquially
and simply as "Fish" by many DOI employees today, manages the
system of national wildlife refuges and safeguards the nation's wild
bird, mammal, and fish populations. The National Park Service is
the governmental bureau charged with both protecting and providing public use and enjoyment of the National Park System—Yellowstone, Yosemite, the Grand Canyon, Shenandoah, the National Mall,
and more than four hundred other sites. Finally, the Bureau of Land
Management, an agency that became the "arid sister" to the Department of Agriculture's Forest Service during the 1960s, oversees vast
tracts of generally dry lands in the Intermountain West, primarily
for grazing and extraction purposes up until Udall's tenure.

Regarding energy and mineral resources, included in the DOI in the 1960s were the offices of Oil and Gas, Coal Research, and Coal Safety, in addition to the Oil Import Administration and Bureau of Mines. The public power distribution firms of the Bonneville, Southeastern, and Southwestern Power Administrations also called the DOI home. With the US Department of Energy an addition during the Carter administration, interior secretaries prior to the late 1970s served as de facto energy secretaries.

The DOI also includes under its big umbrella a historically highly powerful and highly successful dam-building, reservoir-filling, water-managing agency in the Bureau of Reclamation, while the smaller Office of Saline Water oversaw desalinization efforts in the 1960s. Finally, the US Geological Survey (USGS), Bureau of Indian Affairs, Office of Territories, and a few other DOI agencies had their own foci, albeit mainly outside the realm of this publication and its focus on the environment.

Because of this diversity of agencies, the DOI has jokingly been referred to over the years as the Department of Everything Else, while Udall himself was once referred to as "Secretary of Things in General." Jokes aside, with all the agencies, the title of interior secretary included with it ample statutory responsibilities. Furthermore, each natural resource and each DOI agency "touched a special interest group somewhere," which served as "invitations to controversy, targets for writers from the smallest of publications to major dailies and networks," noted one departmental historian.[5]

Conservation Policies Rearrive at the DOI

On the topic of controversy, Udall certainly knew some of the recent interior secretaries preceding him had run things differently from the way he wanted to run them. For instance, the establishment of nature-based and outdoor recreation–based national park units practically came to a standstill in the late 1940s and 1950s, during a time when open lands were shrinking due to suburban sprawl, superlative scenery across the nation was being encroached upon, and the population had more time for leisure and recreation than ever before.

Indeed, President Eisenhower's first interior secretary, Douglas McKay, believed in the scaling back of what he referred to as federal government "socialism." As such, "Giveaway McKay," as his detractors called him, had a general conservation policy of proprivatization and prodevelopment. He pushed for the privatization of federally constructed dams, which many argued against because it would make select businessmen rich off of massive taxpayer-funded projects. Furthermore, many congressmen from western states believed that privatization of public dams would lead to their constituents paying a much higher cost for electricity and water. McKay also opened up dozens of national wildlife refuges to oil and gas development.[6]

The final straw, though, regarding McKay's fate as interior secretary was when one of the largest false mining claims in public lands history was uncovered. When the media and public learned that the Alabama-based Al Sarena Company had been using its mining claim on BLM lands within the state of Oregon to harvest mass quantities of timber rather than minerals, McKay, an Oregonian, was unable to escape the controversy and was forced to resign. His background as a car salesman rather than a conservationist never helped his image with progressives and New Dealers, either. "McKay had little understanding of complex conservation issues," noted historian Donald C. Swain.[7]

Ike's second interior secretary, Fred Seaton, actually pleased many conservationists by helping establish the massive Arctic National Wildlife Refuge in northern Alaska during the final months of the administration. As significant as this was, Seaton seemed to spend most of his energy on the Alaska statehood bill rather than on the growing conservation issues of the day, especially as they related to the lower forty-eight states. Furthermore, in carrying out the wishes of President Eisenhower, Seaton in general did not support federal government spending on conservation and anti-pollution measures.[8]

It's important to note that all of this was occurring in the context of massive suburban growth and prosperity. Because World War II was primarily fought in Europe and the Pacific, the economies and physical infrastructure of several European countries, as well as Japan, were devastated at midcentury; but luckily for the United States, its lands and cities were largely spared these wartime bombings and battles, and thus the country's economy was able to spring ahead while the rest of the countries of "the developed world" were still in the beginning stages of putting themselves back together. And so the late 1940s, '50s, and '60s were an era unlike any other in the country.

With couples often apart during the war years as American servicemen fought overseas, upon the men's return babies were born fast to make up for lost time, giving rise to the baby-boom generation, or the baby boomers. Americans began having larger families, reversing the decades-long trend of decreasing birthrates. These new and growing families needed places to live. Public and private incentives kicked in, and with many residents of the country looking outward from its cities instead of opting to stay and clean them up, suburbs grew at an unprecedented rate.

Popularized by folk singer Pete Seeger in 1963, the song "Little Boxes" satirized this new lifestyle of middle-class, predominantly white Americans. Enjoying unprecedented wealth and prosperity, they moved out into the countryside into standardized tract houses that "all looked just the same" and were constructed using the same materials, jokingly referred to in the song as "ticky tacky." Due to increasing wealth, the homes and yards these people moved into were generally much larger than in the prewar era, and they had all sorts of new kitchen gadgets and gizmos to make their lives easier. Increasing incomes also meant more opportunity for higher education and leisure time.

Seeger's little boxes and golf courses of suburbia grew exponentially as the country's population expanded quickly and as white middle-class and upper-class citizens left cities for the suburbs in record numbers. For instance, Fairfax County, Virginia, primarily a suburb of Washington, DC, grew from 98,557 inhabitants in 1950 to 455,021 people by 1970. The Los Angeles metropolitan area, including not only the city of LA but essentially the entire LA basin, grew from 4,367,911 people in 1950 to 8,463,213 residents by 1970. Finally, the Phoenix metropolitan area grew from 374,961 to 1,039,807 during the same twenty years.[9]

The creation of these suburban areas outside of central cities involved the construction of hundreds of thousands of homes and yards built larger than before the war, thousands of miles of paved roadways and highways, and hundreds of strip malls with large parking lots so that suburban residents could do their shopping, eating, and errands easily. All this led to millions of acres of largely natural land becoming urbanized, which had consequences for the environment. For instance, wild animals were forced to relocate in shrinking open spaces or were killed in the process of development. "Endangered Key deer cannot live in the midst of pizza parlors, and a marsh blacktopped for an airport will not sustain marsh dwellers," bluntly noted Udall's director of the Bureau of Sport Fisheries (US Fish and Wildlife Service), John Gottschalk, in 1968.[10]

In addition, rainwater that once fell onto soil and naturally evaporated or percolated into the soil to recharge groundwater now fell onto impervious surfaces such as rooftops, roadways, and parking lots, thus increasing the amount of dirty stormwater flowing directly into creeks, rivers, and, ultimately, bays and oceans. The increase in the number of cars and amount of time spent driving to and from work led to an increase in harmful emissions. Finally, open spaces simply disappeared at an alarming rate.[11]

All of this, then, was the world that Udall inherited as US secretary of the interior. Higher standards of living and a higher gross national product were certainly beneficial to many people in the country at midcentury, including Stewart Udall, but at what cost environmentally and socially? How could both the economy and the environment prosper, rather than just the economy? How could inhabitants of "little boxes" in suburbia, as well as people left behind in the inner cities, get into the open spaces of the country to enjoy healthful recreation in the great outdoors? These were the questions more and more on Udall's mind as a congressman and now as interior secretary.

To reiterate, the Arizonan believed that very little action had been taken in the Eisenhower administration regarding natural resource stewardship and conservation. Wanting to make up for lost time, the liberal, energetic, ambitious Udall immediately turned 1950s executive branch inaction on these topics into 1960s executive branch action. "This administration has an opportunity to make a record in conservation that would equal or excel that of Theodore Roosevelt," Udall told JFK at the very first cabinet meeting. Indeed, while the Theodore Roosevelt era ushered in the establishment of dozens of national monuments, forests, and national wildlife refuges, and while policies put in place by Franklin Delano Roosevelt reforested eastern woodlands via his Civilian Conservation Corps (CCC) and harnessed great rivers thanks to organizations like the Tennessee Valley Authority (TVA), Udall believed that the 1960s was in need of a "third wave" of conservation.[12]

Kennedy was not as enthusiastic about conservation and environmental protection as Udall was, but he did fully support the policies and ideas of the interior secretary that he had selected. JFK generally had a hands-off style of leadership with his cabinet secretaries, especially the cabinet members not directly involved in Cold War politics. This gave Udall practically a free hand to do what he believed best, and the White House staff in direct contact with Udall were supportive as well; there was no micromanagement of the 1960s interior secretary.[13]

Formulating the backbone of his policy, then, Udall told a group less than two months after he took office that the primary principle of the department would be to seek solutions for problems on the basis of what was best for the nation as a whole: "Decisions will never be made for the purpose of rewarding one special interest group against another, nor for the benefit of one segment of the economy to the detriment of the larger public interest. And we shall try never to forget that the 'larger public interest' includes the welfare of future generations."[14] The need for safeguarding natural resources for the long term—for those yet unborn—as well as the need for sustainably managing and balancing the natural resource needs of all sectors of society would be two recurring, interrelated concerns of Stewart Udall under JFK and LBJ, and in fact for the rest of his life.

With these general thoughts, ideas, and policies of Udall's in place, what was the interior secretary's plan for conservation in the 1960s? In a 1969 interview, he was asked how his progressive conservation plan had begun eight years earlier, and a modest Udall answered that "the thing sort of developed and evolved and grew and gained strength as we began to have some successes, as the country responded and as the country prodded us too—because it works both ways."[15] One of Udall's advisers noted that the interior secretary was extremely interested in expanding the National Park System, increasing recreational opportunities for urban masses, and diminishing pollution from the very beginning.[16]

The Primary Reasons for Udall's Success

But goals cannot become reality unless one succeeds. I believe that Udall succeeded and enjoyed unprecedented accomplishments while serving as interior secretary for at least eight key reasons. Each of these reasons is discussed with specific examples time and time again in the following chapters.

Highly Publicized Conservation Trips
A first reason for Udall's success as interior secretary involved his spearheading of highly publicized tours of proposed park sites and conservation projects. Whether touring the sandy soils of the proposed Fire Island National Seashore on Long Island with area politicians and media representatives, dedicating Northern California's Whiskeytown Dam with President Kennedy, or rafting eleven miles of the Rio Grande and exploring and hiking Big Bend National Park with Lady Bird Johnson, the interior secretary toured many areas, inviting and leading a cadre of journalists, politicians, local officials, and concerned citizens in the process. The journalists would then write about their experiences on these conservation trips, and since these experiences often involved visiting picturesque, sometimes superlative scenery, it generally meant good publicity in newspapers and magazines across the country. The public officials and citizens who attended the tours often thoroughly enjoyed them,

Udall and Lady Bird Johnson in Grand Tetons National Park, Wyoming.
With and without the first lady, Udall toured numerous proposed
and already established national park sites, lobbying for new park
bills in particular and attempting to drum up interest in conservation
in general. Courtesy of the National Park Service.

resulting in their further support of new parks and other conservation projects.

Widespread Public Interest and Bipartisanship on Conservation
Another reason for Udall's success was the fact that the 1960s was
a time when many different individuals and groups really pushed
for and supported conservation and environmental legislation.

This included select local citizens, conservation and environmental groups, and politicians, both Democratic and Republican.

David Brower, the outspoken executive director of the Sierra Club and a frequent visitor to Stewart Udall's office, was one of the most influential activists. However, many other "regular citizens" helped out as well. Indeed, Udall noted that while national parks were established by Congress, "Congress acts only when people demand.... It takes people who love the land and are willing to spend part of their lives to assure its preservation." He continued, "It takes many, many volunteer citizens who will spend their afternoons licking envelopes, and their evenings testifying at hearings, who will study the techniques of preservation, and persuade others to join their cause."[17]

Regarding lawmakers, Senators Henry "Scoop" Jackson (D-WA), Thomas Kuchel (R-CA), Frank Church (D-ID), and Edmund Muskie (D-ME), as well as Representative John Saylor (R-PA), were perhaps the biggest champions of conservation and environmental protection of the decade, according to Udall. It should be highlighted that two of these five politicians were from the Grand Old Party. "In Washington, there was a big tent on the environment," Udall remembered of the 1960s. "Republicans and Democrats, we worked together."[18] In the current day and age, a Republican environmentalist politician, specifically one who is passionately supportive of climate-change legislation, is extremely rare, to say the least. But the importance of Republicans in support of conservation and environmental legislation in the 1960s cannot be overstated.

While Congress held a Democratic majority throughout the decade, several Rockefeller Republicans, who would be referred to today as moderate Republicans, voted for key environmental legislation in the 1960s, much of which would not have passed into law without their support. Named for the political views of Nelson Rockefeller, governor of New York from 1959 to 1973 and vice president of the country under Ford from 1973 to 1977, classic Rockefeller Republicans included Kuchel, Senator Jacob Javits (R-NY), Representative Silvio O. Conte (R-MA), and others.

Several conservative Republicans also lobbied on behalf of the environment. Udall friend Rogers "Rog" Morton (R-MD) was one of these. A representative in the 1960s, Morton later served as chairman of the Republican National Convention as well as Nixon's second interior secretary. He was a conservative Republican with an environmental side. So too were Roman Hruska (R-NE), Wallace Bennett (R-UT), John Saylor, and many others.[19]

Not Afraid to Compromise

The third reason for Udall's great success as interior secretary was the fact that he was not afraid to compromise in order to create new parklands, wilderness areas, and national wildlife refuges. "Insistence upon a purist, 'all or nothing' position on complex issues can only dilute our influence," Udall once wrote. "The resulting inaction will mean lost opportunities in a period of 'last chances.'" Historian Barbara Leunes notes that, to Udall, "The danger was not in making mistakes, but in doing nothing. Therefore, he urged preservationists to be broad-minded and encouraged them to be willing to make temporary, creative compromises."[20]

Exceptional Staff

Besides bipartisanship and widespread public interest in conservation in the 1960s, Udall's conservation trips with the media, and his willingness to compromise, five other reasons for Udall's success are important and perhaps deserve longer explanations. The fourth reason that Udall enjoyed major success was because he surrounded himself with highly capable staff. The interior secretary brought good people with him from his congressional office and also was lucky to get solid political appointees working directly below him.

Udall's immediate office staff members and closest associates included, among others, assistant to the secretary Orren Beaty, whom Udall described as his "right-hand man." Beaty had served as Udall's assistant in Congress. Confidential assistant to the secretary Boyd Finch, a former college friend of Udall's, a lawyer, and fellow for Senator Lee Metcalf, was also an important member of Udall's inner circle.[21]

Regarding political appointees, James Carr was named by Kennedy as undersecretary of the interior, the number-two position in the department behind Udall. A career water and energy engineer and former staff member on both the House Committee on Interior and Insular Affairs and the Bureau of Reclamation, Carr was serving as assistant general manager of the Sacramento Municipal Utility District, an electric power firm, when he became the undersecretary. The Kennedy team believed that since Arizona and California had long disagreed with each other on Colorado River water allocations, and because Udall was from Arizona, then a high-up official of the Interior Department needed to be from California so as to not spark a political fire in the Golden State. Thus, Carr was appointed to the post.[22]

Carr and Udall got along "swimmingly," to quote one official. There was a private hallway between the interior secretary's and undersecretary's offices, and Udall would often walk into Carr's office, take his shoes off, stick his feet up on the desk, loosen his tie, and discuss pressing and controversial issues with Carr in order to get his opinions and thoughts.[23]

Besides Carr, Finch, and Beaty, assistant secretary for public land management (and later undersecretary of the interior) John Carver was also a close confidant of Udall's. Carver had previously led political campaigns in Michigan and had served on the staff of Senator Frank Church. John Kelly, Robert McConnell, D. Otis Beasley, and a few others were also high-up bureaucrats in the department and members of Udall's self-proclaimed "brain trust."[24]

One last Udall team member deserves recognition, his congressional liaison, Bob McCone. As the only Kennedy cabinet member with previous experience in Congress, Udall knew the importance of working well with the legislative branch, and McCone was one of Udall's links to it. McCone was on good terms and had working relationships with many congressmen and senators, including influential politicians Wayne Aspinall of Colorado and Clint Anderson

(D-NM). "[McCone] developed this staff of five or six people and they handled all Congressional contacts, did it extremely efficiently. He was one of the few people who, in effect, had the key to my door, could barge in anytime he wanted to," Udall noted during a 1969 interview. "I think one of the reasons we were highly effective was because he could get all the rumors and all the playbacks. Some of the Congressmen would tell him things they didn't want to tell me and he'd start every morning up there."[25]

The ORRRC's 1962 Report and the
Subsequent Bureau of Outdoor Recreation

A fifth reason the 1960s interior secretary had so much success in conservation and environmental protection was the findings of a 1962 report released by the congressionally chartered Outdoor Recreation Resources Review Commission as well as the subsequent work of the DOI's Bureau of Outdoor Recreation (BOR). With regard to the commission and bureau, back in 1958 President Eisenhower had signed a bipartisan law creating the ORRRC, and the commission was specifically tasked with determining the outdoor-recreation wants and needs of the American people at the present time as well as in 1976 and 2000; the recreational resources of the country available to satisfy those needs in the '60s, in 1976, and in 2000; and, finally, the specific policies and programs that would "ensure that the needs of the present and future are adequately and efficiently met."[26]

The act establishing the ORRRC called for an administering body to be made up of fifteen bipartisan commissioners. Specifically, it called for four members of the US Senate, four members of the US House of Representatives, and seven well-educated citizens to be appointed by the president. The commission, which included Republican John Saylor with Laurance Rockefeller as chairman, was required to issue its report by early 1962 and, at that point, dissolve, as it was not set up to be a permanent federal entity.[27]

In order to make its report accurate, the ORRRC surveyed sixteen thousand citizens as a major component of its research. The survey asked people about their background, economic status, what they did for outdoor recreation, what they wanted to do more of in terms of outdoor recreation, and why they didn't do these things.[28]

Some of the ORRRC report's 1962 findings, of which Udall very much took note, were as follows. First, the report claimed that outdoor opportunities were critically needed in or near metropolitan areas. "Three-quarters of the people will live in these areas by the turn of the century. They will have the greatest need for outdoor recreation, and their need will be the most difficult to satisfy as urban centers have the fewest facilities (per capita) and the sharpest competition for land use," noted the ORRRC. Second, the report noted that "water is a focal point of outdoor recreation. Most people seeking outdoor recreation want water—to sit by, to swim and fish in, to ski across, to dive under, and to run their boats over." Finally, the commission noted that outdoor recreation was a major leisure-time activity in the United States and that it was growing substantially in importance.[29]

The commission recommended several specific actions the country could take to expand recreational opportunities, specifically but not exclusively near metropolitan areas. Central to this was the formation of a new federal agency, the Bureau of Outdoor Recreation, to be established within the DOI in order to manage all recreational programs across federal agencies and to assist state and local governments as well. While National Park Service senior leaders objected to this on the grounds that they believed the BOR would be stepping on their toes (an office within the NPS had been managing outdoor-recreation programs and recommending new park sites for decades), the ORRRC noted that, by establishing the BOR as an agency without the responsibility of directly managing any federal lands like the NPS did, it could focus solely on outdoor recreation and the coordination between agencies thereof.[30] Indeed, according to BOR biographers Edwin Fitch and John Shanklin, NPS recommendations over the years sometimes had trouble materializing due to the fact that the agency, rather than bringing all public land bureaus to the table to talk, tended to act on its own, thus illustrating "the futility of handling problems of interbureau rivalry with unilateral recommendations." Udall agreed that new park-unit planning and recommendations would be more successful if they were overseen by the BOR rather than the NPS.[31]

So that the ORRRC's report wouldn't just be forgotten and ignored after its publication, as so many government reports have been, Udall pushed for the creation of the Bureau of Outdoor Recreation with Kennedy's natural resource adviser Lee White. The eventual result was the establishment of the BOR within the Department of the Interior. And when Udall and assistant secretary John Carver chose Ed Crafts, a high-up official of the US Forest Service, to be the director of the BOR, this nonpartisan selection in part fostered better relationships between the DOI and the Department of Agriculture.[32]

Cooperation Between the Department of the Interior and the Department of Agriculture

As such, a sixth key reason Udall was able to accomplish so much during his eight years was his department's cooperation and close working relationship with the US Department of Agriculture. "Cooperation between Freeman [the secretary of agriculture] and Udall warded off a collision between the two departments and established a relationship no one would have thought possible only a few years before," noted naturalist-writer Frank Graham Jr. in his 1970 publication, *Since "Silent Spring."*[33]

Indeed, historically, the US Department of the Interior and its National Park Service have clashed with the US Department of Agriculture and its Forest Service. This is largely due to a history of forced land transfers between the two departments. For instance, in the early 1900s, Congress transferred the national forests from the Department of the Interior to the Department of Agriculture. Later, many national parks and national monuments were carved out of national forest lands, resulting in large swaths of Forest Service domain transferring to the NPS. Just as sovereign countries do not like giving up land, many Forest Service administrators resented giving away their land to the National Park Service.[34] This inter-bureau bitterness perhaps reached its zenith during the tenure of FDR's interior secretary Harold Ickes, as Ickes publicly lobbied to solve the NPS-USFS dispute by transferring the US Forest Service to the Department of the Interior and then changing the name of the

Interior Department to the Department of Conservation. This made some Department of Agriculture and Forest Service officials even more upset.

Udall actually believed, like Ickes twenty years before him, that the Forest Service, being a public lands agency more than an agricultural and farm agency, ought to be moved from the Department of Agriculture to the Department of the Interior. However, he realized that if he argued for this, other departments could ask why Interior Department bureaus such as the Bureau of Territories were not under the Department of State or why the Bureau of Indian Affairs was not a bureau within the Department of Health and Human Services. In order to get above all this interdepartmental drama, Udall ultimately decided that while the NPS was best suited to administer new national park units, if more recreation areas and natural areas could be established and protected by creating some that were administered by the Forest Service, it would all be for the greater good. As a result, though the relationship was not perfect, Udall and the staff of the BOR ushered in unprecedented cooperation between the DOI and the Department of Agriculture. Udall himself invited Agriculture Secretary Orville Freeman on several conservation trips during the decade, and the duo partnered together on many initiatives.[35]

The Land and Water Conservation Fund

A seventh reason the St. Johns, Arizona, native was able to have so much success as secretary of the interior was his means of paying for many conservation projects: the Land and Water Conservation Fund. Indeed, while some of the new national park units of the decade were carved out of preexisting national forest and BLM lands, many others, primarily in the eastern United States, were carved out of private property, and Udall's LWCF enabled the purchasing of this property without an expansion of the federal budget. Many congressmen would never have approved additional federal allocations for purchasing new federal parklands, but Udall's fund, which he had been lobbying for in some form since his first month in Congress, got around this. Signed into law in September 1964, the LWCF accumulated moneys by way of entrance and user fees on

public land, sales of surplus federal land, and a federal tax on mo-
torboat fuel. While some public land users resented the user fees
and taxes, most went along with them. And additional LWCF moneys
came in 1968, when Udall and Representative John Saylor created
and helped pass an amendment to the LWCF that enabled revenues
from outer-continental-shelf oil taxes to be added to it up to an
annual amount of two hundred million dollars. This was initially
authorized for a five-year period but has since become a regular
source of funding for the LWCF.[36]

Despite its fluctuations in funding over the years due to differing political climates and congressional appropriations, the LWCF
has arguably been one of the most important and successful land-
conservation and outdoor-recreation programs in US history. Since
its beginning, through the purchase of lands for federal government
agencies or by providing matching grants to states, the LWCF has
created and expanded thousands of parks at the national, state,
county, and local levels. Specifically, billions of dollars have been
utilized over the years to acquire lands, create outdoor-recreation
facilities, or update preexisting outdoor facilities.[37]

Administered by the Bureau of Outdoor Recreation, Land and
Water Conservation Fund grants were authorized at the federal
level for the National Park Service, US Forest Service, and US Fish
and Wildlife Service (in the 1970s, the Bureau of Land Management
was authorized to receive LWCF grants).[38] Some of the most note-
worthy federal parklands established and purchased using LWCF
moneys during the decade included Fire Island National Seashore in
New York, Assateague Island National Seashore in Maryland, Padre
Island National Seashore in Texas, and Redwood National Park in
California.[39]

Regarding some specific US Forest Service properties, the Sylvania Tract in the Ottawa National Forest of Michigan, the Major
Realty Tract in the Ocala National Forest of Florida, and the Mineral King Basin in Sequoia National Forest in California were
purchased using LWCF moneys. For the National Wildlife Refuge
System administered by the US Fish and Wildlife Service, Mason
Neck National Wildlife Refuge in Virginia (which was lobbied for

by Udall, though established just after he left office), an expansion of Key Deer National Wildlife Refuge in Florida, and additions to the Patuxent Wildlife Research Center in Maryland were created thanks to LWCF funds.[40] (A discussion of LWCF urban grants is provided in chapter 11.)

His Voice and His Pen: The Quiet Crisis
An eighth significant reason for Udall's success was that he wrote and spoke exquisitely in support of conservation and environmental objectives. That is, he used his typewriter and his voice more passionately and more effectively than any other head of the DOI in history: he was "the articulate voice of environmental preservation," according to Gary Everhardt, former NPS director and historian.[41] To give a few examples from many, Udall attended and spoke at a heated town hall meeting in Indianapolis where he lobbied wholeheartedly for the establishment of Indiana Dunes National Lakeshore, and he wrote a newspaper article pushing for the creation of Redwood National Park in northwestern California.

Arguably Udall's best and most influential piece of writing was published in 1963 in the form of a two-hundred-page book titled *The Quiet Crisis*. With help from key office staff as well as Pulitzer Prize-winning author Wallace Stegner, whom Udall persuaded to leave Stanford University for a semester in order to serve as "writer in residence" at the Interior Department, the publication was one of the first books to chronologically spotlight the country's environmental history, or "the land-and-people story of our continent," as Udall referred to it.[42] The book sold thousands of copies and was on the *New York Times* best-seller list for several weeks. Historian Samuel Schmieding notes that *The Quiet Crisis* was one of the most important books ever written by a sitting politician.[43]

The book's premise involved Udall's conviction that American progress in space and technology, as well as in industrial, commercial, and residential development and expansion, was coming at a tremendous cost to the nation's natural heritage. "America today stands poised on a pinnacle of wealth and power, yet we live in a land of vanishing beauty, of increasing ugliness, of shrinking open space, and of an overall environment that is diminished daily by pollution and noise and blight," the interior secretary wrote. "This, in brief, is the quiet conservation crisis of the 1960s."[44]

Udall believed that the only way to end this quiet crisis was to embrace natural resource conservation and sustainably manage the public domain so that children one hundred years hence could continue to both revere and utilize it. The interior secretary believed that the best way to get the nation on board with this message was to educate it on the history of natural resource abuse as well as conservation in America. Thus, he wrote the book, using time spent traveling on planes, early mornings at his house, and other spare time for the research.

Udall opened *The Quiet Crisis* with a chapter on early American Indians, in which he wrote that, during their long tenure, "the land remained undefiled save for scars no deeper than the scratches of cornfield clearings or the farming canals of the Hohokams on the Arizona Desert." The book then transitioned to "the White Indians" of "Daniel Boone, Jed Smith, and the Mountain Men." *The Quiet Crisis* went on to discuss the 1800s' "raid on resources": specifically, how the American landscape and its natural resources were severally degraded by the lumberman's ax, the farmer's plow, the miner's shovel, and the cattleman's cow.[45]

Udall blamed the destruction of the eastern and northern forests, the removal of topsoil, the slicing of mountainsides, and the resulting pollution of wild rivers on "the myth of superabundance," namely, that white European Americans who settled the United States and pushed westward believed that there was so much land and so many natural resources that the matter of conserving them for the future would never be a problem. Natural resource shortsightedness and ignorance, according to Udall, were primary causes of the country's pending quiet conservation crisis.[46]

Yet even during this era of land degradation, there was, to quote Stegner, a conservation "backfire...burning upwind against the current of claim and grab and raid."[47] Udall wrote about farsighted individuals who put the public long-term good before shortsighted profit. He wrote about the solitary thoughts of Henry David Thoreau at Walden Pond in Massachusetts; the creation of a system of federal forest reserves under early 1890s president Benjamin Harrison and John W. Noble, his interior secretary; and the "big names" of conservation history, including Gifford Pinchot, John Muir, the two Roosevelt presidents, and Aldo Leopold. He touched on urban conservation and the great works of Frederick Law Olmsted, and on philanthropy and environmental nonprofits such as the Nature Conservancy.[48]

At the end of the book, after reiterating the environmental problems of the time—which included increasing air pollution, growing water pollution, decreasing open spaces, and more—Udall issued a new call for conservation and environmental protection. Specifically, he called for the establishment of the Land and Water Conservation Fund in order to round out the National Park System, National Forest System, and National Wildlife Refuge System. He called for a national wilderness system to protect primitive lands for primitive recreation and nature. He called for a permanent conservation corps, similar to FDR's Civilian Conservation Corps, "to rehabilitate and renew our public lands." He called for increased scientific research on the two largest natural resources, the two resources owned by all the people of the world: the oceans and the atmosphere. He called for full-scale collaboration among science, industry, business, and government to "write bright new chapters in the conservation of some resources." He called for "government leadership and government investment...in traditional conservation work." Last but not least, agreeing with pioneering ecologist Aldo Leopold, the interior secretary called for a land ethic. "Beyond all plans and programs, true conservation is ultimately something of the mind," wrote Udall. "We must develop a land conscience that will inspire those daily acts of stewardship.... Only an ever-widening concept and higher ideal of conservation will enlist our finest impulses and move us to make the earth a better home both for ourselves and for those yet unborn."[49]

The popularity of *The Quiet Crisis* helped educate society on conservation, environmental problems, and the need for environmental protection. It also lifted Udall's name and stature, and perhaps the interior secretary's greatest piece of fan mail came from Rachel Carson. Udall fully endorsed Carson's *Silent Spring*, the famous book spotlighting the problems of pesticide use that had been released the year before, and the female scientist fully endorsed Udall's book. She wrote Udall her letter after he sent her a copy. "I found in your book a direct and vital message. We all owe you a debt of gratitude for having written it," Carson wrote Udall, as cancer was overcoming her body and she was nearing a premature death. "I know that I, for one, gained a broader perspective of the history of American conservation, and a deeper admiration and respect for those who struggled so long and faithfully to preserve even remnants of the continent it was.... When will people fully understand and accept the obligation to the future—when will they behave as custodians and not owners of the earth?"[50]

~

UDALL'S GENERAL CONVICTIONS, policies, and reasons for success—including his writings like *The Quiet Crisis*—having now been touched on, and the organization of the Department of the Interior having been discussed, the next several chapters will analyze the 1960s interior secretary's primary conservation work. Beginning with national parks, each chapter covers a specific natural resource or related topic.

Notes

1. Finch, *Legacies of Camelot*, 16.

2. Ibid., 17-18. Finch, an assistant to Interior Secretary Udall, describes Udall's unique friendship with Frost in detail. For more on this friendship, see also Thomas G. Smith, "Robert Frost, Stewart Udall, and the Last Go-Down," *New England Quarterly* 70, no. 1 (1997): 3-32, jstor.org/stable/366525?seq=1#page_scan _tab_contents.

3. Ibid., 23-26. Frost actually prepared a bold, original poem for the Kennedy inauguration, but due to the cold weather and his getting sick, the aging poet decided to read his classic "The Gift Outright" instead.

4. US Department of the Interior, "Organization of the Department of the Interior as of January, 1961," in *The Department of the Interior during the Administration of President Lyndon B. Johnson, November 1963-January 1969*, administrative history, pt. 1, box 151, Udall Papers.

5. Ibid.

6. Sirgo, *Establishment of Environmentalism*, 18. See also Elmo Richardson, "The Interior Secretary as Conservation Villain: The Notorious Case of Douglas 'Giveaway' McKay," *Pacific Historical Review* 41, no. 3 (1972): 333–45, jstor.org /stable/3637862?seq=1#page_scan_tab_contents; Dyan Zaslowsky and T. H. Watkins, *These American Lands: Parks, Wilderness, and the Public Lands*, 173; and Elmo Richardson, *Dams, Parks, and Politics: Resource Development and Preservation in the Truman-Eisenhower Era*.

7. Ibid. For Donald G. Swain, see his *Wilderness Defender: Horace M. Albright and Conservation* (Chicago: University of Chicago, 1970), 302.

8. Richardson, *Dams, Parks, and Politics*, 3, 187–201. See also Martin V. Melosi, "Lyndon Johnson and Environmental Policy," 120. Michael W. Giese gives a more sympathetic summary of McKay and Seaton in "A Federal Foundation for Wildlife Conservation: The Evolution of the National Wildlife Refuge System, 1920–1968" (PhD diss., American University, 2008), 263–73, 307–11. According to Walter R. Borneman in *Alaska: Saga of a Bold Land* (New York: HarperCollins, 2003), 415, soon after becoming interior secretary, Udall was asked to rescind the Arctic National Wildlife Refuge order. He declined to do so.

9. Population numbers according to the US Census Bureau.

10. US Department of the Interior, news release, "Udall Calls for Cooperative Effort to Save Wildlife," July 21, 1968, fws.gov/news/Historic/NewsReleases/1968 /19680721a.pdf.

11. For more on the rise of suburbia in the mid-twentieth century, specifically its negative consequences, see James Howard Kunstler, *The Geography of Nowhere: The Rise and Decline of America's Man-Made Landscape* (New York: Free Press, 1994); and Matthew E. Kahn, "The Environmental Impact of Suburbanization," *Journal of Policy Analysis and Management* 19, no. 4 (2000): 569–86.

12. US Department of the Interior, Office of the Secretary, "A Report for the President on a Proposal for a Kennedy Administration Parks Conservation Program, June 20, 1961, from Secretary Udall," box 88, Udall Papers. For more on JFK's relationship with his cabinet, see Theodore C. Sorenson, *Kennedy*, 260–61, 265, 276.

13. Transcript, Stewart L. Udall oral history interview II, by Joe B. Frantz, May 19, 1969, LBJ Library, lbjlibrary.net/assets/documents/archives/oral_histories /udall/UDALL02.PDF. Graham, in *Presidents and the American Environment*, stresses the point that Kennedy was not that interested in conservation (187–208). Regarding LBJ, Graham believes that the LBJ administration did accomplish a lot. However, he notes that LBJ liked to take personal credit for the work of others (in Congress or otherwise) in terms of conservation (209–21).

14. "We Must Act Now for More National Parks," *Audubon*, March 1961, 77, box 206, folder 7, Udall Papers.

15. Transcript, Udall oral history interview II.

16. Transcript, Orren Beaty Jr. oral history interview III, by William W. Moss, October 31, 1969, JFK Library, archive1.jfklibrary.org/JFKOH/Beaty,%20orren /JFKOH-OB-03/JFKOH-OB-03-TR.pdf.

17. Stewart Udall, introduction to *Wild Peninsula: The Story of Point Reyes National Seashore*, by Laura Nelson Baker.

18. Keith Schneider and Cornelia Dean, "Stewart L. Udall, Conservationist in Kennedy and Johnson Cabinets, Dies at 90," *New York Times*, March 22, 2010.

19. Both Bennett and Hruska voted in favor of the Wilderness Act, Land and Water Conservation Fund, Clean Air Act, and more. Hruska was also a big proponent of expanding the National Wildlife Refuge System.

20. Leunes, "Conservation Philosophy of Udall," 62, 71.

21. Transcript, James K. Carr oral history interview I, November 18, 1970, JFK Library, archive2.jfklibrary.org/JFKOH/Carr,%20James%20K/JFKOH-JKC-01 /JFKOH-JKC-01-TR.pdf. Regarding praise for Orren Beaty Jr., see John A. Carver Jr., recorded interview by William W. Moss, October 21, 1969, 31, JFK Library Oral History Program, archive2.jfklibrary.org/JFKOH/Carver,%20John%20A.,%20Jr /JFKOH-JAC-06/JFKOH-JAC-06-TR.pdf.

22. Ibid. See also transcript, Orren Beaty Jr. oral history interview IV, by William W. Moss, November 7, 1969, JFK Library, archive2.jfklibrary.org/JFKOH /Beaty,%20Orren/JFKOH-OB-04/JFKOH-OB-04-TR.pdf. Ian Robert Stacey, in "The Last Conservationist: Floyd Dominy and Federal Reclamation Policy in the American West" (PhD diss., University of Montana, 2013), claims that Carr created many problems for Udall and was in some cases even insubordinate. However, I have not seen other sources claiming this.

23. Ibid.

24. Transcript, Beaty oral history interview III.

25. Transcript, Udall oral history interview II.

26. Edwin M. Fitch and John F. Shanklin, *The Bureau of Outdoor Recreation*, 60.

27. Ibid., 61–62.

28. Ibid., 64.

29. Outdoor Recreation Resources Review Commission, "Outdoor Recreation for America: A Report to the President and to the Congress by the Outdoor Recreation Resources Review Commission." For Udall's endorsement of the ORRRC report, see US Department of the Interior, Office of the Secretary, news release, "Secretary Udall Pledges Support of ORRRC Proposals," February 1, 1962, fws.gov /news/Historic/NewsReleases/1962/19620201b.pdf.

30. Fitch and Shanklin, *Bureau of Outdoor Recreation*, 49, 69. See also Ney C. Landrum, *The State Park Movement in America: A Critical Review* (Columbia: University of Missouri Press, 2004), 187–89.

31. Ibid. The Department of the Interior's Bureau of Outdoor Recreation was relatively short-lived, however. In 1978 it morphed into the Heritage Conservation and Recreation Service. In 1981 the Reagan administration dissolved this agency and transferred its duties back to the National Park Service.

32. John A. Carver Jr., oral history interview IV, by William W. Moss, September 23, 1969, 18–23, JFK Library, archive2.jfklibrary.org/JFKOH/Carver,%20John%2 0A.,%20Jr/JFKOH-JAC-04/JFKOH-JAC-04-TR.pdf.

33. Frank Graham Jr., *Since "Silent Spring"* (Boston: Houghton Mifflin, 1970), 232.

34. Ironically, the initial national forests, known as forest reserves, were actually administered by the Interior Department. In 1905 they were transferred to the Department of Agriculture.

35. Transcript, Stewart L. Udall oral history interview I, by Joe B. Frantz, April 18, 1969, LBJ Library, lbjlibrary.net/assets/documents/archives/oral_histories /udall/UDALL01.PDF. Though not 100 percent controversy free, the relationship between the two departments in the 1960s culminated in the so-called Treaty of the Potomac, a meeting between Interior Secretary Udall and Agriculture Secretary Orville Freeman in 1963, in which they agreed to have their bureaus work together, cooperate, and assist each other.

36. Thomas G. Smith, "John Kennedy, Stewart Udall, and New Frontier Conservation." For more on the political drama behind the passing of the LWCF, see Richard A. Baker, "The Conservation Congress of Anderson and Aspinall, 1963-1964," *Journal of Forest History* 29, no. 3 (1985): 104-19, jstor.org/stable/4004822?seq =7#page_scan_tab_contents. See also Thomas G. Smith, *Green Republican: John Saylor and the Preservation of America's Wilderness*, 245.

37. Fitch and Shanklin, *Bureau of Outdoor Recreation*, 89; Carol Hardy Vincent, "Land and Water Conservation Fund: Overview, Funding History, and Current Issues," Congressional Research Service, July 10, 2006, digital.library.unt.edu/ark :/67531/metacrs9469/m1/1/high_res_d/RL33531_2006Jul10.pdf. The National Park Service now manages the LWCF, and its extensive database listing all projects can be found at waso-lwcf.ncrc.nps.gov/public/index.cfm.

38. Specifically, LWCF funds were authorized for the Bureau of Sport Fisheries and Wildlife, a subagency within the US Fish and Wildlife Service. This subagency eventually morphed into the US Fish and Wildlife Service.

39. Fitch and Shanklin, *Bureau of Outdoor Recreation*, 89, 96, 127.

40. Ibid.

41. William C. Everhart, *The National Park Service*, 38.

42. Stewart L. Udall, *The Quiet Crisis*, viii; Wallace Stegner to Udall, December 7, 1963, azmemory.azlibrary.gov/cdm/singleitem/collection/uoaslu/id/20/rec/1.

43. Samuel J. Schmieding, *From Controversy to Compromise to Cooperation: The Administrative History of Canyonlands National Park* (Washington, DC: National Park Service, 2008), 85-88.

44. Udall, *The Quiet Crisis*, viii.

45. Ibid., 4, 25, 54-68.

46. Ibid., 54, 178-79.

47. Wallace Stegner, *Marking the Sparrow's Fall: The Remaking of the American West*, 136.

48. See Udall, *The Quiet Crisis*, 39-53, 69-172.

49. Ibid., 173-91.

50. Rachel Carson to Udall, November 12, 1963, University of Arizona Special Collections Department Special Exhibition, September 2014.

4 | Expanding the National Park System in the US West

What I wanted…and also believed in, too,
was that Tucson should be surrounded
by protected areas, with native wilderness areas,
and that was true in the end.

OF ALL THE DUTIES that Stewart Udall had as interior secretary, perhaps his favorite was serving as the "steward-in-chief" of the National Park System. Having a passion for the great outdoors, Udall saw the need to preserve superlative examples of America's landscapes, flora, fauna, and history before they were consumed by post–World War II industrial, commercial, and residential development. He also wanted to secure "backyard" outdoor recreation sites for inner-city and suburban masses, as the Outdoor Recreation Resources Review Commission recommended. As such, he put the expansion of America's system of federal parklands high on his list of priorities. And he succeeded in this expansion, helping push through more additions to the National Park System than any other US secretary of the interior in history. Udall helped create a record sixty-four new national park units from 1961 to early 1969. In comparison, Harold Ickes, FDR's interior secretary and the longest-serving such secretary in history, helped establish fifty-one national park units from 1933 to early 1946, while the US secretary of the interior with the third-highest number of national park units was Cecil Andrus, President Jimmy Carter's conservation crusader. From 1977 until early 1981, Andrus helped establish forty-seven new units, many of which were in Alaska.[1] "More park land and more irreplaceable natural resources were preserved for public use during [Udall's] term of office than under any other Secretary of the Interior," noted historian Barbara Leunes in 1977. "By act of Congress or by executive proclamation, 246,000 acres of land were placed in the national park system during the Kennedy years and 3,605,000 acres during the Johnson administration." As a result, Leunes notes that in the autumn of 1966, while signing new conservation and national park bills, LBJ told the press, "The person mainly responsible for it all is Secretary Udall."[2]

As the history of the National Park System and National Park Service has been well documented, this chapter begins with only a brief background on the subject. The chapter then delves into approximately a half-dozen examples from around the western portion of the country of Udall's involvement in and successes with establishing new national park units. It might be interesting for the reader to determine which of the eight reasons for Udall's success spotlighted in the previous chapter are at play in each park example below.

Brief Background on the National Park System

From the establishment of the US National Park Service in 1916 to the early 1930s, the system of national park units included both national parks and national monuments. Established by Congress and the president, national parks tended to be created in order to protect and promote large tracts—generally more than fifty thousand acres—of remote and scenic lands. Differentiated from national parks were national monuments, which could be established by the president's signature without the consent of Congress thanks to the powers vested in him or her by the 1906 Antiquities Act. National monuments were established, by and large, on smaller land tracts in order to protect specific archaeological, historical, or scientific features. Stephen Mather, the charismatic and energetic first director of the fledgling NPS, largely contained the National Park System to these two administrative-unit types.[3]

Mather's successor, Horace Albright, expanded the National Park System drastically. With the backing of Interior Secretary

TABLE 4.1. National park units established during Stewart Udall's years as secretary of the interior

Agate Fossil Beds NM	John F. Kennedy NHS
Alibates Flint Quarries NHS	John Muir NHS
Allegheny Portage Railroad NHS	Johnstown Flood NMem
Amistad NRA	Lake Chelan NRA
Appalachian NST	Lake Meredith NRA
Arbuckle NRA (later expanded and reclassified as Chickasaw NRA)	Lincoln Boyhood NMem
	Mar-a-Lago NHS (later declassified)
Assateague Island NS	Marble Canyon NM (later absorbed
Bighorn Canyon NRA	into Grand Canyon NP)
Biscayne NP	Nez Perce NHS
Buck Island Reef NM	North Cascades NP
Canyonlands NP	Ozark NSR
Cape Cod NS	Padre Island NS
Cape Lookout NS	Pecos NHS
Carl Sandburg Home NHS	Pennsylvania Avenue NHS
Chamizal NMem	Pictured Rocks NL
Curecanti NRA	Piscataway Park
Delaware Water Gap NRA	Point Reyes NS
Eisenhower NHS	Redwood NP
Fire Island NS	Roger Williams NMem
Fort Bowie NHS	Ross Lake NRA
Fort Davis NHS	Russell Cave NM
Fort Larned NHS	Sagamore Hill NHS
Fort Smith NHS	Saguaro NP–West
Fort Union Trading Post NHS	Saint Gaudens NHS
Frederick Douglass NHS	San Juan Island NHP
George Rogers Clark NHS	Saugus Iron Works NHS
Guadalupe Mountains NP	Theodore Roosevelt Birthplace NHS
Hamilton Grange NMem	Theodore Roosevelt Inaugural NHS
Herbert Hoover NHS	Whiskeytown NRA
Hubbell Trading Post NHS	Wolf Trap NP for the Performing
Indiana Dunes NL	Arts

Note: Unless otherwise noted, the listing above reflects the current name of each national park unit. A few of the parks were established in the 1960s under a different name or park classification and then renamed or reclassified.

Note: Park title abbreviations are as follows: NHP, National Historical Park; NHS, National Historic Site; NL, National Lakeshore; NM, National Monument; NMem, National Memorial; NP, National Park; NRA, National Recreation Area; NS, National Seashore; NSR, National Scenic Riverways; NST, National Scenic Trail.

Harold Ickes, Albright, a history enthusiast, orchestrated the transfer of numerous Department of War–administered battlefield and fort memorials to the NPS, in addition to all of Washington, DC's national parks. Just afterward, between 1933 and the mid-1940s, several new national parks and monuments were established thanks to the conservation leadership of Ickes, FDR, and others. Following this, at midcentury, a new class of national park units known as national recreation areas slowly evolved, based largely on the concept of reservoir, water-based recreation.

By and large, though, in the 1950s, America's population, cities, suburbs, commerce, and industry all expanded rapidly and significantly, yet there was little expansion of nature-based and recreation-based units of the National Park System. Udall observed this and reversed course as interior secretary. He pushed for a major uptick in each of the various kinds of national park units—national parks, national monuments, national recreation areas, national historical parks, national historic sites, and so on—and orchestrated new types. To Udall, if the National Park System couldn't expand in the 1960s to protect additional natural and recreation areas, it never would; the land would be lost to commercial, industrial, and residential development forever due to a societal emphasis on and belief in post–World War II progress.

Canyonlands National Park

Just a few weeks after becoming interior secretary, Udall received a joint request from Senator Frank Moss, Representative David King, and Representative Morris Blaine Peterson to determine the possibility of establishing a national park or national recreation area in the Canyonlands country of southeastern Utah.[4] With significant state and local interest in increasing mineral extraction in the area, the delegation, by contrast, thought that the land might be more valuable as a national park unit. Udall responded to their request by leading a highly publicized tour of the area and then throwing his full support behind the national park campaign. The result of these efforts was the 1964 establishment of the 237,000-acre Canyonlands National Park, a place of such beauty that the secretary of the interior referred to it as "one of the most magnificent places in the United States."[5]

As backstory, it should be noted that a national park unit for the area had first been studied in the 1930s, with an additional survey in the 1950s, and NPS director Conrad Wirth publicly supported the establishment of a national recreation area based on the principle of multiple use. Wirth attempted to please all the area interests by permitting grazing, hunting, and mineral, oil, and gas extraction— in addition to recreation—in the proposed national recreation area. Even so, the Department of the Interior's own Bureau of Land Management as well as Utah's state park system administrators didn't want an official recreation area. The Canyonlands country was actually situated on BLM lands, and BLM administrators at the time didn't want to change anything. Meanwhile, Utah state park authorities were looking to expand their system of state parks, and the Needles, an area named for its standing-up rock formations and situated in the heart of the proposed national recreation area, was at the top of their list of new acquisitions. It should be noted, as well, that Utah managed its system of state parks at the time in multiple-use fashion. This was the state of disarray upon Udall's becoming interior secretary, and hence three of Utah's four federal politicians asked the interior secretary to jump into the fray and help sort out what was best for the area.[6]

As luck would have it, at the end of a preplanned work trip to southeastern Utah in April 1961 Udall's eyes gazed out over the Canyonlands area. With Bureau of Reclamation director Floyd Dominy and others, Udall had been on the ground at Rainbow Bridge National Monument, studying the effects that Glen Canyon Dam's rising backwaters were having on the soil and sandstone beneath the natural bridge. Afterward, en route from Page to Denver aboard Dominy's private jet, the duo gazed out over Canyonlands country from roughly ten thousand feet in the air. While Dominy excitedly explained his plans to Udall for additional large-scale dam projects along the Colorado River in the area, Udall looked out his window and saw the need for something else: "My goodness, that's a national park!" the interior secretary thought excitedly. While he did not tell Dominy his thought at the moment, Udall was utterly impressed by what he had seen.[7]

In fact, so enthralled was Udall with Canyonlands that "after returning to Washington he began to move the political mountains necessary to create a national park in the region," notes National Park Service historian Samuel Schmieding.[8] The secretary of the interior did this by first planning out a five-day summertime exploration of Canyonlands country. He invited area politicians and representatives from influential media venues, including but not limited to *Life* and *National Geographic* photographers and writers; the three Utah congressional delegates who were in favor of the park, and who wanted Udall to announce Kennedy administration support; Utah governor George Dewey Clyde; National Park Service officials; the secretary of agriculture, Orville Freeman; Lee Udall; and others. Bates Wilson, a legendary Canyonlands character, superintendent of nearby Arches National Park, full supporter of the new national park, and soon-to-be friend of Udall's, prepared the trip's itinerary and essentially led the group in the field.[9]

In July the entourage spent the better part of a week venturing through the proposed national park unit. By jeep, by boat, by military helicopter, and by hiking boots, Udall and company explored such scenic areas as Anderson Bottom, Grandview Point, Upheaval Dome, Dead Horse Point, Chesler Park, Elephant Canyon, Druid Arch, Salt Creek Canyon, Angel Arch, and Cave Spring. The group was blessed with unseasonably pleasant rather than hot weather, and almost everyone became utterly impressed with the landscape.[10] "The diversity and beauty of the area had an extraordinary impact on the writers that came along," Udall remembered years later.[11]

At a wrap-up press meeting in Moab, just outside the proposed park, on the last day of the trip, Udall and many others expressed their dreams and plans for establishing Canyonlands National Park. Practically the only person not enamored with the national park idea was Clyde, the governor, and he showed this by lapsing into

Udall played a significant role in the establishment of southeastern Utah's
Canyonlands National Park. Seen here is the view through Mesa Arch,
located in the Island in the Sky district of the park. Photo by author.

complete silence during most of the press conference. When one of
the journalists put Clyde on the spot by asking him why he didn't
approve of the national park, Clyde publicly responded by saying,
"You see, we could need the land for building stones one day."[12] Such
visions of natural resource extraction in the area were the primary
reason compromises were fleshed out and the national park took
three more years to officially be created.

Indeed, while the Utah governor eventually approved of the national park bill, he and Senator Wallace Bennett of Utah, as well as
local mineral, energy, and grazing interests, were the main antipark
factions. Canyonlands was in a remote area, and although uranium
mining, cattle grazing, and oil and gas development did not reign
supreme over the land, they still had a presence.

In opposing the park, Bennett, Clyde, county officials, and others
argued that rugged country protected itself. They also used a classic
argument, namely, that setting aside land as a national park would
close it to economic interests and thus deplete the local economy.[13]
Herein lies a recurring theme in the history of the National Park

Additional view of Canyonlands National Park. Photo by author.

Service and its National Park System: the lockout argument. Time and time again, numerous residents living near proposed parkland have largely opposed the establishment of national park units in their areas because they see them as closing off the land to their economy. Five or ten years after the park is established, though, communities on the peripheries of national parks find their economies more diversified and better off than before the establishment of the park, thanks to tourism.[14] National park units attract tourists, and tourists require gas for their vehicles, food for their bellies, and hotel rooms for their sleep, thus leading to expenditures in the local economy surrounding the national park. As Stewart's brother Morris once put it, "I've been through legislation creating a dozen national parks, and there's always the same pattern. When you first propose a park, and you visit the area and present the case to the local people, they threaten to hang you. You go back in five years and they think it's the greatest thing that ever happened. You go back in twenty years and they'll probably name a mountain after you."[15] At any rate, the writers and photographers who tagged along

on the Udall trip marketed the positive experience as well as the
need for a national park in national media outlets. But the opposition, especially Bennett, was still a major challenge to passing the
national park bill.

One primary debate centered on the size of the park. Udall and
Senator Moss claimed that the minimum amount of land needed for
Canyonlands National Park was 330,000 acres. Ideally, though, they
wanted a 1-million-acre park. Nevertheless, understanding political realities, they submitted bills for the 330,000-acre park. Bennett
and Clyde, on the other hand, pushed for a significantly smaller national park. One of Bennett's proposals called for a meager 11,000-
acre park, with three small units to it, each separated from the
others. Another Bennett bill called for no national park at all but a
parkway, or highway with scenic views, running through the area.
Bennett was actually openly verbally hostile toward Udall, telling
a group of Utah citizens not to listen to the interior secretary's
proposals unless they wanted the state to "become a Udall-created
wasteland."[16]

Udall, unfazed, and with the backing of David Brower and the
Sierra Club, commissioned the University of Utah's School of Business Research to complete an economic study of the benefits of
the national park. The completed study, which foresaw significant
economic improvements to the surrounding area due to tourist expenditures, was then released publicly. Udall also commissioned
Charles Eggert, an award-winning photographer and filmmaker,
to produce a documentary film on the proposed national park. The
film, titled *The Sculptured Earth*, received accolades. It premiered in
Salt Lake City in a seven-hundred-seat theater, and Udall personally
introduced it beforehand.[17]

After much debate, in 1964 Congress took up the cause of Canyonlands National Park in earnest. With Bennett's proposals overshadowed in part by will of the majority Democratic Congress,
compromises were nonetheless hammered out.[18] The boundaries of
the park shrank to allow mining and energy exploration just outside
it rather than inside it, and in select areas of the park grazing was
permitted for a multiple-year period before an ultimate phaseout.

Udall and others who had seen the area firsthand knew that grazing was not a big business in the area, and with lack of water, grasses, and extreme summer heat, the "hoofed locusts," as California naturalist John Muir called them, would not really do significant damage to the park's natural resources.[19]

As a result of these compromises, the bicameral legislature passed the 237,000-acre Canyonlands National Park bill, and on September 12, 1964, Lyndon Baines Johnson signed the bill into law.[20] This proved a major victory for Udall and, over the long haul, National Park System enthusiasts, hikers, campers, four-wheel-drive adventurers, and nature and geology students. It also proved a benefit for southeastern Utah's economy, as a modern-day visit to Moab, Utah—the closest town to Canyonlands as well as to Arches National Park—will convey. Eventually, the park was lightly developed to include formalized hiking trails, a couple of small campgrounds, and a couple of visitor centers and employee housing areas. Canyonlands was also later expanded in size and now includes the 330,000 acres once proposed by Udall and Moss.[21]

Saguaro National Park–Tucson Mountain District

While Udall gained an interest in Canyonlands just after becoming interior secretary, he supported the establishment of another southwestern national park unit as a congressman and then saw it through to fruition during the first year of the Kennedy administration. Establishing this park unit would protect unique Sonoran Desert flora and fauna as well as petroglyphs inscribed in rock on Signal Hill by prehistoric Hohokam peoples. The park encompassed a range of mountains just five miles west of downtown Tucson and was no doubt an area that Udall hiked while going to college and practicing law there. Thanks to Stewart Udall, this landscape would be preserved forever as part of Saguaro National Monument, later reclassified and hereafter referred to as Saguaro National Park.

Since 1961 Saguaro National Park has been unique in that it has consisted of two units, the Saguaro East–Rincon Mountain District, just east of Tucson, and the Saguaro West–Tucson Mountain District, just west of Tucson. While Saguaro East was established by

Herbert Hoover during his final days in office, Saguaro West was established by the signature of John F. Kennedy. This process began two years before the JFK administration, though, when Representative Stewart Udall discovered that a senior official within the Department of the Interior had, without warning, prior public notification, or prior debate, authorized the leasing of 7,600 acres by a private company to develop a massive open-pit mine on mountainous land just west of Tucson.[22]

The mining land made up the northern portion of Tucson Mountain Park, a park under long-term lease to Pima County by the Department of the Interior's Bureau of Land Management. While small-scale open-shaft mining had a history in the Tucson Mountains, some residents became livid when word got out about the massive open-pit mine proposal, as it threatened to mar the landscape and diminish the seemingly pristine views. Congressman Udall sounded the alarm on behalf of his constituents. "I strongly protest the August 25 order signed by Assistant Secretary Ernst which opened up 7,600 acres of land in Tucson Mountain Park for mineral location," Udall wrote in a telegram to Interior Secretary Fred Seaton. "This order has caused consternation in Tucson as this is a major recreational asset of this community and adequate notice or hearing was not given of the proposed change of land use status. In my opinion the overriding public interest requires that the August 25 order be rescinded and a full scale hearing be held in Tucson where all interested parties and public agencies can be heard. I urge that you take such action without delay."[23]

Fortunately, a Tucson hearing was exactly what happened, and support to cancel the mining order was almost unanimous. "Let lands of equivalent mineral value be substituted if need be, but away from our backyard," argued a retired US Air Force veteran and resident of Tucson. Udall himself argued on behalf of the area's unique nature. "The area contains, in a virgin setting, one of the best Saguaro forests in the United States," he told the crowd. Udall also told the group about his vision for having the proclaimed mining area in Tucson Mountain Park designated as a national monument and having in this bill a no-mining clause.[24]

While federal protection in the form of a national monument would give the mountains much more official and permanent protection than if they remained a Pima County park, Senator Barry Goldwater (R-AZ) and others protested Udall's plan. "Pima County is capable of taking care of its own park," Goldwater claimed.[25] Because of this faction, the national monument bill Udall wrote and proposed to Congress in 1960 didn't pass. Be that as it may, after Udall became interior secretary in early 1961, he again pushed for national monument status.

In doing so, he had to delicately maneuver around Representative Wayne Aspinall (D-CO), the powerful chairman of the House Interior and Insular Affairs Committee and an individual whom Udall saw as both a personal mentor and a dictator. Aspinall wasn't necessarily against new national park units, but he believed the authority should come from Congress, not the executive branch (perhaps because he was in Congress and not the president). That is, Aspinall was fully against presidential use of the Antiquities Act to create national monuments. On the other hand, though, Udall knew that the legislative process for establishing a new national park unit could take considerable time, and he was adamantly against further mining in the Tucson Mountains. In the end, Udall maneuvered around Aspinall, and Kennedy added the Saguaro West addition to Saguaro National Park. "I went to President Kennedy's people and told them I wanted to do this for my hometown, for Tucson, and I told them Aspinall wouldn't like it. Then I went to Aspinall and told him I was going to do it and this was my backyard, and he couldn't seriously object. What I wanted…and also believed in, too, was that Tucson should be surrounded by protected areas, with native wilderness areas, and that was true in the end."[26]

Indeed, with Kennedy in full support of his interior secretary's preservation and conservation initiatives, the president signed Proclamation 3439, "Enlarging the Saguaro National Monument, Arizona," on November 22, 1961. Thus, he established what is today known as the fifteen-thousand-acre Saguaro National Park–West, or Saguaro National Park–Tucson Mountain District. There is no mining in the park, only significant Sonoran Desert beauty.[27]

Guadalupe Mountains National Park

"My mouth is still part way open," expressed Udall, with a kid-on-Christmas-morning expression, after touring and hiking through the Guadalupe Mountains of western Texas in 1964. "I expected something spectacular but this exceeds my expectations. With canyons that deep and the escarpment, the area certainly will make a good addition to the National Park System if Congress approves it." Indeed, on another proposed national park unit mission to see the land for himself and drum up interest, Udall was all in on the proposal while discussing a Guadalupe Mountains National Park with western Texas and southeastern New Mexico officials.[28]

The main impetus for establishing Guadalupe Mountains National Park was a land donation: in the late 1950s aging oil geologist Wallace Pratt approached the NPS and offered his fifty-six-hundred acres. Retired at an early age, Pratt and his wife lived on the edge of their Guadalupe Mountains property in a long, rectangular house they called "Ship on the Desert." The bulk of their landholding was in McKittrick Canyon, a deep, rugged canyon revered today for its fall foliage and the year-round waters of its trickling stream. The NPS accepted Pratt's donation in three easements, and after showing Udall his property in 1964, the oil geologist then went to DC and, with the interior secretary by his side, testified to Congress about the beauty of the area and the need for the mountains to be established as a national park. "The cause of conservation needs a new generation of outdoor philanthropists," Udall pleaded in a 1961 newspaper article. One outdoor philanthropist that the conservation movement got was Wallace Pratt.[29]

While the NPS was obtaining Pratt's property, it learned around the same time that the bordering and much larger landholdings of J. C. Hunter Jr. were for sale. Hunter's father had purchased the property, and while both father and son had managed a cattle ranch on generally the flatter portion of their land, they had kept the rugged mountainous terrain, comprising most of the seventy-two-thousand-acre ranch and including the highest peaks in Texas, at elevations between eight and nine thousand feet, largely in its

Udall also successfully lobbied for the establishment of Guadalupe Mountains National Park in western Texas. Seen here is the massive rock outcropping of El Capitan, one of the highest peaks in the park—and in the state of Texas. Photo by author.

natural state. In light of this, an NPS report was released, opting for a twenty-seven-thousand-acre national park, including about a third of Hunter's land in addition to Pratt's. However, when a high-up official in the NPS notified Udall that all of Hunter's property was for sale, and furthermore that Texas contained very little public land, Udall came to envision a larger park.[30]

All of this activity occurred in the early 1960s, before the Land and Water Conservation Fund had passed. As such, Udall first attempted to get Texas philanthropic organizations to purchase Hunter's land and then donate it to the NPS. While this plan did not pan out, Udall was happy to learn that practically all West Texas politicians supported idea of the national park, as it would be a cause for state pride. Moreover, unlike the local opposition to Canyonlands National Park, El Paso, Carlsbad, and other communities around the proposed Guadalupe Mountains National Park saw it as a boon for their economies. In fact, during Udall's 1964 visit to the region,

J. C. Hunter met the interior secretary with a handshake and a tour of his property rather than with a shotgun; supposedly Udall was met with the latter during a visit to the proposed Prairie National Park in Kansas.[31]

After holding various meetings in the nation's capital with Hunter's real estate agent, Texas governor John Connally, and progressive representative Ralph Yarborough, the national park plan was firmed up and the stars aligned: Yarborough introduced the bill in Congress, and the LWCF Act passed. Then, after a controversy over oil-drilling rights was resolved and the park bill passed both houses of Congress, LBJ authorized the establishment of Guadalupe Mountains National Park on October 5, 1966. Hunter's property was then purchased in parcels using the Land and Water Conservation Fund, as were other small parcels of private property. The national park was officially dedicated and opened to the public a few years later. With its outstanding hiking opportunities, expansive views, and diverse ecosystems, Guadalupe Mountains is one of my favorite parks in the National Park System today.[32]

Ozark National Scenic Riverways

Moving east from arid West Texas, across the Texas plains, and into the dense forestlands of eastern Oklahoma, Arkansas, and southern Missouri to an area of the country known as the Ozarks, one finds a national park unit very different from Guadalupe Mountains, established in the 1960s. This park had, as its backbone, clean, clear, cool water. Indeed, the Ozark National Scenic Riverways, established on the Jacks Fork and Current Rivers in southern Missouri, is unique in that it was the first series of rivers in the United States to be federally protected in its free-flowing state. Who had a major hand in helping establish the national park unit? Stewart Udall.

Learning of the push to establish a special river park in the area by then Jefferson National Expansion Memorial superintendent George B. Hartzog Jr., whom Udall would bring to the nation's capital just months later as the new NPS director, the interior secretary visited the area during the autumn of his first year as a cabinet member. For two days, Udall, Hartzog, Ozarks author and environmentalist Leonard Hall, fervent anticommunist congressman Richard Ichords (who had actually invited Udall to come down to the rivers), and others explored the Jacks Fork and Current Rivers.[33] The group enjoyed white-water rafting, fishing, drinking springwater directly out of the earth, swimming, and even skinny-dipping late at night. The interior secretary was thoroughly impressed with the undammed clean-water rivers, and he became excited about the opportunity for establishing a unique park. "The main feature would be conservation, the preservation of a great rivers system, a system that our Geological Survey calls the finest group of 'untouched' rivers in the country," Udall said in a press release before heading back to DC. "I think that this could be one of the most valuable additions to the park system we could have in the next few years. The springs, the type of mountain, the animals, the plant growth all are distinctive."[34]

Establishing a national park unit, as well as the larger national forest preceding it in the 1930s, was seen by many southern Missourians as a way to boost the area economy, as the Ozarks had been in economic decline and actually losing population due to logging firms pulling out after exhausting the timber supply in the early 1900s. Still, during his tour of the rivers, the interior secretary observed signs on certain sections of the riverbank reading, "Udall: Go home!"[35] When asked about the signs by the media, the interior secretary noted, "Most of the opposition to this thing comes from people who don't have their facts straight.... I predict that the people who are opposed [to the park site] may someday find they're the chief beneficiaries of such a monument or park."[36]

As it turned out, the main opposition stemmed from the belief that if the area was turned into a national park or monument, area residents would lose their hunting rights. Seeing that hunting was a staple part of Ozarks culture and heritage, instead of pushing for national park or national monument status for the rivers—national park unit designations generally outlawed hunting—Udall and the NPS pushed for a more recreation-oriented, national riverways designation, allowing hunting. With this, local opposition became mostly local support.[37]

While much of the national park unit was slated to be carved out of preexisting national forest lands, one other debate, besides the one about hunting, concerned the lands along the river, specifically whether the government should purchase private inholdings along the waterways or turn them into scenic easements. While Representative Thomas Curtis submitted a bill to Congress in support of the easements, which meant allowing private property owners along the rivers to keep doing with the land what they had been doing before the park was established, eventually all of Missouri's congressional delegation united in favor of purchasing the inholdings. Thus, the more comprehensive park became the winner.[38]

The riverways legislation was helped along by Kennedy when he endorsed its establishment during a broad conservation speech to Congress in 1962. Of course, Udall and his staff were the ones who actually proposed and then wrote the speech.[39]

For these reasons and more, Ozark National Scenic Riverways was established in 1964, thus protecting 140 miles of the rivers as well as their banks and immediate surroundings. For the first time, the federal government permanently preserved a river in its wild state, thus initiating a balancing of dam building with the preservation of free-flowing water. Indeed, in 1971 Udall would note that the creation of the Ozark National Scenic Riverways "was a pioneering concept for conservation which led to the enactment in 1968 of the Wild and Scenic Rivers System Act."[40]

Whiskeytown National Recreation Area

A couple thousand miles west of the Ozarks, just west of the Northern California city of Redding, lies Whiskeytown-Shasta-Trinity National Recreation Area. The establishment of this unique three-units-in-one recreation area in the early 1960s represented a new era in cooperation between the Department of the Interior and its National Park Service and the Department of Agriculture and its Forest Service.

First, some background: the mountains just west and north of Redding, where the national recreation area is located today, were mined extensively during the California Gold Rush era. Then, as gold mining faded and farming the fertile Central Valley took hold, California farmers and city officials, wanting to make sure they had water for their growing populations, looked for a new kind of gold: water. As a result, from the mid-1930s to the early 1960s, Shasta Dam was built with California's largest reservoir, Shasta Lake, filling in behind it; Trinity Dam was built, creating Trinity Lake behind it; and in the same area, Whiskeytown Dam was built, creating its namesake reservoir.[41]

At the time that Udall became interior secretary, some government reports had proposed a national recreation area centered on the three lakes in order to provide water-based recreation to the populace. Learning of this, Udall approached Agriculture Secretary Orville Freeman about creating the recreation area. In March 1961, the two cabinet members had pitched a five-point conservation plan to Kennedy that included new programs to "develop the full recreational potential" of both the national forests and the National Park System.[42] Udall, Undersecretary James Carr, who was a native son of the Whiskeytown region, and NPS officials worked with Freeman and USFS officials on a plan for the recreation area that would meet both goals. In the end, it called for a Forest Service–administered Shasta-Trinity National Recreation Area, since the Forest Service already managed the lands in and around the two lakes. It also recommended the purchasing of lands around Whiskeytown Lake and then turning the area into an NPS-administered national recreation area.[43]

While this settled things as far as government officials were concerned, it was not okay with some of the people living inside the proposed Whiskeytown National Recreation Area. Not wanting to give up their mountain homes and livelihoods for the establishment of the recreation area, they complained. One N. D. Nelson told a newspaper that Udall was "empire building," while Whiskeytown resident Norma Vergnes contended that Udall and Representative Harold "Bizz" Johnson, the local congressman and an additional supporter of the national recreation area, were "playing footsie with Khrushchev; they're selling us down the river to serfdom and slavery."[44] Of course, Udall didn't turn Vergnes into a slave, but eminent domain did claim her house and property.

But it was for the greater good, arguably. On a conservation trip through the western United States arranged by Udall, President Kennedy, with the interior secretary sitting behind him, dedicated Whiskeytown Dam in September 1963. A couple of years later, Congress authorized and LBJ signed the recreation area into law. Today, more than eight hundred thousand people visit Whiskeytown National Recreation Area annually, primarily to escape the intense summer heat of the northern Sacramento Valley by boating and swimming on the reservoir. Included in this number of visitors are hundreds of area fifth graders, who spend a night away from home obtaining healthy doses of the great outdoors at Whiskeytown Environmental School.[45]

Notes

1. A listing of national park units by date of authorization and establishment can be found in US National Park Service, *The National Parks: Shaping the System*, 1991.

2. Leunes, "Conservation Philosophy of Udall," 87.

3. The history of the National Park System and its National Park Service has been exceptionally well documented over the years, and I didn't think it needed substantial repetition in this publication. NPS history has been a deep interest of mine, however. For thorough NPS histories, see Alfred Runte, *National Parks: The American Experience* and *Allies of the Earth: Railroads and the Soul of Preservation* (Kirksville, MO: Truman State University Press, 2006); Douglas H. Strong, introduction to *Nature and the American: Three Centuries of Changing Attitudes*, by Hans Huth; Richard West Sellars, *Preserving Nature in the National Parks: A History*; Horace Albright, Russell E. Dickenson, and William Penn Mott Jr., *National Park Service: The Story Behind the Scenery* (Whittier, CA: KC Publications, 1978); Robert Shankland, *Steve Mather of the National Parks* (New York: Alfred A. Knopf, 1954); Donald C. Swain, *Wilderness Defender: Horace M. Albright and Conservation* (Chicago: University of Chicago Press, 1970); Kim Heacox, *The Making of the National Parks: An American Idea* (Washington, DC: National Geographic Society, 2001); and Lary M. Dilsaver, ed., *America's National Park System: The Critical Documents* (Lanham, MD: Rowman & Littlefield, 1994).

4. US Department of the Interior, *The Department of the Interior during the Administration of President Lyndon B. Johnson, November 1963–January 1969*, administrative history, pt. 2, box 151, 83, Udall Papers.

5. National Park Service, "Stewart Udall Speaking at Grand View Point, Canyonlands National Park, July 6, 2006," nps.gov/cany/learn/historyculture /stewartudall.htm.

6. Samuel J. Schmieding, *From Controversy to Compromise to Cooperation: The Administrative History of Canyonlands National Park* (Washington, DC: National Park Service, 2008), 85–88. In the early 1960s, NPS director Conrad Wirth proposed Canyonlands as a national reserve rather than a national recreation area. He almost got it right…In today's somewhat confusing National Park System nomenclature, national reserves refer to National Park System units that are actually administered by state governments—Idaho's City of Rocks National Reserve, for instance. National preserves are national park units that, in general, allow hunting, some mineral and energy extraction, and subsistence uses. The concept of a national preserve was popularized in the 1980 Alaska National Interest Lands Conservation Act legislation, in which many of Alaska's national parks gained official national preserve areas. And so Wirth's proposal, by allowing multiple uses, is more in line with a national preserve designation. For more on National Park System nomenclature, see Laura B. Comay, "National Park System: What Do the Different Park Titles Signify?," Congressional Research Service, February 20, 2013, fas.org/sgp/crs/misc/R41816.pdf.

7. National Park Service, "Stewart Udall Speaking at Grand View Point."

8. Schmieding, *From Controversy to Compromise to Cooperation*, 96.

9. National Park Service, "Stewart Udall Speaking at Grand View Point." See also Jen Jackson Quintano, *Blow Sand in His Soul: Bates Wilson, the Heart of Canyonlands* (Moab, UT: Friends of Arches and Canyonlands Parks, 2014), 88–90. Arches was technically a national monument during the time of Wilson. It was reclassified as Arches National Park in the early 1970s.

10. Schmieding, *From Controversy to Compromise to Cooperation*, 96–97.

11. National Park Service, "Stewart Udall Speaking at Grand View Point."

12. Ibid.

13. Ibid. See also Schmieding, *From Controversy to Compromise to Cooperation*, 97–100.

14. See Jared Hardner and Bruce McKenney, *The National Park System: An Economic Asset at Risk* (Washington, DC: National Parks Conservation Association, 2006).

15. Morris K. Udall, Bob Neuman, and Randy Udall, *Too Funny to Be President*, 77–78.

16. Schmieding, *From Controversy to Compromise to Cooperation*, 98.

17. Ibid., 99–100.

18. The specific session of Congress is remembered as the Conservation Congress due to the significant conservation and environmental bills it passed. This list of bills includes the Wilderness Act, the Lands and Water Conservation Fund, bills establishing several national park units, and more.

19. National Park Service, "Stewart Udall at Grand View Point."

20. Schmieding, *From Controversy to Compromise to Cooperation*, 106.

21. Ibid., xiii.

22. National Park Service, *History of Mining in Saguaro National Park, West* (site brochure).

23. Western Union telegram, Udall to Fred A. Seaton, US secretary of the interior, September 12, 1959, box 54, folder 7, Udall Papers. For general information on the history of Tucson Mountain Park and Udall's "Saguaro National Park–West" involvement, see Sam Negri, *Movers and Shakers: The Creation of Tucson Mountain Park*. For specific information on Saguaro West, see Berle Clemensen, *Cattle, Copper, and Cactus: The History of Saguaro National Monument*, Historic Resource Study (Washington, DC: National Park Service, 1987), and Douglas S. Kenney and Doug Cannon, "Saguaro National Park Case Study," University of Colorado–Boulder Natural Resource Law Center, 2004, scholar.law.colorado.edu/cgi/view content.cgi?article=1022&context=books_reports_studies.

24. See newspaper clippings in box 3, folder 3, Udall Papers.

25. Jim Cooper, "Udall's National Park Idea Is Opposed by Goldwater," *Tucson Daily Citizen*, October 29, 1959, newspapers.com/newspage/23031132/.

26. Negri, *Movers and Shakers*, 26.

27. Ibid., 28. Ironically, there is a small memorial in the Saguaro National Park–West visitor center dedicated to Stewart Udall's brother Morris Udall; someone seems to have mixed up the two brothers, as Morris did much for conservation over his career, but the creation of Saguaro National Park–West primarily involved Stewart, not Morris. The memorial should be changed to honor Stewart.

28. "Udall Impressed by Visit to Guadalupe Mountains" (unidentified newspaper), December 12, 1964, box 119, folder 14, Udall Papers.

29. Judith K. Fabry, "The Role of Wallace Pratt," in *Guadalupe Mountains National Park: An Administrative History* (Washington, DC: National Park Service, December 1988), npshistory.com; "Noted Geologist 'Does Something' About America's Natural Beauty," *Arizona Daily Star* (Tucson), July 28, 1965.

30. Judith K. Fabry, "National Park Service Interest in the Guadalupe Mountain Ranch" and "Legislative History," in *Guadalupe Mountains National Park*.

31. Hugh Morgan, "Udall Visits Canyon, Attends Barbecue: Secretary Impressed by Area," *El Paso (TX) Times*, December 13, 1964. See also Monte Latimer Monroe, "Glenn Biggs and the Crusade for Guadalupe Mountains National Park" (master's thesis, Texas Tech University, 1991), repositories.tdl.org/ttu-ir/bitstream /handle/2346/59780/31295006177579.pdf?sequence=1.

32. Fabry, "Legislative History."

33. Donald L. Stevens Jr., *Homeland and a Hinterland: The Current and Jacks Fork Rivers*, Ozark National Scenic Riverways Historic Resource Study (Washington, DC: National Park Service, 1991), 202.

34. Dale Freeman, "Said the Secretary: 'At Least Nobody Shot at Us'—Interior Chief Jumps into Row over Scenic Ozark Rivers Park," *Springfield (MO) News and Leader*, September 24, 1961, box 156, folder 6, Udall Papers.

35. Ibid.

36. Marsh Clark, "Not Merely Monument: Udall Is Strong for Ozarks as Site for National Park," *St. Louis Globe-Democrat*, September 24, 1961, box 156, folder 6, Udall Papers.

37. James E. Price, "The Preservation of Two Wild and Scenic Ozark Rivers," National Park Service, nps.gov/ozar/learn/historyculture/establishment.htm; Tim Palmer, *Endangered Rivers and the Conservation Movement* (New York: Rowman & Littlefield, 2004), 162. See also George B. Hartzog Jr., *Battling for the National Parks*, 59–69.

38. Stevens, *Homeland and a Hinterland*, 201–2.

39. Transcript, Stewart L. Udall oral history interview II, by Joe B. Frantz, May 19, 1969, LBJ Library, lbjlibrary.net/assets/documents/archives/oral_histories /udall/UDALLO2.PDF.

40. Stewart L. Udall, *America's Natural Treasures: National Nature Monuments and Seashores*, 41.

41. Anna Coxe Toogood, *Whiskeytown National Recreation Area Historical Resource Study* (Washington, DC: National Park Service, 1978), npshistory.com/publications /whis/hrs/contents.htm.

42. "A Report for the President on a Proposal for a Kennedy Administration Parks Conservation Program," June 20, 1961, JFK Library, online copy.

43. Al M. Rocca, *Whiskeytown National Recreation Area: A History* (Scotts Valley, CA: CreateSpace, 2010).

44. "Federal Land Grabbing," *Sacramento Union*, December 25, 1961; "Shasta Board Hears Protests on US Recreation Control," *Sacramento Bee*, March 20, 1962, box 156, folder 8, Udall Papers.

45. Jim Milestone, introduction to *Whiskeytown National Recreation Area*, by Rocca, 9.

5 | Expanding the National Park System in the US East

*I was impressed beyond my imaginings
by the superb quality of the remaining beaches,
dunes, natural vegetation, and wildlife habitat.*

THIS CHAPTER'S OPENING QUOTE from Udall, spoken during the congressional debates over whether to establish Indiana Dunes National Lakeshore, represents the interior secretary's belief in the "necessity of now." To the St. Johns native, America's booming economy during the post–World War II era did some great things for the country, but this increasing industrial, commercial, and residential development also caused massive amounts of previously undeveloped land to be paved and built on at an unprecedented rate. Udall believed that additional lands needed to be protected in perpetuity for scientific, recreational, and ecological purposes, and that if they didn't get preserved in the 1960s, they never would.

With the country east of the Mississippi River being, in general, more populated and developed than the west, the secretary of the interior believed this "necessity of now" was especially true with the partially wild landscapes of the east. The Outdoor Recreation Resources Review Commission and National Park Service were suggesting a series of national seashores and lakeshores to protect much of the last remaining wild shoreline across the Great Lakes, Atlantic Seaboard, and Gulf Coast for outdoor recreation and natural resource preservation, and Udall was fully in favor.

Since European Americans primarily settled the East Coast and eastern half of the country before the western portion, there are tens of millions more acres of wild federally owned lands in the West than the East. Due to this, the Department of the Interior has been more associated historically with the West. Udall has been given ample credit, though, for increasing the DOI's responsibilities in the eastern United States and, in so doing, making it a truly national department. A primary method for Udall bringing the DOI more into the eastern United States was through new national park units.

Two of the first national parklands that Udall lobbied for after becoming interior secretary were Massachusetts's Cape Cod National Seashore and Texas's Padre Island National Seashore. Perhaps strategically emphasized by Udall in order to get presidential and vice presidential support for his general conservation plans, these two parks represented, respectively, JFK's and LBJ's home states. Certainly, the president and vice president appreciated Udall's assistance in the matters, as it's generally seen as a feather in the cap for any sitting politician to get a national park unit in his or her state while serving in office.

Every national park unit establishment story can be fascinating, and the interior secretary also had a great role in the creation of Assateague Island National Seashore, Fire Island National Seashore, and Indiana Dunes National Lakeshore. In addition to looking at the origins of these three units, this chapter analyzes Udall's involvement in the establishment of the Appalachian National Scenic Trail and passage of the National Trail System Act. Last, it looks at the improvements Udall helped oversee in the National Park Service, the government agency composed of the employees who administer and staff the national parks. With these examples of Udall's involvement with the national parks in the east, in addition to the western parks, it should become even clearer what an impact he had on the establishment of new national parks and what a passion he had for the National Park System, a passion I share.

Assateague Island National Seashore

A national seashore three hours east of the nation's capital and Baltimore, located on the eastern shore of Maryland, Assateague Island National Seashore today is an expanse of relatively wild sandy shoreline complete with habitat for various shorebirds and wild ponies. It's also a place where Marylanders and urbanites can escape to for a day of sand, sun, and fun. Sea fishing and beach relaxing are the most popular pastimes. Perhaps ironically, this mostly wild landscape, whose sands are subtly but constantly changing due to storms and wind, was actually slated to become a massive housing development in the 1950s.

Real estate developers during this time acquired the land and subdivided it successfully, resulting in the sale of eight thousand lots to approximately thirty-six hundred owners. But while a road and street signs were constructed, only about fifty beach houses were ever built. This was primarily due to the remoteness of the area. Access to Assateague Island was only by ferry at the time, and, furthermore, the real estate developers didn't follow through in developing island infrastructure outside of neighborhood roads and housing-tract foundations. This resulted in most of the property owners dragging their feet in building their homes.[1]

Add to this scenario a major winter storm in 1962 that wreaked havoc across the Eastern Seaboard, including the Assateague area. Half the beach homes were destroyed, and eerie photos showed the island's roads mostly covered in sand. Additional storms throughout the next two years caused repeated infrastructure damage and beach erosion. These factors led some to believe that the island might not be best utilized as a residential area. What could the sandy area be used for instead?[2]

Secretary Udall and the governor of Maryland agreed in June 1962 to have the Bureau of Outdoor Recreation make a study of the area to determine its best use. When the analysis was complete, the BOR recommended that the area should be a national seashore for public recreation. Udall fully endorsed this plan.[3] While the interior secretary argued that a public seashore would be for the greater good, a few argumentative island home owners opposed the plan. Both sides of the debate were spotlighted in a *Washington Post* article in 1963:

ASSATEAGUE ISLAND, Md., June 24—Secretary of the Interior Stewart Udall stood ankle deep in sand on a remote dune here today and argued face-to-face with an angry group of Worcester County officials and landowners who oppose Federal acquisition of the land.

"You sir, are on our land, and you're trying to use our money to take it away from us," Philip King, president of the Ocean Beach Club, which represented the Island's 3,200 land owners, said as he shook a finger in Udall's face....

Udall hopes to have the Federal Government acquire the underdeveloped island from its present 3,200 owners, build a system of dunes to prevent further erosion and turn it into "one of the finest beach areas between Cape Cod and Cape Hatteras."

To sell his program to Worcester County and members of Congress, Udall set upon the island with an airborne task force of Interior officials, two Senators, four Congressmen and a host of newsmen.

They were loaded in two helicopters and five jeeps at Wallops Island, after a flight from Andrews Air Force Base, for a sightseeing tour of the Virginia and Maryland sections of Assateague.

At 11 A.M., the helicopters and jeeps converged on a spot that moments before had been as desolate as any other on the island, and Udall's group met with the Worcester officials....

"Let me take a few minutes to explain 'this invasion,'" Udall said. "We should have learned something from the past of this island. Unless the right kind of job of dune stabilization is done, the island will soon be in a dangerous situation."

He recommended a continuation of the wildlife refuge on the Virginia section of the island and "some recreational accessories and a beach up to National Park standards," for the Maryland section....

Worcester officials prefer a program of private development with a public beach front.

"I don't see anything wrong with letting Americans build
on their own land," King, a former National Parks official, told
Udall. "If things had been done as you say, the Pilgrim Fathers
would have had to go back to Holland. You want to keep the
whole place a wilderness," King added.

"If your attitude had prevailed," Udall shouted back, "there
would be no National Park System."[4]

While the news column probably overdramatized the controversy surrounding Udall's visit, fortunately for Udall and admirers
of Assateague Island National Seashore today, most of the interior
secretary's entourage agreed with his sentiments. Senator Daniel
Brewster of Maryland said after Udall's speech that he was "tremendously impressed with the sincerity of the Secretary's words and
the wisdom of his project." Representative Rogers C. B. Morton, also
of Maryland, a Republican, friend of Udall's, and future interior secretary himself, as well as James Glenn Beall, also a Republican and at
the time a legislator for Maryland and a future US senator, thought
the national seashore was a good idea, too. The article noted that
Beall "thoughtfully squirted 'OFF!,' an insect repellant, on members
of the tour as Udall gave the initial briefing." Indeed, Assateague
Island is well known for its summertime mosquitoes.[5]

Newspaper article and mosquitoes aside, Udall and his staff
wrote the first draft of the national seashore bill and then sent it
onward to Congress, where Morton then introduced it. Debates
were heated, though, with continued opposition from Worcester
County officials and home owners. The result was two years of back-
and-forth in the legislature, with the original bill being amended
several times.[6]

In the end, the bill that President Lyndon Baines Johnson signed
into law on September 21, 1965, which authorized Assateague
Island National Seashore and allowed for its lands to be purchased
from private owners, included, for better or worse, some compromises from all sides. For instance, the remaining few homes were

permitted to remain on the island, though Udall argued successfully against having an access road the entire length of Assateague Island. Also, Maryland created and kept a portion of Assateague Island as its own state park. Finally, a bridge was constructed over the northern portion of the island to allow visitors and residents easy access to the national seashore and state park.[7]

Fire Island National Seashore

Up the coast from Assateague, past Atlantic City and the Jersey Shore and just northeast of New York City on Long Island, is a national park unit that Udall once referred to as a "Central Park by the sea."[8] This is Fire Island National Seashore, a twenty-six-mile stretch of natural dune fields, maritime forest, and coastal waters, bordered by private housing developments. During summertime it's one of the most popular areas on Long Island and in the New York City area for spending time on the beach.

The major push to create this national seashore occurred after the same 1962 storm that wreaked havoc on Assateague Island infrastructure destroyed portions of Fire Island. NPS reports of the mid-1950s had recommended the establishment of Fire Island National Seashore, and after the severe storm Udall urged that immediate thought be given to this concept in order to provide public use and natural resource protection of the shoreline. At the interior secretary's direction, a committee of federal, state, and local officials made an aerial study of the shoreline and then recommended that a seven-mile seashore be protected for public recreation purposes. In response, the NPS and Bureau of Outdoor Recreation conducted further research and found that a national seashore was warranted.[9]

Udall's stance was similar to his approach to the Guadalupe Mountains, in that he approved of the national seashore but pushed for a larger one. He particularly eyed the primitive northeastern portions of the long, linear barrier island and envisioned the seashore stretching all the way up to the village of Southampton. This undeveloped area, Udall believed, could complement the southwestern half of the national seashore, which was slated to run in parcels between preexisting island communities. To the secretary's delight,

New York senators Kenneth Keating and Jacob Javits, as well as Representative John Lindsay, all Republicans, introduced bills conforming to his views of the larger park, consisting of seventy-five hundred acres of land. Yet there were challenges in swiftly establishing the national seashore, and these challenges involved Robert Moses, Lee Dennison, and others.[10]

Moses, a renowned urban planner, master builder, and long-time Long Island State Park commissioner, and Dennison, a Suffolk County executive, were both endorsers of large-scale shoreline engineering and development. As such, during the meeting with Udall, they pushed for a developed seashore with an access highway running its full length and connecting the island's small communities. Moses, in particular, also pushed for significant dredging work to be completed in surrounding water channels and for the dredged soil to then be built into a large flood wall, or dike, to protect the island from future storms. Finally, Moses and Dennison argued that the cost of purchasing the larger stretch of seashore would be too expensive. Thus, the duo and others recommended a smaller seashore than the one Udall and the Republican lawmakers envisioned, encompassing only fifteen hundred acres. For all these reasons, Udall left his first visit to the island discouraged. "It may well be that we are 20 years too late, as they say," the interior secretary lamented. "I can't get support in Washington if there is no local support for such a park."[11]

Udall was adamantly against the highway and dredging projects. "We need to provide for the preservation of natural open spaces free of automobile traffic, parking lots, and hot-dog stands," the interior secretary wrote to Fire Island communities.[12] In his mind, the island would lose its mostly natural character by building the road, and, regarding protecting the island and its residents from future major storms, Udall believed that small-scale dune-stabilization projects needed to be undertaken rather than massive engineering feats.[13]

In order to push Congress to create the park, as well as to push the public to push Congress to create the park, Udall wrote an article for the New York Times at the height of the seashore debate. "A Century ago a landscape architect named Frederick Law Olmsted was ridiculed when he suggested that the dreary flats in the middle of Manhattan could one day become a magnificent area of municipal greenery," the interior secretary wrote. "Yet because of Olmsted's foresight millions of New Yorkers now find relaxation and recreation in the verdant acres of Central Park." He continued:

> Today, by an accident of geography, we have an opportunity comparable to Olmsted's. Right now we can save Fire Island for future generations. We can preserve a superb stretch of unspoiled coastline which will become a seashore sanctuary for the citizens of the nation's largest metropolis....
>
> It is up to Congress to act. It is last call for the shorefront of Long Island. If Congress does not act swiftly the beaches will be pre-empted for private use—and a Central Park by the sea will be lost for all time.[14]

Congress did act, but only after Udall gave up on the push for a larger national seashore. Having lobbied for the fifty-two-mile beachfront park up to and through much of the congressional hearings and debates, the interior secretary finally realized that if he didn't soften there would be no Fire Island National Seashore, and thus he agreed to dropping much of his proposed northeastern portion. However, when Moses suddenly resigned amid the debates, Udall was able to scrap the highway and dredging propositions. As a result, a fifty-eight-hundred-acre park bill passed Congress, and LBJ signed Fire Island National Seashore into law on September 11, 1964, with Udall officiating at the ceremony.[15]

Directly afterward, a small team of NPS officials from Cape Cod National Seashore moved into an office on Fire Island. After they purchased and claimed title to the authorized national seashore lands using Land and Water Conservation Fund moneys, Udall, in 1966, again traveled up to the barrier island, this time to officially break ground at Watch Hill to mark the start of construction of the national seashore's first public facility. During this visit, Udall also accepted the donation of the Sunken Forest.[16]

Perhaps the most unique ecosystem of Fire Island National Seashore, Sunken Forest comprises an old-growth maritime holly forest, surrounded by sand and saltwater. In a later book he wrote, Udall referred to it as an "unusual" forest, with "virgin woods located a little below sea level. Here may be found unusually large serviceberry, birch, black gum, and gnarled American holly trees, some of which are several hundred years old, with ferns and azalea growing beneath them."[17]

The Sunken Forest Preserve, Inc., purchased the fifty-acre parcel of forest in the 1950s to protect it in perpetuity but then donated it to the National Park Service in 1966, knowing it would be in good hands. After Udall's remarks at the ceremony, the Sunken Forest Preserve's president read a poem that he had written in honor of the interior secretary:

> To you whose "Quiet Crisis" shows the nation
> The dark, but hopeful path of conservation,
> Who makes with staunch support and forceful speech
> A nation's seashore of the Great South Beach,
> We bring the thought that you have gained security
> For the Sunken Forest's measureless futurity,
> So man and flora, fauna, one and all,
> Will sing the praise of Stewart L. Udall.[18]

Today, the national seashore, which includes the Sunken Forest, welcomes approximately one million visitors per year. They come primarily in the summer to play in the surf, swim in the ocean, tan on the beach, relax, hike, and explore. The seashore remains relatively wild and without ample development, in part due to Udall.

Indiana Dunes National Lakeshore

At the same time that the Assateague Island and Fire Island fights were taking place, a battle pitting industry leaders versus conservation forces was occurring just east of Chicago in the area that is now primarily Indiana Dunes National Lakeshore.

Stephen Mather, the charismatic and energetic first director of the National Park Service, had proposed and lobbied for an Indiana Dunes National Park as far back as 1916. Unsuccessful in the national park endeavor due to the expansion of industry into the area, Mather and others then lobbied successfully for a much smaller Indiana Dunes State Park. The state park was a great asset to recreationists in the area, but the idea of a larger Indiana Dunes National Park never totally died down. And as urban populations in and around Gary, Indiana, and Chicago expanded in 1950s and '60s America, so too did the need for additional lakeside recreation.

Dune preservationists and recreationists found their "four-star generals" in citizen activist Dorothy Buell, who founded and then became president of the Save the Dunes Council in 1952; Paul Douglas, Illinois's senior senator, who, because of his passion for saving Indiana Dunes, came to be called "the third senator of Indiana"; and Stewart Udall. Yet even with the trio's intense lobbying efforts, it took five long years for Indiana Dunes National Lakeshore to come to fruition once Udall became secretary. This is due to the fact that on the other side of the arena were the metal industries of the area and their supporters. "It's like the battle of Manassas, only this time it's the people against the steel companies," Douglas claimed around the centennial of the Civil War battle.[19]

As historian James Michael Bailey notes, "Most Hoosier politicians, sparked by the St. Lawrence Seaway's 1959 opening, supported increased industrial development in the region. To do any less would jeopardize Indiana's tax base." Specifically, they wanted a large industrial port in the very heart of the proposed national seashore, as Indiana included only a small portion of Great Lakes shoreline and the lakes served as major arteries of traffic for shipping industries. Another reason for opposing the federal lakeshore was the fact that many Indiana residents resented Chicago residents intervening in their state's affairs. "Let us do with our state what we please, and you do with your state what you want" might well have been their battle cry.[20]

For conservationists, Bailey notes, "Something had to be done before the expanding steel and utility industries swallowed all remaining dune land surrounding the small Indiana Dunes State Park."[21] What was done was a meeting in the dune fields by Buell, Douglas, Udall, National Park Service director Conrad Wirth, and other officials and journalists in the summer of 1961. Even though it happened to be a rainy day, Douglas enjoyed showing off his "back-yard" to the interior secretary, who in turn was awestruck with the area, which he had never seen before. "I was impressed beyond my imaginings by the superb quality of the remaining beaches, dunes, natural vegetation, and wildlife habitat," Udall told reporters on his way back to Washington. "Nowhere else have I seen the story of dune formation and stabilization so graphically and scenically portrayed."[22]

A couple of months later, a hearing in Indianapolis about the lakeshore park proposal occurred. "Today you are considering the future of one of America's irreplaceable resources," he told the audience. "Natural shoreline is a true scarcity today. The day is past when public administrators can sign away natural landscape, as they have done so bountifully in our recent past. Now we public men must consider human values, and social values, in determining the best interests of our Nation. We can no longer afford to be irresponsible with a natural resource, and claim that 'someone else' will save a similar resource 'next time.' The time for there to be a 'next time' is already gone."[23]

Udall believed that one of the best justifications for the lakeshore was that there was no unit of the National Park System within two hundred miles. He also believed that it didn't have to be all or nothing for either the steel industry or the conservationists; a compromise could be worked out and was the best option. Yet it did not bode well for compromise when Bethlehem Steel, in 1962, began removing a series of sand hills that had been ten thousand years in the geological making—the Central Dunes were lost forever, some conservationists lamented.[24]

As it turned out, in the case of Indiana Dunes, one individual refused to compromise. Representative Charles Halleck didn't want a square inch of national lakeshore created but rather wanted all the land to go to the steel industry. Halleck, in large part, caused the delay in national seashore legislation. It didn't help the matter that Udall and Halleck apparently despised each other, having once, during Udall's congressional years, gotten into a shouting match on the floor of Congress.[25]

Rainy day at Indiana Dunes National Lakeshore. The lakeshore,
surprisingly, is one of the most biologically diverse national park units
in the country, including not only dunes and beaches but also several
different forest types, rivers, marshes, and even a bog. Udall played
a major role in the establishment of this national park unit as well as
many other national seashores and lakeshores in the eastern
United States. Photo by author.

After several years passed with no results from Congress and
after additional visits to rally support in favor of the dunes seemed
to go nowhere, Udall got annoyed. Bailey notes, "By late September 1966, it seemed that Secretary Udall had finally lost his patience
with the languid legislative process, mostly because Indiana politicians had allegedly allowed Bethlehem Steel to fill in another 300
acres of lakeshore for industrial use." When the interior secretary
threatened to withdraw administration support for the park, his
warning appeared to be the trick needed to speed up the legislative
process. Speaker of the US House of Representatives John McCormack was urged to push the national seashore bill through, and he
did so by initiating a "shrewd political maneuver."[26]

McCormack saw that the Indiana Dunes National Lakeshore
bill would be defeated because it was scheduled for a final hearing
and vote on a day when many of its endorsers were back home in
their respective districts campaigning for reelection. In a "shrewd
move of parliamentary brilliance," McCormack went to Halleck and
proposed to him that the bill's vote be rescheduled for later in the

same week. Halleck, believing that the majority of the proseashore faction would be absent on a Friday and thus that the bill would be defeated, agreed to vote for the legislation on that day. The problem for Halleck was that McCormack scheduled the national lakeshore vote the same day as the vote for one of LBJ's major Great Society programs, the Demonstration Cities and Metropolitan Development Act. "Johnson used every means possible short of brutal physical coercion to summon the presence of as many sympathetic, urban, liberal congressman as possible. They voted for the 'Model Cities' bill, and for Indiana Dunes."[27]

In the national lakeshore legislation that was written by Paul Douglas, the "third senator from Indiana" made sure that the highly desired Port of Indiana could come only with the authorization of Indiana Dunes National Lakeshore, not beforehand. As a result, thanks to the two sides finally working together and compromising, the national lakeshore essentially includes two main areas, with the private industrial port separating the two.

Today, there is a picturesque national lakeshore on Lake Michigan in Indiana. The lakeshore includes not only dunes and coastline but also oak savannas, swamps, bogs, marshes, prairies, rivers, and forests—an incredibly lush and biologically diverse array of ecosystems. Indiana's national lakeshore is home to more plant species— eleven hundred—than almost any other national park unit.[28]

The National Trails System Act
and Appalachian National Scenic Trail

While Udall 100 percent supported the establishment of a series of national lakeshores and seashores to protect natural shoreline and increase recreational opportunities and experiences for the human populace, the interior secretary also became a major advocate for a series of long-distance hiking trails during his years in the cabinet. One of the most famous of these trails was the Appalachian Trail, or AT, as it is commonly referred to.

The AT stretches from Georgia to Maine, and the "father of the trail," Benton MacKaye, an early 1900s forester and regional planner, in large part conceived of the long-distance hiking trail and made it a reality. Volunteers then constructed the trail. But while the western United States had ample federal lands, the East had little in comparison. Thus, controversies over property rights had erupted along the AT by the 1960s. "The trail was nibbled away or reduced to a rutted, muddy track through zones of commerce," notes Bill Bryson.[29]

Indeed, in a section of his highly acclaimed, hilarious account of attempting to trek the trail as an overweight, out-of-shape non-outdoorsman, Bryson, in *A Walk in the Woods*, describes the problems with the Appalachian Trail at midcentury, as well as how Stewart Udall helped protect the trail in perpetuity:

> In 1958, twenty miles were lopped off the southern end from Mount Oglethorpe to Springer Mountain. By the mid-1960s, it looked to any prudent observer as if the AT would survive only as scattered fragments—in the Smokies and Shenandoah National Park, from Vermont across to Maine, as forlorn relic strands in the odd state park, but otherwise buried under shopping malls and housing developments. Much of the trail crossed private lands, and new owners often revoked informal rights-of-way agreements, forcing confused and hasty relocations onto busy highways or other public roads—hardly the wilderness experience envisioned by Benton MacKaye.... The AT looked doomed.
>
> Then, in a timely piece of fortuitousness, America got a secretary of the interior, Stewart Udall, who actually liked hiking. Under his direction, a National Trails System Act was passed in 1968. The law was ambitious and far-reaching.... It envisioned 25,000 miles of new hiking trails across America, most of which were never built. However, it did produce the Pacific Crest Trail [PCT] and secured the future of the AT by making it a de facto national park. It also provided funds for the purchase of private lands to provide a wilderness buffer alongside it.[30]

Udall, an interior secretary "who actually liked hiking," was, as Bryson notes, a key figure in the establishment of the National

Trails System as well as the Appalachian National Scenic Trail. During his years in the Department of the Interior, Udall knew that the population of the United States was expanding at an unprecedented rate. He also knew that both the middle class and workers' rights were expanding, resulting in increasing amounts of leisure time for the average citizen, meaning more time when they were not at work or school. Thus, as the Outdoor Recreation Resource Review Commission reported, citizen interest in outdoor recreation was increasing drastically, and development of new outdoor recreation infrastructure was of utmost importance in order to keep up with this interest.

Udall and Lyndon Johnson both believed that trails encouraged healthy living and exercise, outdoor exploration, and, ultimately, a culture of conservation. Asked by the president in 1965 to work to establish a system of national trails, the interior secretary and his highly capable US Department of the Interior management team needed no further guidance to hit the ground running. After Johnson's directive, Udall asked the Bureau of Outdoor Recreation to take a leadership role in undertaking a comprehensive study on the feasibility of establishing a nationwide trails system. In coordination with the Forest Service and the National Park Service, director Edward Crafts of the BOR and his staff completed a far-reaching report, published under the title *Trails for America*, in 1966. In it the BOR recommended a series of national scenic trails and national historic trails to promote outdoor recreation, exercise, and the learning of and appreciation for US history.[31] "Those of us who endorsed the [National Trails System Act] legislation wanted to make it possible for Americans to share some of the adventure, the toil and even a bit of the danger experienced by our forebears—native people, explorers and settlers," recalled Udall years later.[32] The BOR and Udall also called for major increases in urban trail systems nationwide (a topic that is discussed in more depth in chapter 10).

The BOR recommended that four national scenic trails be established at once, and that individual studies for several national historic trails then be undertaken. Udall wholeheartedly embraced the BOR's report and studied its findings fully. The interior secretary and the BOR director then lobbied Congress to implement the report during a series of hearings. Udall and Crafts pushed for immediate national scenic trail status for the Pacific Crest Trail, extending from the US-Mexico border up the spine of the Sierra Nevada and Cascade Range to the Canadian border; the Continental Divide Trail, hugging the crest of the Rocky Mountains from the US-Canada border in Glacier National Park, Montana, to Silver City, New Mexico; the Appalachian Trail; and, finally, the Potomac Heritage Trail, a series of long-distance hiking trails bordering the Potomac River and a couple of its tributaries, from where the Chesapeake Bay meets the Atlantic Ocean to its headwaters in the highlands of West Virginia, Virginia, and Pennsylvania.[33]

While practically all of the PCT and AT had been constructed by the 1960s, Udall and the BOR believed that official federal government recognition and funding were needed for safeguarding hiker rights-of-way as well as trail views. "There are, Mr. Chairman, as you know, some serious problems facing the Appalachian Trail," Udall told Colorado's Wayne Aspinall during congressional hearings.

> In many instances the trail moves across areas where landowners have simply given permission in the past for the trail to pass through. Naturally with rising land prices, with growth pressures and everything else, you must acquire trail easements or acquire a trail corridor outright in order to protect the continuity of the trail. We estimate that we will need $4.6 million for acquisition purposes for the Appalachian Trail in order to protect it, to complete the right-of-way, and to give it the full development that it needs. This is one of the main features in this bill today, to help save the Appalachian Trail.[34]

Udall and the BOR proposed that acquisition funds come from the Land and Water Conservation Fund. They also proposed that AT administration and trail maintenance be shared among federal, state, and local governments as well as partnership organizations such as the historic Appalachian Trail Conference (today known as the Appalachian Trail Conservancy), an advocate for official federal protection of the trail since the 1920s.[35]

Because it primarily traveled through public lands, specifically through national forests, the Pacific Crest Trail, by and large, did not have as many threats posed by economic interests as the AT. However, in order to give the PCT official recognition and support, as well as to ensure high-quality trail design and maintenance standards, it was included in the national trails system proposal.[36]

Udall submitted to Congress a draft of the trails system bill, and thanks to ample congressional support for national trails, most noticeably, perhaps, from Senator Gaylord Nelson of Wisconsin, the future founder of Earth Day, the bill gained steam. After it was known that acquisition, maintenance, and construction costs would primarily come out of the LWCF and not the government's general funds, and after some modifications to the bill were made, Congress passed the National Trails System Act in 1968. President Johnson signed it into law on the second day of October.[37]

The act immediately established the Appalachian National Scenic Trail as an official unit of the National Park System, to be managed in a unique partnership among various entities, primarily but not exclusively the National Park Service and the Appalachian Trail Conservancy. It also provided for funding to reclaim and define rights-of-way. In addition to the AT, the National Trails System Act also immediately put the Pacific Crest Trail under the control of the US Forest Service. Next, the act called for studies to be conducted on a series of potential additions to the National Trails System. Many of these trails, including the Trail of Tears, Lewis and Clark Trail, Oregon Trail, Mormon Trail, North Country Trail, Natchez Trace, and others, later became additions to the system, albeit not as hiking and backpacking trails as first proposed by Udall and others but rather as primarily driving trails on preexisting highways and "only on paper" trails.[38] Nevertheless, the National Trails System today offers recreation to millions of hikers, drivers, travelers, and adventurers. As Udall himself noted in 2008, on the fortieth anniversary of the National Trails System Act, "a national trail is a gateway into nature's secret beauties, a portal to the past, a way into solitude and community. It is also an inroad to our national character. Our trails are both irresistible and indispensable."[39]

National Park Service Accomplishments: Ecology, Human Diversity, and International Conservation

The several preceding pages have tried to establish the fact that Udall was a major player in creating an unprecedented number of new national park sites in the 1960s. These new national seashores, lakeshores, recreation areas, monuments, parks, and trails, after being carefully and thoughtfully developed by landscape architects and others so as to generally have their roadways and visitor facilities intrude on the landscape as little as possible, invited healthy living in the form of outdoor recreation. At the same time, they provided protection for hundreds of thousands of acres of unique American flora, fauna, and landscapes.

In addition to new park sites, Udall, both directly and indirectly in his eight years as interior secretary, significantly modernized the National Park Service, the governmental agency that oversees the National Park System. He did this specifically, though not exclusively, through supporting the growing field of ecology; making an exceptional choice for the position of new NPS director; helping to diversify the agency's workforce; and, finally, supporting international conservation and diplomatic efforts.

A progressive person and growing promoter and endorser of science and sound research, Udall quickly embraced and directed a major uptick in scientific research in the national parks. The impetus for this was a report handed to him by the NPS chief of natural resources that showed why a stronger science program was needed. Udall read and embraced the report, and, as bureau historian Richard West Sellers notes, in 1962 he called for a thorough study of the Department of the Interior's resource management practices, including how to make federal agencies under his control focus more on ecology. Udall personally persuaded A. Starker Leopold, a biology professor at the University of California–Berkeley and the son of pioneering ecologist Aldo Leopold, to lead the research efforts.[40]

The result of this comprehensive study, which came to be called the Leopold Report, was that the NPS, as well as all other public land management agencies within the department in the 1960s, became much more ecologically and biologically focused. The Leopold Report did this in a number of ways. For starters, the report called for the termination of the long-standing practice of predator control, or pest control, namely, the killing of wolves, mountain lions, and coyotes because they killed small quantities of stock animals. The ecological thinking of the age held that all native animals of an ecosystem deserved to be there and were integral to the web of life. "The problems of today must be met with an ecological approach based upon the husbandry of all wildlife," noted the interior secretary. "This includes even those species which, at certain times and places, are either misplaced by land use or are concentrated in such numbers as to be regarded as pests."[41]

Second, the Leopold Report called for an end to the policy of eradicating all forest fires. Sound science was proving that fires were actually a natural part of forest life cycles and that they were even beneficial to the land.[42] The Leopold Report touched on many more issues. The bottom line, though, is that Udall directed the NPS—as well as the Bureau of Land Management and US Fish and Wildlife Service, the other land-managing agencies within the DOI—to put their recommendations into permanent practice. The agencies did and have done so ever since.

It was easy for Udall to grasp, embrace, and support an increased emphasis on science and ecological management. Among the reasons for this were that he was an avid reader and a progressive. Furthermore, one of the interior secretary's idols was Aldo Leopold (1887–1948), whom he wrote about in *The Quiet Crisis*. One of the earliest ecologists, Leopold posthumously released *A Sand County Almanac*, an ecological classic, which Udall referenced often in his speeches as secretary of the interior.[43]

Another thing that Udall did in the 1960s was to begin diversifying the workforce of the National Park Service. When he became interior secretary, there was a single African American park ranger in a bureau that consisted of 474 rangers.[44] Udall and his second NPS director set policies in place to bring in employees more truly representative of the face of America. Several dozen African American citizens were employed by the NPS by the end of 1968. According to Orren Beaty, Udall's assistant, the DOI in the 1960s was especially successful in bringing in African American law students to complete summer internships, working out of the DOI solicitor's office and the NPS's law office.[45]

Robert Stanton, National Park Service director from 1997 to 2001, credits Udall with his career in the NPS, as Stanton was recruited by Udall's staff in the 1960s. Moving up the career ladder through the decades, Stanton remains the only African American head of the agency to date.[46]

Outside of pushing ecology and diversity, Udall, among other things, succeeded in hiring an extremely capable new National Park Service director: the cigar-smoking, hardworking, sometimes angry George Hartzog Jr. Even though Udall and the prior director, Conrad Wirth, were never the best of friends, upon Wirth's retirement in 1964 he sent to Udall a list of his top five candidates for the directorship. On this list was Hartzog, whom Udall then appointed.[47]

Hartzog served as director until 1972, becoming one of the last nonpolitically appointed directors in NPS history.[48] Having a great working relationship with Udall, Hartzog expanded the interrelated fields of interpretation and environmental education. He also formalized and grew volunteer efforts within the National Park System by creating the Volunteer-in-Parks program. With tens of thousands of interns and volunteers contributing tens of thousands of hours, the NPS today could not survive without VIPs. Hartzog was also instrumental in the creation of the National Park Foundation, the NPS's nonprofit fund-raising partner; diversifying the workforce; and establishing dozens of new national park units. "They made a formidable team," notes historian Steve Dunsky in describing Udall and Hartzog.[49]

One final major success for Udall regarding the NPS was his support in creating, soon after becoming interior secretary, the agency's small but highly important Office of International Affairs (OIA). The office was set up to handle and promote international coordination and cooperation on matters of conservation and the national parks. Udall envisioned the day when park managers, rangers, and field experts would be exchanged between various countries of the world "in order to assist and learn from each other's busy summer season," and this day came to fruition.[50]

While the OIA usually had to gain funding from and work under the auspices of the US Agency for International Development, an agency with which Udall was dissatisfied because it gave a low priority to parks, NPS employees nevertheless traveled to Jordan, Greece, Turkey, and other locales in the 1960s. At these locations, they set up master plans for each country's newly established national parks. The OIA had additional successes in 1965, when hundreds of foreign national park and nature reserve employees came to the United States to attend the International Seminar on the Administration of National Parks and Equivalent Reserves, an annual summer course bringing over about thirty representatives at a time to complete specific university courses as well as extensive tours of US national parks. By the early 1970s, conservationists from seventy different countries had attended the seminar.[51]

Udall himself was instrumental in setting up the First World Conference on National Parks with the OIA. Hundreds of national park and public land employees from around the world attended the weeklong conference in Seattle during the summer of 1962. The interior secretary served as keynote speaker, and in his opening remarks he noted that unchecked technological development and increasing human population were the main dangers to federally protected areas worldwide, as they could lead to overcrowded, underpreserved national parks. Udall also spoke of the economic value of parks—through tourist expenditures for local economies—and how this needed to be weighed with watershed, scientific laboratory, and aesthetic values. "We know now that upriver forests and downriver cultivation will produce more crops than a land completely cultivated but without watershed protection," Udall told his international audience. "We know also that our wildlands form the only perfect wildlife habitat, and constitute an irreplaceable science laboratory where we can measure the world in its natural balance against the world in its man-made imbalance."[52]

～

UDALL'S NATIONAL PARK SYSTEM and National Park Service legacy is a strong one. The 1960s interior secretary orchestrated the establishment of an unprecedented number of new national park units, diversified the NPS workforce, brought ecology to the forefront, and helped expand international conservation efforts. Yet this book serves as a broad environmental biography of Udall, and the US Department of the Interior is composed of several bureaus and offices. Udall's success was not limited to just one agency or topic.

Notes

1. US Department of the Interior, *The Department of the Interior during the Administration of President Lyndon B. Johnson, November 1963-January 1969*, administrative history, pt. 2, 1:75–76, box 151, Udall Papers.

2. Ibid.

3. Ibid.

4. Richard Homan, "Udall, Landowners Argue over Assateague's Future," *Washington Post*, June 24, 1963, pqasb.pqarchiver.com/washingtonpost/search.html.

5. Ibid.

6. US Department of the Interior, *Department of the Interior during the Administration of Johnson*, 76–78. See also Barry Mackintosh, *Assateague Island National Seashore: An Administrative History* (Washington, DC: National Park Service, 1982), 5–20.

7. Ibid.

8. Udall, "What the Big Outdoor Boss Has in Mind," *Life* [?], [1963?], box 211, Udall Papers.

9. Lee E. Koppelman and Seth Forman, *Fire Island National Seashore: A History* (Albany: State University of New York Press, 2008), 58.

10. William M. Blair, "Bill Urges Park for Fire Island," *New York Times*, April 1963, box 156, Udall Papers; Koppelman and Forman, *Fire Island National Seashore*, 67–71. Javits served in the US Senate from 1957 to 1981 and was known as one of the most liberal of the liberal Republicans of the twentieth century.

11. Kirk Price, "Udall Ready to Drop Fire Isle Park Plan," *Newsday*, June 4, 1962, box 103, folder 2, Udall Papers; Koppelman and Forman, *Fire Island National Seashore*, 73.

12. Warren Weaver Jr., "Fire Island Plan Opposed by Udall: He Rebuts Moses Plan for Road and Boat Channel—Would Keep Open Space," *New York Times*, June 21, 1962, box 130, folder 2, Udall Papers.

13. Udall, "What the Big Outdoor Boss Has in Mind."

14. Ibid.

15. Koppelman and Forman, *Fire Island National Seashore*, 74–75.

16. Ibid., 154–55.

17. Udall, *American Natural Treasures*, 192.

18. Poem, Sunken Forest Preserve president to Udall, 1967, box 199, folder 1, Udall Papers.

19. Ron Cockrell, *A Signature of Time and Eternity: The Administrative History of Indiana Dunes National Lakeshore, Indiana*. See also National Park Service, "Indiana Dunes National Lakeshore Story," nps.gov/indu/historyculture/establishment .htm; and newspaper clippings, box 93, folder 3, Udall Papers.

20. James Michael Bailey, "The Politics of Dunes, Redwoods, and Dams: Arizona's 'Brothers Udall' and America's National Parklands, 1961–1969," 99.

21. Ibid.

22. See newspaper clippings, box 93, folder 3, Udall Papers.

23. US Department of the Interior, "Statement by Stewart L. Udall, Secretary of the Interior, for Presentation at the Hearing Concerning Interim Report on Burns Waterway Harbor, Indiana," August 30, 1961, box 155, folder 10, Udall Papers.

24. "Udall Sees Dunes Win for All," *Gary (IN) Post Tribune*, July 24, 1961, box 93, folder 3, Udall Papers.

25. Bailey, "Politics of Dunes, Redwoods, and Dams," 120. See also transcript, Orren Beaty Jr. oral history interview III, by William W. Moss, October 31, 1969, JFK Library, archive1.jfklibrary.org/JFKOH/Beaty,%20Orren/JFKOH-OB-03/JFKOH -OB-03-TR.pdf.

26. Bailey, "Politics of Dunes, Redwoods, and Dams," 133.

27. Ibid., 135; J. Ronald Engel, *Sacred Sands: The Struggle for Community in the Indiana Dunes* (Middletown, CT: Wesleyan University Press, 1986), 279–80.

28. National Park Service, "Indiana Dunes National Lakeshore Story"; National Park Service, "Nature and Science," nps.gov/indu/naturescience/index.htm.

29. Bill Bryson, *A Walk in the Woods* (New York: Broadway Books, 1998), 111.

30. Ibid., 112.

31. US Department of the Interior, Bureau of Outdoor Recreation, *Trails for America: Report on the Nationwide Trails Study*, 14.

32. Stewart L. Udall, "Trails Tell Tales," *Montgomery (AL) Advertiser*, June 4, 2008, montgomeryadvertiser.com/apps/pbcs.dll/article?AID=/20080607/OPINION 0101/806040374/1006/opinion.

33. US Department of the Interior, Bureau of Outdoor Recreation, *Trails for America*, 14; US House of Representatives, *Nationwide Trails System: A Hearing Before the Subcommittee on National Parks and Recreation of the Committee on Interior and Insular Affairs, Ninetieth Congress: First Session on H.R. 4865, and Related Bills, to Establish a Nationwide System of Trails*, March 6, 1967, fs.fed.us/cdt/pdf_documents /natl_trails_system_hearing_hr4865_1967.pdf.

34. US House of Representatives, *Nationwide Trails System*, 27.

35. Ibid., 26.

36. US Department of the Interior, Bureau of Outdoor Recreation, *Trails for America*.

37. Ibid.

38. US House of Representatives, *House Report No. 1631: National Trails System Act*, fs.fed.us/cdt/pdf_documents/natl_trails_system_house_report_no_1631.pdf.

39. Udall, "Trails Tell Tales."

40. Sellers, *Preserving Nature*, 170, 200. See also US Department of the Interior, Office of the Secretary, news release, "Secretary Udall Names Board to Advise Him on Wildlife Management," April 25, 1962, fws.gov/news/Historic/NewsReleases/1962/19620425.pdf.

41. US Fish and Wildlife Service, Bureau of Sport Fisheries and Wildlife, news release, "Secretary Udall Approves Predator and Rodent Control Work," June 16, 1965, fws.gov/news/Historic/NewsReleases/1965/19650616a.pdf; A. S. Leopold et al., *Wildlife Management in the National Parks: The Leopold Report*, March 4, 1963, craterlakeinstitute.com/online-library/leopold-report/complete.htm.

42. Leopold et al., *Wildlife Management in the National Parks*.

43. The "book on tape" for *A Sand County Almanac* was voiced by none other than Stewart Udall.

44. Smith, "Kennedy, Udall, and New Frontier Conservation," 342.

45. Transcript, Beaty oral history interview III.

46. "Robert Stanton," History Makers, thehistorymakers.com/biography/robert-stanton-38.

47. Conrad Wirth, *Parks, Politics, and the People*, 301–3. Regarding Hartzog and Udall, both men had major respect for each other. Udall actually wrote the foreword to Hartzog's 1988 book, *Battling for the National Parks*. The book discusses Hartzog's NPS career, including his years and experiences as director. In the book, Hartzog thanks Udall "for giving me the best job in the world."

48. While almost all NPS directors served multiple presidential administrations—both Republican and Democrat—between 1916 and 1972, this changed after Hartzog. With the exception of Russell Dickenson, NPS director from 1980 to 1985, new NPS directors have come in with each new presidential administration that represents a change in political party.

49. Steve Dunsky, review of *Reshaping Our National Parks and Their Guardians: The Legacy of George B. Hartzog Jr.*, by Kathy Mengak, *Environmental History* 18, no. 2 (2013): 435–36.

50. Stewart Udall, "Address at the First World Conference on Parks, Seattle, Washington," July 4, 1962, library.arizona.edu/exhibits/sludall/speechretrievals/addressparksx.htm.

51. Everhart, *The National Park Service*, 201–3.

52. Udall, "First World Conference on National Parks," 17; Udall, "Nature Islands for the World," 1–10, archive.org/stream/firstworldconferooadam/firstworldconferooadam_djvu.txt.

6 | Protecting Wildlife and Expanding the National Wildlife Refuge System

Before irrevocable decisions are made, the quiet values of singing bird and sloshing marsh should be given their full day in court.

A PROGRESSIVE LIBERAL and supporter of the growing field of ecology, the well-read Udall, as a relatively young interior secretary, was one of Rachel Carson's biggest supporters. It might have helped that the female science writer had formerly been a Department of the Interior employee for a number of years. In any case, Udall invited the famous science writer to dinner at his suburban Virginia home, had her present on pesticides at a meeting with Robert F. Kennedy himself and other public figures at RFK's home, and was even a pallbearer at Carson's funeral at the Washington National Cathedral.[1] In light of Udall's connections with Carson, perhaps it was only natural for the politician to work toward improving the plight of wildlife.

Indeed, second only to National Park System expansion, Udall put great emphasis in his years as a cabinet member on the protection of wildlife, specifically though not exclusively through his work with the Department of the Interior's US Fish and Wildlife Service. Udall successfully oversaw a major increase in the number of national wildlife refuges, pushed for increased environmental awareness of and protection for wild animal species threatened with extinction, and lobbied for a decrease in pesticide use nationwide.

The USFWS is the main government agency charged with managing and protecting wildlife, primarily through its system of more than five hundred national wildlife refuges. Begun as two separate governmental bureaus in the late 1800s, the USFWS, Udall believed, had by the 1960s developed its game-management techniques into a science, in which "hunters 'crop' only the annual increase" of wildlife and thus kept wild critters within the carrying capacities of their refuges.[2]

Expanding the National Wildlife Refuge System

Yet the system as a whole and the sizes of the various refuges were not keeping up with postwar industrial, commercial, and residential development, thus leading to decreasing habitat and wild animal populations. In a 1963 newspaper article, Udall noted that "the main threat today arises from the side effects of advancing civilization. The draining of each swamp, the building of each road, the indiscriminate broadcast of pesticides, the widening circle of pollution, and the destruction of open space on the edges of our cities are now the clear and present danger to wildlife."[3]

In order to battle this, Udall, almost immediately upon becoming interior secretary, began a massive expansion of the National Wildlife Refuge System. He knew that by increasing the amount of public land dedicated to wildlife habitat conservation, more wildlife could be saved, and he knew that national wildlife refuges were set up for this exact purpose. With this in mind, Udall served as an active chairman of the Migratory Bird Conservation Commission, a congressionally chartered entity created in 1929 to decide on and oversee new additions to the National Wildlife Refuge System. Working with fellow commissioners, including Representative Silvio O. Conte (R-MA, who served sixteen terms), Senator Roman Hruska (R-NE), Senator Lee Metcalf (D-MT), Secretary of Agriculture Orville Freeman, Commerce Secretary John Conner, and others, he helped establish almost sixty new national wildlife refuges during his tenure. With the exception of Harold Ickes, FDR's interior secretary, no other secretary of the interior has ever had as many wildlife refuges established during their time in office (and Ickes had more than twelve years in office compared to Udall's eight).[4]

TABLE 6.1. National wildlife refuges established during Stewart Udall's years as secretary of the interior

Alamosa, CO	Eastern Neck, MD	Pahranagat, NV
Amagansett, NY	Eufaula, AL	Pee Dee, NC
Anahuac, TX	Flint Hills, KS	Prime Hook, DE
Ankeny, OR	Grays Lake, ID	Rachel Carson, ME
Arapaho, CO	Grulla, NM	Ridgefield, WA
Baskett Slough, OR	Harris Neck, GA	San Bernard, TX
Bear Lake, ID	Hatchie, TN	San Luis, CA
Brazoria, TX	Hobe Sound, FL	Seatuck, NY
Browns Park, CO	John Heinz Tinicum, PA	Seedskadee, WY
Buck Island, USVI	Kootenai, ID	Sherburne, MN
Cedar Island, NC	Lake Woodruff, FL	St. Vincent, FL
Cedar Point, OH	Las Vegas, NM	Target Rock, NY
Choctaw, AL	Lee Metcalf, MT	Togiak, AK
Cibola, AZ	Maxwell, NM	Toppenish, WA
Clarence Cannon, MO	Merritt Island, FL	Ul Bend, MT
Clarence Rhode, AK	Moody, TX	Wapanocca, AR
Conboy Lake, WA	Muscatatuck, IN	Washita, OK
Cross Creeks, TN	Ottawa, OH	William L. Finley, OR
Delevan, CA	Oyster Bay, NY	Wyandotte, MI

Note: The list above reflects the current names of the national wildlife refuges. Some were established under a different name and later reclassified.

While some national wildlife refuges were created thanks to private donations from hunting and fishing clubs, and while others were established by way of federal agency land transfers and reclassifications, most of the National Wildlife Refuge System's expansion in the 1960s occurred thanks to moneys accrued from the federal duck-stamp program, the long-standing program wherein hunters who wish to hunt on national wildlife refuge lands pay a fee and then receive a permit, or "stamp," to do so.[5]

As can be seen in table 6.1, expansion to the system in the 1960s occurred in practically all parts of the United States. In general, though, refuges were established primarily on the four North American flyways, including the Atlantic Flyway, Mississippi Flyway, Central Flyway, and Pacific Flyway. These flyways each involve broad swaths of land, water, and sky that waterfowl and other birds utilize during their south-to-north migrations in spring and north-to-south migrations in fall.

Some examples of specific national wildlife refuges created under Udall's watch include the almost 10,000-acre Anahuac National Wildlife Refuge near Galveston, Texas, established to protect dwindling populations of canvasback ducks and other bird species, and, farther west, Delevan National Wildlife Refuge in the Central Valley of California, created as an important winter nesting ground for waterfowl of the Pacific Flyway.[6]

Elsewhere, just outside Toledo, Ohio, Udall accepted a land donation from the North American Wildlife Foundation, which had received the gift of land from the Cedar Point Hunting Club. The land became Cedar Point National Wildlife Refuge, which Udall proclaimed as "the best wildlife refuge left on the Great Lakes" after an on-the-ground visit.[7]

One of the larger wildlife preserves to be established in the 1960s came into being during the final weeks of the Johnson administration. In late 1968, after conferring with and getting the recommendation from Alaska-based US Fish and Wildlife Service staff, Udall announced the establishment of the 265,000-acre Cape Newenham National Wildlife Refuge on the rugged coastline of the Bering Sea. Later expanded and reclassified as Togiak National Wildlife Refuge, the protected area included, according to the press release, "rocky islands, coastal cliffs, tundra, tumbling rivers, and interior mountains." It also preserved the home of "what may be the greatest bird city on the American mainland—1,000,000,000 nesting murres, puffins, and kittiwakes.... Mammals include grizzly bears, seals, and sea lions. Spectacular runs of salmon swim the rivers. In all, it is considered a showcase of Arctic wildlife at its varied best."[8]

On the opposite side of the country from Alaska, one final example of Udall working to establish national wildlife refuges involved a marshland known as the Great Swamp, bordering the New York City metropolitan area. Learning of plans to construct an airport on the mostly natural, biologically diverse area, local conserva tionists, consisting of an amalgam of hunters, fishermen, outdoor recreationists, and nature students and led by local resident-activist Helen Fenske, banded together to protect the Great Swamp from development. Udall joined the debate shortly after becoming interior secretary, coming to the side of the conservationists after a DOI official notified him of the matter.[9]

While a small Great Swamp National Wildlife Refuge was established thanks to conservationists' fund-raising efforts in late 1960, Udall both encouraged and challenged the organizations and individuals to raise money to purchase 3,000 acres of additional land to then donate to the DOI. Only with the larger wildlife refuge established could the airport plans be stopped once and for all, Udall believed. Working through the North American Wildlife Foundation, conservationists raised the additional funds, purchased the land, and donated it for the national wildlife refuge cause. Dedicating the refuge on behalf of the US government in 1964, Udall praised the work of "ordinary citizens" in their successful effort to preserve a "most unique and important parcel of public land, Great Swamp National Wildlife Refuge." To date, 244 bird species as well as an array of mammals, fish, and amphibians have found refuge there.[10]

Combating Pesticides and Writing the Endangered Species Preservation Act

Regarding the preservation of wildlife on the verge of extinction, the American bald eagle, to use just one example of many, was drastically decreasing in numbers in the mid-1900s. While hunting and habitat loss were reasons for eagle decline, pesticides were another major culprit, as Rachel Carson's 1962 *Silent Spring* made clear. Utilized in agriculture to get rid of pest species that destroy crops, pesticides brought into contact with soil, plants, and the air filter directly into streams and ponds. When bald eagles and other wildlife then drink from the streams and ponds and devour fish from the water, they get poisoned. Fortunately, Udall stepped in on behalf of the bald eagle and other vanishing wildlife species before it was too late.

With fewer than five hundred nesting pairs of bald eagles left in the entire world, the secretary of the interior's first action involved banning the aerial shooting of both bald and golden eagles from Department of the Interior–administered lands.[11] He then further protected bald eagles by requiring a one-square-mile no-public-access zone at each of their nesting sites.[12] But perhaps the best thing Udall did in order to begin bringing back bald eagle populations and other wild critters from the brink of extinction was to ban pesticides, including DDT, from use on DOI-administered lands.[13]

The progressive Udall was in fact the first Kennedy administration official to speak out boldly and publicly against the widespread use of pesticides, thus helping force the pesticide debate into the open, specifically into the halls of government. Indeed, at a pesticide hearing orchestrated by Senator Abraham Ribicoff (D-CT), Udall testified, noting the significant amount of chemical residue found inside fish deep within the ocean. The Department of the Interior's own Bureau of Commercial Fisheries had gathered the data that Udall spoke about, although naturalist and writer Frank Graham Jr. noted that the bureau had been reluctant to share its findings. "Can we afford to use these persistent toxic chemicals if we cannot control the movement of their residues after use? From my point of view, the answer is an unequivocal 'no,'" the interior secretary claimed.[14]

Rachel Carson wrote a masterpiece, Senator Abraham Ribicoff lobbied for pesticide control, and JFK, who had a love for the sea, ordered his Science Advisory Committee to conduct a special study on pesticide use in the early 1960s.[15] As a culmination of these factors and more, funding for pesticide research increased, and the US Fish and Wildlife Service became the primary government agency studying the effects that DDT, endrin, dieldrin, aldrin, and lindane had on land, water, and wildlife.

As part of the Patuxent Wildlife Research Center, a unique national wildlife refuge just north of the nation's capital set up primarily for wildlife research and study, a high-tech pesticide research laboratory was built during the era. At its dedication ceremony, Udall noted that the facility would hopefully "prevent or halt the spread of 'silent springs' that stalk the earth." The interior secretary continued:

Pesticides have done much good. There is no doubt about that. But evidence of the price we have paid is around us. We cannot longer ignore the unanswered questions. What are we doing to our total environment by spreading millions of pounds of deadly chemicals over the land? Are we in danger of losing part of our precious wildlife heritage? What price can we put on the song of a bird? The answers to these and other problems cannot arrive too soon, it is already late evening on the conservation front.[16]

Outside of protecting bald eagles and pushing for a decrease in pesticide use, Udall had many more successes in terms of wildlife protection, one of which involved his role in the passage of a bill that sought to bring back species from the brink of extinction. Listening to USFWS officials as well as concerned citizens, he lobbied for a policy to protect all endangered wild animals of the United States, including the Key deer, Gila trout, Sonoran pronghorn, grizzly bear, Kirtland's warbler, whooping crane, timber wolf, and more.

While Udall had been trying to acquire refuges to protect endangered species as early as 1962, in 1965 Udall and his staff actually wrote the first draft of the Endangered Species Preservation Act and then submitted it to Congress. For a year, the interior secretary lobbied for passage of the act, referred to by some as the Udall bill. He argued that the continued existence of all species was imperative. "Every species, being unique, may prove essential in current and future scientific research into the mystery of life itself," Udall said. "Each species is a part of the food chain which supports other species, and each has a function to perform. Man is a part of the vast web of life and cannot escape the natural consequences of his action."[17]

The result of Udall's and others' lobbying was the Endangered Species Preservation Act of 1966, which authorized the secretary of the interior to place endangered domestic fish and wildlife species on an official, publicized endangered species list. The Departments of Interior, Agriculture, and Defense were then required to preserve the habitats of the listed species on all of the lands that they managed. The act also permitted the US Fish and Wildlife Service to spend up to fifteen million dollars per year per endangered species to buy additional habitat for each animal's protection. In March 1967, after careful research and study by USFWS staff, state officials, conservation organizations, and scientists, Udall placed seventy-eight species of endangered wildlife on the list (see table 6.2).[18]

TABLE 6.2. 1967 Endangered Species List

In accordance with section 1(c) of the Endangered Species Preservation Act of October 15, 1966 (80. Stat. 926; 16 U.S.C. 668aa(c)) I find after consulting the States, interested organizations, and individual scientists, that the following listed native fish and wildlife are threatened with extinction.

Mammals: Indiana Bat (Akohekohe), Delmarva Peninsula Fox Squirrel, Timber Wolf, San Joaquin Kit Fox, Grizzly Bear, Black-Footed Ferret, Florida Panther, Caribbean Monk Seal, Guadalupe Fur Seal, Florida Manatee (Florida Sea Cow), Key Deer, Columbian White-Tailed Deer, Sonoran Pronghorn

Birds: Hawaiian Dark-Rumped Petrel, Hawaiian Goose (Nene), Aleutian Canada Goose, Tule White-Fronted Goose, Laysan Duck, Hawaiian Duck (Koloa), Mexican Duck, California Condor, Florida Everglade Kite (Small Florida Kite), Hawaiian Hawk, Southern Bald Eagle, Akiapolaau, Crested Honeykeeper (Akohekohe), Kauai Nukupuu, Laysan Finchbill, Nihoa Finchbill, Ou, Maui Parrotbill, Bachman's Warbler, Kirtland's Warbler, Dusky Seaside Sparrow, Attwater's Greater Prairie Chicken, Masked Bobwhite, Whooping Crane, Yuma Clapper Rall, Hawaiian Common Gallinule, Eskimo Curlew, Puerto Rican Parrot, American Ivory-Billed Woodpecker, Hawaiian Crow (Alala), Small Kauai Thrush (Pusiohi), Nihoa Millerbird, Kauai Oo (Oo Aa)

Reptiles and Amphibians: American Alligator, Blunt-Nosed Leopard Lizard, San Francisco Garter Snake, Santa Cruz Long-Toed Salamander, Texas Blind Salamander, Black Toad (Inyo County Toad)

Fishes: Shortnose Sturgeon, Longjaw Claco, Plute Cutthroat Trout, Greenback Cutthroat Trout, Montana Westslope Cutthroat Trout, Gila Trout, Arizona Trout (Apache Trout), Desert Dace, Humpback Chub, Little Colorado Spinedace, Moapa Dace, Colorado River Squawfish, Cui-ui, Devils Hole Pupfish, Commanche Springs Pupfish, Owens River Pupfish, Pahrump Killifish, Big Bend Gambusia, Clear Creek Gambusia, Gila Topminnow, Maryland Darter, Blue Pike

Source: Stewart L. Udall, *Secretary of the Interior*, February 24, 1967, F.R. Doc. 67-2758; Filed, Mar. 10, 1967; 8:48 a.m.

Known as the "Udall bill," the 1966 Endangered Species Preservation
Act put the grizzly bear as well as dozens of other species near
extinction on the pathway to recovery. Photo by author.

Largely overshadowed in history by the 1973 Endangered Species
Act, which protected endangered wildlife across all federal departments and created important additions to the original bill, the 1966
act was an important step for the federal government in its drive for
endangered species preservation. "Some people think that environmental protection began with Earth Day in 1970, but a lot of action
led up to that," Udall claimed in the 1980s.[19] Practically ignored and
forgotten today, the Endangered Species Preservation Act is a case
in point.

Thanks in large part to the 1966 act, the US Fish and Wildlife
Service was able to conduct significant research on endangered
species in the late '60s. They also began raising wildlife in research
centers to bolster wild populations. Finally, acreage was purchased
and added to specific national wildlife refuges to protect specific
endangered species. For instance, almost twenty-five hundred acres

of additional land was added to Key Deer National Wildlife Refuge in southern Florida to protect the endangered Key deer, a unique dwarf subspecies of the white-tailed deer.[20]

~

AS A RESULT OF UDALL'S strong record on wildlife protection, the Wildlife Society awarded him, in 1968, their most prestigious award, the Aldo Leopold Medal for Outstanding Service to Conservation. That same year, the National Audubon Society awarded Udall the Audubon Medal.[21]

Notes

1. Rachel Carson to Dorothy Freeman, October 25, 1962, in *The Letters of Rachel Carson and Dorothy Freeman, 1952–1964: An Intimate Portrait of a Remarkable Friendship*, edited by Martha Freeman (Boston: Beacon Press, 1994), 415; Mark Stoll, "Rachel Carson's *Silent Spring*: A Book That Changed the World," Environment and Society Portal, Virtual Exhibition, 2012, environmentandsociety.org/exhibitions/silent-spring/us-federal-government-responds; Jack Doyle, "Power in the Pen: *Silent Spring*, 1962," February 21, 2012, pophistorydig.com/topics/tag/rachel-carson-senate-hearings/; Frank Graham Jr., *Since "Silent Spring"* (Boston: Houghton Mifflin, 1970), 89.

2. Udall, "To Save Wildlife and Aid Us, Too," *New York Times Magazine*, September 15, 1963, box 207, folder 2, Udall Papers. No scholarly book yet exists on the full-scale history of the US Fish and Wildlife Service, but for basic information, see the extensive timeline at training.fws.gov/history/USFWS-history.html; Zaslowsky and Watkins, *These American Lands*, 151–93; Lynn A. Greenwalt, "A Brief History of the National Wildlife Refuge System," in *America's National Wildlife Refuges: A Complete Guide*, by Russell D. Butcher (Lanham, MD: Taylor, 2008), 11–22; and Robert L. Fischman, "The National Wildlife Refuge System and the Hallmarks of Modern Organic Legislation," *Ecology Law Quarterly* 29, no. 457 (2002): 458–501, repository.law.indiana.edu/cgi/viewcontent.cgi?article=1225&context=facpub. For a thorough political history of the USFWS from the 1920s to the 1960s, see Michael W. Giese, "A Federal Foundation for Wildlife Conservation: The Evolution of the National Wildlife Refuge System, 1920–1968" (PhD diss., American University, 2008). For US wildlife conservation history, see E. Donnall Thomas Jr., *How Sportsmen Saved the World: The Unsung Conservation Efforts of Hunters and Anglers* (Guilford, CT: Lyons Press, 2010).

This chapter is specifically focused on Udall's work within the Bureau of Sport Fisheries and Wildlife, one of two bureaus constituting the US Fish and Wildlife Service in the 1960s. The other agency was the Bureau of Commercial Fisheries. Seemingly out of place in the Interior Department, the Bureau of

Commercial Fisheries was located more properly within the Department of Agriculture prior to moving over to the Department of the Interior. In 1970 the bureau then moved to the newly created National Oceanic and Atmospheric Administration within the Department of Commerce.

3. Ibid.

4. US Fish and Wildlife Service, "Refuge Establishment Dates," training.fws.gov/history/ListsRefugeDates.html.

5. Thomas, *How Sportsmen Saved the World*, 89–93; US Fish and Wildlife Service, Federal Duck Stamp Office, fws.gov/duckstamps/Info/Stamps/stampinfo.htm.

6. US Department of the Interior, Office of the Secretary, news release, "Secretary Udall Announces Creation of Two New Wildlife Refuges, Enlargement of Two Other Protective Areas," March 6, 1962, box 154, folder 1, Udall Papers.

7. Ibid.

8. US Department of the Interior, Office of the Secretary, news release, "Interior Seeks Designation of 1,265,000 Public Land Acres as Wildlife Refuge Areas," December 19, 1968, fws.gov/news/Historic/NewsReleases/1968/19681219.pdf. See also US Fish and Wildlife Service, Jim King oral history transcript, April 18, 2006, 6–7, digitalmedia.fws.gov/cdm/ref/collection/document/id/1868.

9. Stewart Udall, "Open Space: Our Legacy to Future Generations," in *The Benefits of Open Space*, edited by Leonard W. Hamilton (Morristown, NJ: Great Swamp Watershed Society, 1997); Stewart Udall, keynote address at the meeting of the Great Swamp Committee of North American Wildlife Foundation, Sommerville, NJ, November 27, 1962, box 104, folder 8, Udall Papers.

10. Ibid.; US Department of the Interior, Office of the Secretary, news release, "Great Swamp in New Jersey, Donated to Government, to Be Dedicated," May 25, 1964, fws.gov/news/Historic/NewsReleases/1964/19640525b.pdf; US Fish and Wildlife Service, Great Swamp National Wildlife Refuge brochure.

11. US Department of the Interior, Office of the Secretary, news release, "Federal Rules Tighten Protection for Bald Eagles and Golden Eagles," January 28, 1963, box 154, folder 2, Udall Papers; US Fish and Wildlife Service, "Bald Eagle Fact Sheet: Natural History, Ecology, and History of Recovery," fws.gov/midwest/eagle/recovery/biologue.html.

12. US Fish and Wildlife Service, news release, "Secretary Udall Orders New Steps to Protect the Bald Eagle," January 27, 1966, fws.gov/news/Historic/NewsReleases/1966/19660127b.pdf.

13. "Udall Limits Use of Pesticides," *St. Petersburg (FL) Times*, September 6, 1964, news.google.com/newspapers?nid=888&dat=19640906&id=MrpSAAAAIBAJ&sjid=DnoDAAAAIBAJ&pg=3599,2683717&hl=en.

14. John W. Finney, "Udall Asks a Ban on Key Pesticides," *New York Times*, April 9, 1964, nytimes.com/1964/04/09/udall-asks-a-ban-on-key-pesticides.html. See also transcript, Stewart L. Udall oral history interview V, by Joe B. Frantz, December 16, 1969, LBJ Library, lbjlibrary.net/assets/documents/archives/oral_histories/udall/UDALL05.PDF; and Graham, *Since "Silent Spring,"* 110.

15. Graham, *Since "Silent Spring,"* 74–78; Doyle, "Power in the Pen"; John W. Finney, "Ribicoff Offers Pesticide Curbs," *New York Times*, May 1, 1964, nytimes.com /1964/05/01/ribicoff-offers-pesticide-curbs.html.

16. US Department of the Interior, Office of the Secretary, news release, "Secretary Udall Dedicates New Federal Research Laboratory; Warns of Pesticides Hazards," April 25, 1963, fws.gov/news/ShowNews.cfm?ID=5B96B2EB-ED61-7C3A-30728 d37e63074d7.

17. Eric Wentworth, "From O'Os to Cui-uis, Rare Wildlife May Be Saved by Federal Plan," *Wall Street Journal*, August 10, 1965, box 154, folder 2, Udall Papers; "Man, the Endangered Species," *New York Times*, January 27, 1966, ibid.

18. US Department of the Interior, Office of the Secretary, *Native Fish and Wildlife Endangered Species*, Fed. Reg., Doc. 67-2758, February 24, 1967; US Department of the Interior, "40 Years of the Endangered Species Act: Remarkable Origin, Resilience, and Opportunity," January 14, 2013, doi.gov/sites/doi.gov/files/migrated /ppa/upload/40-Years-of-the-Endangered-Species-Act.pdf.

19. Stewart L. Udall, interview in Tim Palmer, *Endangered Rivers and the Conservation Movement* (New York: Rowman & Littlefield, 2004), 166.

20. US Department of the Interior, news release, "Udall Calls for Cooperative Effort to Save Wildlife," July 21, 1968, fws.gov/.

21. Leunes, "Conservation Philosophy of Udall," 95.

7 | Transitioning the Bureau of Land Management to Multiple Use

The increase in [grazing] fees which has been under consideration would be substantial because in the past the charges have been purely nominal.

IN 1961 THE Bureau of Land Management's official emblem depicted a miner, rancher, logger, and surveyor, each individual complete with their gear and specialized tools. Behind these natural resource extractors and users, train tracks, covered wagons, and industrial development dominated the scene. By the middle of the decade, the BLM had a new logo that depicted a winding river, grassland, conifer, and mountain—"snowcapped as a result of mountain climber Udall's suggestion," remembered BLM director Charles Stoddard. The difference between the old and new emblems, with the old depicting "private initiative, natural resource development, and human progress" and the new promoting conservation, multiple use, and multiple landscapes, symbolizes the major changes brought about within the bureau in the 1960s.[1] A Department of the Interior agency that, according to its official biographers, had much soul-searching and shifting to do in the decade, the BLM, with Udall's help, turned from a "giveaway" bureau with short-term policies into a public lands conservation bureau with a long-term view of land retention and protection.[2]

First known as the General Land Office, the BLM, for much of its history, served as the biggest real estate agent in the world. Indeed, while the Louisiana Purchase and Treaty of Guadalupe Hidalgo gave the US government hundreds of millions of acres of new land in the first half of the nineteenth century, it was the GLO that orchestrated public disposal of these lands at minimal prices to homesteaders, miners, and railroad tycoons. Then, in the first several decades of the twentieth century, the GLO transferred sizable acreage to the US Forest Service, National Park Service, armed forces, and other government entities. In 1946 the GLO combined with the US Grazing Service to form the BLM, and by 1961, despite the newly named agency's one-hundred-year policy of land disposal, it still administered tens of millions of acres of land throughout the US West, primarily but not exclusively in dry, vast, remote areas of Nevada, Utah, Wyoming, and Alaska.

The lands administered by the BLM had many problems by 1961. Stemming from years of slow bureaucracy, the agency had a backlog of sixty thousand land-acquisition applications upon Udall's arrival as interior secretary. Furthermore, for decades, BLM grazing policies had allowed for widespread soil exhaustion and depletion. Because BLM lands had been used primarily for grazing and mineral extraction, the agency was both critically and jokingly referred to by its detractors as the Bureau of Livestock and Mines. This was the state of the Bureau of Land Management when Udall arrived as its "head sheriff."[3]

Fortunately, eight years later, the BLM was on a much better track. According to bureau historians James Muhn and Hanson Stuart, Udall tackled the bureau's problems head-on in the 1960s:

> Inspired by the conservation accomplishments of Theodore and Franklin Roosevelt, Secretary Udall launched the nation's "Third Conservation Wave" by requesting a new legislative mandate for the public lands from Congress. Part of this agenda included formal recognition of multiple use management on BLM lands, patterned after the Forest Service's Multiple Use Sustained Yield Act of 1960. Other components centered on getting BLM a more flexible land sale authority and repealing outdated settlement acts.
>
> But more than a push for legislation, the Third Conservation Wave was a philosophy—one that viewed natural resources as finite, interrelated, and vulnerable components of

larger systems. According to Udall, the Interior Department had "the prime function of planning for the future of America and working to conserve the natural resources which sustain its life." The Department's 1961 Annual Report spoke of a "quiet crisis" facing America's citizens, the result of unplanned progress and explosive growth—something that threatened the nation's natural resources and its citizens' quality of life. Careful management of America's public lands could turn the tide, and this could only be done with extensive planning and involvement from the public.[4]

While the BLM was not 100 percent backward before Udall, and while it didn't become 100 percent perfect because of Udall, the agency did evolve and progress by leaps and bounds in the 1960s, as Muhn and Stuart suggest. Specifically, with direction from Congress, the Bureau of Land Management surveyed its land, decided to permanently retain much of it, and then classified it into specific multiple-use categories. Udall was significantly involved in this process. He was also a key figure in the battle to increase grazing fees on BLM lands, thus resulting in increased funds for rangeland conservation and restoration efforts.[5] This chapter spotlights these developments within the BLM, specifically as they relate to the main subject of this book, Stewart Udall.

The Classification and Multiple Use (C&MU) Act

Regarding the land-application backlog, shortly after becoming interior secretary, Udall issued an eighteen-month freeze so that the BLM could take a step back and figure out a more efficient system of processing and implementing the applications. Karl Landstrom, Udall's first BLM director, largely oversaw the overhaul of the system, which resulted in a reduction by half in the amount of time needed to process applications. Yet Congress, much of the American public, many BLM land users, and Udall wanted the agency to be more than just a land-giveaway bureau, and therefore in 1964 Congress passed the BLM's Classification and Multiple Use Act.[6]

The act called for the BLM to survey and then classify its land, and the BLM did just this. Through the surveying, BLM employees determined which land the agency should hold as part of its public lands system and which it should dispose of and sell (the selling was specifically completed through the Public Land Sale Act, passed the same time as the C&MU).[7] "Lands were to be disposed of if they were either required for the orderly growth and development of a community or [if they were] chiefly valuable for residential, commercial, agricultural, industrial, or public uses or development," a 1970s Interior Department report asserted. Otherwise, BLM lands were to be retained and managed by the agency not just for cattle grazing and mineral extraction, but also for fish, wildlife, and watershed protection and management; outdoor recreation; and wilderness preservation. For the first time in its history, then, the BLM officially began disposing of its land-disposal policy.[8]

Knowing that its holdings involved many different users and interests, the BLM sought extensive local and community input in every step of its land-classification and multiple-use recommendation processes. The BLM's ultimate findings concluded that there was "broad local support" for the federal agency retaining the vast majority of its lands and managing them for multiple uses. State resource agencies as well as all of the board members of the Western Region of the National Association of Counties fully supported the BLM's retaining and categorizing its lands. In fact, BLM proposals to transfer lands out of federal ownership often met with sharp resistance, as in several cases in southern Arizona.[9]

After the surveying and decision about retention came land classification. Based largely on the Forest Service's policy of multiple use, which was seen as highly successful and forward thinking for the time, Udall, Interior Undersecretary John Carver, and high-level BLM bureaucrats developed a system of land categories based on each land unit being managed for one primary use. As such, scientific natural areas, later reclassified as research natural areas, were established in the 1960s to preserve examples of each ecosystem found on BLM lands for comparative research and scientific study and to ensure the survival of animal and plant species. Another land classification involved recreation. As the name suggests, these were land parcels set aside primarily for outdoor exercise and fun in the form of hiking, horseback riding, hunting, and sightseeing. Udall established Red Rocks Recreation Area in 1967 as the first such land unit. Located just outside Las Vegas, today the area is known as Red Rock Canyon National Conservation Area and attracts more than one million visitors annually. Other BLM lands were set aside in the 1960s as wildlife management areas, resource conservation areas, primitive areas (which were to be managed as de facto wilderness areas), and more. Historian James Skillen notes that many of these lands that were first protected and classified in the 1960s were redesignated as national monuments, a more prestigious and protective title, in the 1990s and early 2000s by President Bill Clinton. He did so with the urging of Bruce Babbitt, his interior secretary and the second cabinet member in history from the state of Arizona.[10]

While most lands overlap in their uses and cannot simply be classified for one specific use, the steps taken in the 1960s by the BLM represented progress. One move that Udall made that petered out over the years, though, was naming BLM lands "national resource lands." Indeed, for most people, today as in the 1960s, national park units, national forests, and to a lesser extent national wildlife refuges—the three other major types of US public lands—are much easier to recognize than public lands administered by the BLM. This is because these first three categories have roadside signs in place demarcating the land as such—Inyo National Forest, Mount Rainier National Park, and so on. Furthermore, national park units and often national wildlife refuges and national forests show up in special colors on tourist and state maps. BLM lands, on the other hand, are not widely known by people outside of their key stakeholders. One major reason for this is that the BLM's lands do not have an official name. For instance, the National Park Service has its lands classified as national parks, national monuments, national recreation areas, and so forth, and the US Forest Service has its national forests, but what does the BLM have? Udall noted this exact problem and pushed for general BLM lands to be classified as "national resource lands." The primary reason for naming BLM lands as national resource lands was, according to Udall, "to provide easy identification of these areas and help in familiarizing the public with lands administered by the BLM."[11]

However, while the "national resource lands" nomenclature was implemented by BLM employees under Udall, it has fallen out of fashion since the 1970s. And so to this day, with the exception of BLM-administered national monuments, federal wilderness areas, and other lands constituting its relatively new "National Landscape Conservation System," the BLM does not have an official name for the majority of its lands.

BLM Challenges and Controversies

During the BLM's land-classification era, a major power struggle developed between the agency and Representative Wayne Aspinall of Colorado. Aspinall, described as an autocrat in his chairmanship of the House committee focused on DOI affairs, believed that such duties as land classification should be controlled by the legislature rather than the executive branch of government, perhaps because he himself was a legislator. Additionally, Aspinall was generally in favor of utilization and development of public lands in terms of mining, grazing, reclamation, and more. Ironically, perhaps, in a decade in which many Republicans joined Democrats and voted in favor of environmental and conservation legislation, Aspinall, essentially a conservative Democrat, often single-handedly held up much of the legislation for weeks, months, and years on end.[12]

Another BLM controversy of the decade involved the agency's management of wild horses. Considered feral animals under the law and therefore unqualified for wildlife protection of any kind, wild horses were resented by many rangeland managers and cattlemen because they competed with stock for the already limited grass supply. BLM staff also knew that the majority of horses roaming the public lands had until recently been domesticates; they were displaced into the "great wide open" by America's increasing mechanization, as the tractor replaced the horse-drawn plow and the automobile replaced the horse-drawn carriage in the early and mid-1900s. Yet with decreasing wild horse populations due to increasing BLM-sponsored roundups, and with these roundups often ending in horses being taken to a slaughterhouse, ground up, and then used as animal feed and pet food, the climate became ripe for protest.[13]

Led by Nevada resident Velma Johnston, who witnessed a particularly bloody and violent BLM roundup, opposition to what was perceived as the inhumane treatment of wild horses grew. Wild Horse Annie, as Johnston is remembered, founded the International Society for the Protection of Mustangs and Burros in 1965.[14]

As a result of the push to protect the lives of wild horses, and also the broadening concept of multiple-use management within the BLM, Udall, Nevada's BLM state director, the commander of Nellis Air Force Base, and the Nevada Fish and Game Commission (now known as the Nevada Department of Wildlife) worked out an agreement and established the Nevada Wild Horse Range in 1963. The wild horse range was set aside as a 435,000-acre refuge on the land within the base. Udall told the press, upon the establishment of the Nevada Wild Horse Range, that "preserving a typical herd of feral horses in one of the nation's most isolated areas may prove difficult, but we will make an effort to assure those of us who admire the wild horse that there will always be some of these animals. To many people, the wild horse is a symbol of an inspiring era in the west." Indeed, after Udall's announcement, a newspaper quipped that President Kennedy's "New Frontier has taken steps to preserve a bit of the old frontier."[15]

By interior secretary order, Udall established an additional horse refuge in Montana. The Pryor Mountains Wild Horse Range was created in 1968. Both of the wild horse ranges were then managed so as to maintain their carrying capacity while at the same time enabling grazing to continue on adjacent lands.[16]

All in all, land classification—whether wild horse range or otherwise—and the switch to multiple use "changed BLM forever," noted Muhn and Stewart. The agency no longer classified lands on a case-by-case basis arising from petitions and permit requests. Instead, the BLM began planning for and managing all of its lands. As Muhn and Stewart wrote, "The bureau no longer managed its holdings along individual program lines; it integrated each activity into land use plans that would [in Udall's own words] 'best meet the present and future needs of the American people.'"[17]

Grazing-Fee Increase
for Increased Land Restoration

Aside from working to classify lands, organize them under specific use categories, and protect some of the most scenic and biologically diverse areas, Udall helped successfully push for a substantial increase in grazing fees on BLM lands. He did this due to a push from federal politicians outside the states with significant BLM lands. The reason for increasing the grazing fees was to expand the moneys dedicated to soil conservation and protection on these lands in order to make them sustainable.

"The increase in fees which has been under consideration would be substantial because in the past the charges have been purely nominal," the interior secretary told a large group of cattlemen at the annual convention of the American National Cattlemen's Association in Las Vegas in 1963. While some of the cattlemen didn't approve of the fee increase and actually walked out in the middle of Udall's speech, some also knew they had been getting a bargain deal and that an increase in fees was inevitable. The Forest Service charged over 150 percent more for its grazing fee, and Udall, Agriculture Secretary Orville Freeman, and others believed it was time for the BLM to get its fee system more in line. "People who use the public domain should help pay the costs. We think that is true if you use the land for grazing livestock," Udall told the cattlemen at the meeting.

> The present 19-cent [grazing] fee does not seem realistic. It does not appear to represent value delivered. It does not seem to provide adequately for range improvement. It could constitute a possible source of major trouble from an irate public. Forest Service fees average more than 50 cents per animal....
>
> Fees [obtained by the BLM] brought in about $3 million in 1962; [yet] we spent over $12 million for management and

maintenance. Fees won't bring in much more this year, yet we
are faced with spending around $17 million. If the rancher who
has economic dependence on public lands is to get his forage,
his part-time landlord, the Government, must produce it. It
is obvious that the rancher should pay a fair share for the resource which benefits him.[18]

To Udall, the revenue accrued from the increase in grazing fees
could help combat "the gullies and erosion which have resulted
from overgrazing." Moreover, the fee increase could help stop the
"invasion of millions of acres by noxious and poor quality brush and
weeds," including cheatgrass, greasewood, select species of catclaw,
and other invasive nonnative plant species that outcompete native
grasses and plants.[19]

Despite some opposition from those who stood to lose profits due
to the fee increase, the increase succeeded and the BLM's grazing
fee shot up to $0.33 per animal per month (animal unit month, or
AUM). Later in the decade, after the BLM and USFS completed a joint
six-year study of grazing fees that included gathering information
from 218 financial institutions, ten thousand interviews, and fourteen thousand questionnaires to determine a fair price for federal
grazing permits, Udall and Freeman pushed through a plan for a
uniform grazing fee of $1.23 per AUM on BLM and USFS lands. The
cabinet members announced the increase to occur in phases over a
ten-year period.[20]

As a result of more moneys for the BLM in the 1960s, significant
rangeland revitalization and conservation occurred. One important
improvement was the creation of conservation plans, or, more formally, allotment management plans, developed jointly by individual
cattlemen and livestock operators as well as BLM officials. Many of
these plans called for and implemented rest-rotation grazing systems: just as a thoughtful farmer allows his field to remain fallow
for part of the year in order to let the soil regain its health and nutri-
ents, cattlemen keep their cattle off the range for extended periods
each year to let the rangeland recover.[21]

The BLM took other steps in the 1960s in its transition from a de facto Bureau of Livestock and Mines to an actual land-management and conservation agency. As in the NPS, science came to the forefront, reflected in the increasing number of professional biologists within the BLM and the creation of new divisions dedicated to wildlife, watersheds, and recreation.[22]

Along these same lines, BLM and Arizona wildlife officials worked together to reintroduce pronghorn antelope on public lands in the Arizona Strip, a remote corner of the state between the Grand Canyon and the Utah border. "The world's record prong-horn trophy" was taken from the area in 1878, noted a news release from Udall's office, but by the early 1920s, due to overhunting, the fast-moving mammal had been extirpated from the land. Udall announced in 1961, though, that twenty to forty pronghorns were to be released in the aptly named Antelope Valley area and that "the local ranchers and sportsmen and State and Federal officials who have worked out the long-sought establishment of antelope in the Strip deserve long applause for their hard work in the cause of conservation."[23]

Though a minority of the populace resented the expanding role of the federal government in general and the BLM in particular, most of America approved. This, in tandem with LBJ's Great Society and BLM grazing-fee increases, led to major funding and staffing increases for the BLM during the Udall years. From 1960 to 1966, BLM's workforce grew from twenty-five hundred to four thousand employees, while its budget grew from thirty-five to eighty-eight million dollars.[24]

Rebuttal to the Backlash Against the BLM

While the vast majority of citizens and elected officials approved of increased BLM land protection, revitalization, and management in the 1960s, a small windstorm of opposition was growing. Certain ranchers, elected officials, and others despised the increased grazing fees and didn't like the US government telling them what they could and could not do. Udall referred to these individuals cumulatively as "antifederalists," or, more fully, "the anti-federal government movement of the West." Fundamentally a liberal Democrat in that he believed in the helping hands of "big government" to improve the environmental and social wellness of the country, Udall believed that antifederalists suffered from "Zane Grey Syndrome," that is, an oversimplified worldview in which they believed that there were only "bad bureaucrats" and "good individualists."[25]

Antifederalism and the push for states' rights in public lands management in the West perhaps culminated with Ronald Reagan's election as president and the so-called Sagebrush Rebellion of the 1980s, in which the movement attempted (but spectacularly failed) to transfer BLM lands to state governments. However, more than a decade and a half before this time, Udall argued strongly against the antifederalist belief system. "States' rights and other anti-federal slogans have taken the same form in the West as in the South. The federal government's role as proprietor of the public estate is attacked as forcefully by some western spokesman as the federal government's role as the protector of civil rights is attacked by the southern segregationists," Udall told a University of New Mexico audience in 1964. "To remind these westerners that the federal activities and appropriations have underwritten much of the West's progress is about as fruitless as to remind the South that only as all Americans enjoy civil rights can we realize our full potential as an equal-opportunity society that revitalizes America each generation."[26]

According to Udall, the antifederalists' warnings of federal land grabs, federal "lockups" of resources, and "the insidious encroachments of the agents of big bureaucracy" were ignorant and unfounded. "Let us begin with the essential facts," the interior secretary said.

> It is indeed a fact that half the land of the eleven westernmost contiguous states is in federal ownership. It is also a fact that in these eleven states, three quarters of these 400 odd million federal acres are managed by the Forest Service and Bureau of Land Management for mineral, forage, timber, and outdoor recreation values. The other quarter contributes to the na-

tional welfare as areas reserved for national parks, military reservations, and Indian reservations....

The truth of the matter is that the federal government maintains, conserves, and develops these lands as a common estate that each of you, if you obey the rules, can use at will. In a very real sense we are all owners and proprietors of the public lands. Take it from one who is of late a fenced-in easterner, your ownership of and ready access to these spacious, scenic lands at your back door is a precious heritage that includes a special brand of personal freedom![27]

Continuing his strong stance against antifederalist beliefs, Udall asserted that it was ironic for these individuals to ignore how important a role the federal government had played in the development and settlement of the West. "To listen to some latter day orators, one might think that the federal government had nothing to do with the development of the West. That kind of talk, of course, does not reckon with the daring diplomacy of Thomas Jefferson, John Quincy Adams, and James K. Polk; each presided over an acquisition of territory now included in the Western states," the interior secretary exclaimed. "Lewis and Clark and later army officers explored the West. Others reconnoitered the prospective railroad routes more than a century ago. Federal land grants made transcontinental railroads possible. Government geologists King, Powell, and Hayden systematically reported the mineral wealth. Congress passed settlement laws, the Homestead Act, the Desert Land Act, the Timber and Stone Act, and the mining laws." Udall continued on, listing more benefits that the federal government provided the West. Also on this list were the massive dam-building projects completed by the Bureau of Reclamation and US Army Corps of Engineers, which enabled new farm fields to be cultivated, much to the benefit of western farmers.[28]

The secretary of the interior concluded that the federal government had lent a massively helpful hand in the settlement and management of the western half of the country and that the antifederalists would do well to realize this.

To sum up, I submit that whether one measures it by the conservation objectives achieved, by living values attained, by the economic consequences of our federal-state-people program of cooperation, or by the future opportunity the West has not only to grow but to grow right, the federal government has been a creative partner this century in the development of the West.

There is much unfinished work, and we cannot afford the luxury of anti-federalism. It is my hope that in the years ahead the people of the West will reject the sterile doctrines of anti-federalism and build a bright future based on the patterns of action and cooperation of the past.[29]

Notes

1. James Muhn and Hanson R. Stuart, *Opportunity and Challenge: The Story of BLM*, 51, 116.

2. Ibid., 104–6.

3. Ibid., 122. See also James R. Skillen, *The Nation's Largest Landlord: The Bureau of Land Management in the American West*, 28–39.

4. Muhn and Stuart, *Opportunity and Challenge*, 104.

5. Samuel Hays also gives Udall ample credit for initiating improvements to the BLM in the 1960s. See his *Beauty, Health, and Permanence: Environmental Politics in the United States, 1955–1985*, 128.

6. Muhn and Stuart, *Opportunity and Challenge*, 106, 108, 111, 112–13.

7. D. Michael Harvey, "Public Land Management under the Classification and Multiple Use Act," *Natural Resources Lawyer* 2, no. 3 (1969): 242, jstor.org/stable/40921619?seq=9#page_scan_tab_contents.

8. US Department of the Interior, *Final Report of the Task Force on the Availability of Federally Owned Mineral Lands*, 62–63. See also Charles Davis, "The Politics of Grazing on Federal Lands: A Policy Change Perspective," in *Punctuated Equilibrium and the Dynamics of U.S. Environmental Policy*, edited by Robert Repetto and James Gustave Spethe (New Haven, CT: Yale University Press, 2006), 236. Finally, see Richard H. Jackson, "Federal Lands in the Mountainous West," in *The Mountainous West: Explorations in Historical Geography*, edited by William Wyckoff and Lary M. Dilsaver, 267.

9. Harvey, "Public Land Management," 246–47.

10. Skillen, *Nation's Largest Landlord*, 154, 206; Muhn and Stuart, *Opportunity and Challenge*, 113.

11. Harvey, "Public Land Management," 249.

12. Skillen, *Nation's Largest Landlord*, 47–49. For better or worse, most of these 1990s national monument designations called for continued administration

by the BLM rather than transfer to the National Park Service, the organization that already had the experience, expertise, and history in managing national monuments.

13. Muhn and Stuart, *Opportunity and Challenge*, 142–50.

14. Craig C. Downer, "Women's Biographies: Velma Bronn Johnston, a.k.a. Wild Horse Annie," University of Nevada–Reno, unr.edu/nwhp/bios/women/johnston .htm; Muhn and Stuart, *Opportunity and Challenge*, 146–47.

15. "At Last, U.S. Acts to Save Wild Horses: Haven Established in Nevada Wilds," *Chicago Tribune*, February 11, 1963, archives.chicagotribune.com/1963/02/11/page /51/article/at-last-u-s-acts-to-save-wild-horse.

16. US Department of the Interior, Bureau of Land Management, "About the Prior Mountain Wild Horse Range," blm.gov/mt/st/en/fo/billings_field_office /wildhorses.html. See also Muhn and Stuart, *Opportunity and Challenge*, 149–50.

17. Muhn and Stuart, *Opportunity and Challenge*, 112.

18. US Department of the Interior, Office of the Secretary, news release, "Excerpts from Remarks by Secretary of the Interior Stewart L. Udall Before the 66th Annual Convention of the American National Cattlemen's Association," January 30, 1963, box 110, folder 1, Udall Papers.

19. Ibid.

20. Skillen, *Nation's Largest Landlord*, 75–76.

21. Muhn and Stuart, *Opportunity and Challenge*, 133.

22. Ibid., 116, 150.

23. US Department of the Interior, Office of the Secretary, news release, "First Antelope to Return to Northern Arizona in Half Century," September 24, 1961, box 154, folder 1, Udall Papers.

24. Skillen, *Nation's Largest Landlord*, 38.

25. Stewart L. Udall, "The West and Its Public Lands: Aid or Obstacle to Progress?"

26. Ibid. While the 1980s Sagebrush Rebellion and the more recent 2016 short-lived occupation of the Malheur National Wildlife Refuge are the modern examples of a small faction trying to make certain federal lands transfer to the states, these factions have been present for decades. David H. Stratton, in *Tempest over Teapot Dome: The Story of Albert B. Fall* (Norman: University of Oklahoma Press, 1998), writes extensively on Fall's states'-rights stance of the early 1900s when Fall was a New Mexico politician.

27. Udall, "West and Its Public Lands."

28. Ibid.

29. Ibid.

8 | Establishing Wild Rivers and Supporting Reclamation

Water in rivers should be as clean as possible,
not as unclean as admissible.

UDALL'S ACCOMPLISHMENTS and policies as interior secretary in terms of national parks, wildlife, and changes to Bureau of Land Management policy have been analyzed in the last four chapters. Another major responsibility of the Arizona native was "all things water." Indeed, when it comes to water, in the 1960s the Department of the Interior held under its umbrella the Bureau of Reclamation, Office of Water Desalinization, and, beginning in the middle of the decade, the Federal Water Pollution Control Administration (FWPCA). Udall also became the chairman of the Water Resources Council. As the ultimate head of many water-based federal agencies, and as a passionate advocate of conservation and environmental protection, Udall was heavily involved in the works of the water agencies and in broadscale water policies in the 1960s. This chapter focuses on Udall's involvement in the establishment of both wild rivers and dams and his work on water conservation and energy-efficiency projects, reclamation diplomacy, and, finally, water-pollution control.

Dam Dilemmas

In 1967, after ample study, the secretary of the interior issued a statement declaring his rejection of Alaska's Rampart Dam project. The dam, proposed by the US Army Corps of Engineers along the mighty Yukon River in an area known as the Yukon Flats, would have created the largest man-made reservoir in the world. Backing up water for 280 miles along the Yukon, the reservoir would have been larger than Lake Erie. After it became clear to Udall that this massive reservoir and dam project would destroy the river that was home to more waterfowl than all national wildlife refuges combined, he opted for no Rampart Dam, and the dam was never built.[1]

Perhaps if Udall had been an Alaskan politician, he might have come out in favor of the dam. But Udall took his jobs seriously; when he served in the US House of Representatives, he represented and supported Arizona, but as interior secretary for the whole country and as a member of the executive branch of government, Udall had to make decisions based on what was best not just for Arizona or Alaska but for the entire country. In addition, in the 1950s and especially the 1960s the country was at a crossroads with regard to dam building.

Though large-scale reclamation projects had been endorsed for decades by the majority of society, with the increase in ecological awareness of the time, environmental concerns regarding dam building were growing. These included the fact that by altering downstream water flow, dams altered stream-side habitat and biodiversity. Dams also trapped nutrient-rich sediment behind them instead of dispersing its life-supporting soil particles downstream. Next, dams altered water temperatures and oxygen levels, thus affecting fish and other aquatic wildlife species. Finally, one could argue that man-made dams simply marred the views of wild landscapes. These were the general arguments against dams, and they all played heavily in Udall's decision against the Rampart Dam on the Yukon River.[2]

Arguments for dams included the fact that they provided cheap, reliable energy and stored water behind them in massive reservoirs that could then be used to irrigate farm fields and provide water to suburbia and the cities. Furthermore, reservoirs offered water-based recreation opportunities, which the ORRRC report said were incredibly popular among American citizens. Interestingly, there was little recognition at the time of the clean, renewable-energy benefits of dams—they do not emit carbon dioxide into the atmosphere.

While Udall ultimately came out against Rampart Dam, one can see his challenges regarding reclamation policy as a whole. On one side of the equation, he managed a powerful federal agency in the Bureau of Reclamation with a powerful, politically connected director named Floyd Dominy, whose battle cry might well have been "Dam, dam, dam." At the same time, Udall oversaw the National Park Service, an agency with nonprofit groups, including the Sierra Club, National Parks Conservation Association, and others, watching over it closely and generally keen on preserving national park natural resources as they were. These environmental organizations subscribed to a general "no-dam" policy. What could and should Udall have done in overseeing both a reclamation bureau and a nature protection bureau?

He supported both. Udall balanced dam-building projects with river-preservation projects, thus promoting dams in some cases and wild rivers in many others. While some might call this a cop-out, Udall consistently and successfully promoted compromise throughout the 1960s and beyond, and his balancing of dams with wild rivers was a classic example. In fact, the art of compromise was one of the major reasons Udall accomplished so much good as interior secretary.

This balancing act and compromising with both conservationists and dam proponents were major changes from the policies of Representative Stewart Udall, who had been seemingly a full-fledged supporter of dam building in the state of Arizona. In the 1960s, "Udall personified the upheaval happening in water development philosophy," notes historian Tim Palmer in *Endangered Rivers and the Conservation Movement*. "He had supported dams that were the epitome of river destruction and that rallied conservationists to the cause of river protection." But in his first year as interior secretary, "with the help of people who were working to save their rivers, by experiencing these waterways personally from a canoe or a raft, and with the statesman's regard for his job," Udall came to see the need for balancing dam building with river preservation. "This man stood uniquely as a river developer and a river saver both, bearing the complications and compromises inherent in the holding of two opposite views at once."[3]

Indeed, four specific things happened to Udall in 1961 that caused his shift from proreclamation to balancing river preservation with river development. First and foremost, he became interior secretary. Whereas US representatives and senators represent a specific state, members of the executive branch of government, such as cabinet-level secretaries, are supposed to represent the entire nation. In a 1983 interview with Palmer, Udall remembered that in early 1961, "Suddenly I had the national responsibility, and that put on my shoulders the burden of thinking for the nation and not just for Arizona, which is what a congressman would do when it comes to water."[4]

Second, Udall joined Senator Edmund Muskie (D-ME) on a canoe trip on northeastern Maine's Allagash River. The duo took a little floatplane, landed on the river, and then toured the wilderness waterway. Muskie and Udall went canoeing during the height of the controversy over the proposed Rankin Rapids Dam. Muskie and much of Maine wanted the river left in its natural state, and the senator invited Udall to experience the river firsthand to see what would be lost if the dam were to be built. The experience left a lasting impression on the interior secretary; there weren't many rivers in Arizona, and the Allagash trip was actually the first canoeing experience of Udall's life. "The Allagash was identified as one of the finest wild rivers in the eastern part of the country, and the fact that the people in Maine wanted to save it left an impression on me," he remembered.[5]

A third catalyst for Udall changing from a prodam politician to a believer in the need for balance between dams and wild rivers was his 1961 involvement in the push to establish Ozarks National Scenic Riverways, which resulted in southern Missouri's Jacks Fork and Current Rivers being preserved in their natural state. Udall toured these wilderness waterways, a precursor to the National Wild and Scenic River System, much like he did Maine's Allagash (see chapter 4).[6]

Finally, conservation and fishing groups asked Udall to intervene and help stop the Bruce's Eddy Dam (now known as the Dworshack Dam) on Idaho's Clearwater River just weeks after he became interior secretary. The fishermen's argument against the dam— namely, that the dam would destroy mass quantities of fish—was a strong one, according to Udall, and the secretary of the interior was also amazed by the beauty and wildness of the river. While it was too late to stop the dam from being built, Udall did manage to work with congressmen to add an amendment to the bill that prohibited additional dams along the Clearwater. Though this amendment was removed before the vote, "the Clearwater case led Udall to reconsider nothing less than the philosophy of dam building, and he suddenly became committed to balancing the federal water program," notes Palmer.[7]

The National Wild and Scenic Rivers System

Regarding wild rivers, the Ozark National Scenic Riverways was the first national park unit dedicated to protecting clean, dam-free rivers. However, the year before the riverways' 1964 establishment, Udall and Agriculture Secretary Freeman created a federal wild rivers study team to survey the state of rivers throughout the United States and look at the feasibility of keeping some of them forever wild and free-flowing rather than developed. The leader of the study team was Frank Craighead, a cutting-edge scientist who had proposed a river classification system in a magazine article and whom Udall had hand-selected for the role.[8]

The result of Craighead's study was Udall's writing and then submitting to Congress a draft bill to establish a "National Wild Rivers System."[9] The bill was then pushed for by Senators Frank Church of Idaho and Walter Mondale of Minnesota as well as Representative John Saylor, Republican of Pennsylvania.[10] Conservative Democrat Wayne Aspinall, a devout reclamation advocate, was a formidable foe of the bill in the beginning, but Udall and Saylor hammered Aspinall so much that the Colorado congressman eventually came around. Aspinall did see to it, however, that essentially no pending dam projects would be affected by the wild rivers bill's passage. Regarding other reclamation proponents, Udall believed that "the dam people who didn't like it just weren't in a frame of mind yet to fight it. I had been pretty good to them, giving them some of the things they wanted."[11]

During congressional hearings for the wild rivers system, Udall argued that a network of undammed rivers would significantly benefit water quality, trout fishing, and more. Yet many citizens who owned property bordering waterways came to strongly oppose the bill. In their minds, they feared that their land would be taken or that they would be given a strict set of laws for managing it. Other citizens pushed for the bill, though, because they wanted to ensure the protection of their favorite rivers. As a compromise between the two factions, many of the rivers that ultimately came to be officially protected were on public or state-owned lands rather than in areas with large-scale private property.[12]

The bill called for immediate federal protection of significant portions of Idaho's Salmon River as well as the Middle Fork of the Clearwater, Oregon's Rogue River, New Mexico's upper Rio Grande, Wyoming's Green River, and the entire length of Georgia and Florida's Suwanee River, from its source in Okefenokee Swamp to the Gulf of Mexico.[13] While these last two rivers never gained National Wild and Scenic River status, the Clearwater, Salmon, Rogue, and upper Rio Grande, in addition to Wisconsin's Wolf River and St. Croix River, California's Feather River, and Missouri's Eleven Point River, were immediately protected with the passage of the National Wild and Scenic Rivers Act on October 2, 1968.[14]

"A few summers ago, after Secretary Udall took his lovely family on a float trip of high adventure down the turbulent Colorado River, he returned to Washington and said that every individual and every family should get to know at least one river," President Johnson remarked upon the signing of the bill, which passed the House of Representatives by a bipartisan margin of 265 to 7. "Today we are initiating a new national policy which will enable more Americans to get to know more rivers." He continued:

At Udall's urging, the Rio Grande in northern New Mexico was federally designated as a wild and scenic river in 1968. Today this section of river forms the backbone of the BLM's Rio Grande del Norte National Monument, established by President Obama. Photo by author.

An unspoiled river is a very rare thing in this Nation today. Their flow and vitality have been harnessed by dams and too often they have been turned into open sewers by communities and by industries. It makes us all very fearful that all rivers will go this way unless somebody acts now to try to balance our river development.

So we are establishing a National Wild and Scenic Rivers System which will complement our river development with a policy to preserve sections of selected rivers in their free-flowing conditions and to protect their water quality and other vital conservation values....

This is really a monument to you, Secretary Udall. Our children will remember your great adventures and pioneering.[15]

The National Wild and Scenic Rivers Act authorized the use of LWCF funds to acquire a one-quarter-mile protective corridor on both sides of designated rivers in cases where private property was present. It also outlawed federal dam projects on all officially designated wild and scenic rivers. Finally, it listed three types of protected rivers, with the designations still in place today. Wild rivers protected vestiges of primitive, remote America and had minimal human development along their borders. Scenic rivers were similar but had some road access for recreational purposes. Both wild rivers and scenic rivers had zero dams of any size along them. The third classification was recreational rivers, which were a bit more accessible and could have some development and possibly some past water-diversion or impoundment projects along their banks.[16]

The National Wild and Scenic Rivers Act, in addition to immediately protecting the aforementioned eight rivers as well as four portions of tributaries, called for additional studies to detemine rivers to be included in the system. As a result, in a little more than forty years, the National Wild and Scenic Rivers System has expanded from its initial eight to include over two hundred waterways across the nation.[17]

Water Reclamation and
the Kennedy Conservation Trips

As previously mentioned, on the other side of the "wild river coin" are dams, some of which Udall lobbied for and dedicated during the decade. During the Johnson administration alone, the Bureau of Reclamation built forty storage and power-producing dams, and the associated reservoirs, off-shoot canals, and piping systems provided irrigation services to more than one million acres of farmland. Furthermore, water infrastructure was developed to provide an additional ninety-nine billion gallons of water for municipal and industrial use in cities.[18]

Prior to LBJ, several reclamation projects were in the works during the Kennedy administration, as the era in general represented a peak in large federal dam-building projects—these were the "go-go years" of the Bureau of Reclamation, according to one agency employee.[19]

In order to drum up citizen interest in conservation, Udall actually talked JFK into going on two nationwide trips with him where they toured and dedicated reclamation projects as well as national park units.[20] During their first trip together, in September 1962,

Kennedy and Udall dedicated the Oahe Dam on the Missouri River near Pierre, South Dakota, in a special "Power-on-the-Line Ceremony." Creating a reservoir 231 miles long and stretching all the way to Bismarck, the dam project provided major flood-control, irrigation, and navigation services, in addition to offering a large supply of relatively cheap, clean electric power for the north-central states. Out west in California, later on in the same trip, Kennedy and Udall broke ground for the San Luis Dam in Los Banos. This agricultural area receives fewer than ten inches of rain per year, so water storage was a major benefit of the dam. During the trip, the duo also spoke at rallies on behalf of Senator George McGovern and Governor Pat Brown of California, as it was an election year and both of the popular politicians wanted to help ensure victory.[21]

A year later, just two months before Kennedy's fateful day in Dallas, Udall and JFK again traveled together on a conservation trip.

Udall, President Kennedy, and two others studying a model of Oahe Dam in South Dakota just before the dam dedication ceremony in August 1962. At Udall's urging, JFK took two conservation trips with his interior secretary to the western United States in order to drum up interest in conservation. Courtesy of the John F. Kennedy Library and Museum.

Udall and President Kennedy at the dedication of Whiskeytown Dam
in Northern California. To JFK's left is Undersecretary James K. Carr,
a native of Northern California and Udall's second in command at the
Department of the Interior during part of the decade. The photo was
taken only a month and a half before Kennedy's fateful day in Dallas.
Courtesy of the John F. Kennedy Library and Museum.

They visited Grey Towers, the Pennsylvania home of renowned
forester Gifford Pinchot; the newly established Apostle Islands National Lakeshore in Wisconsin; and the Yellowtail Dam construction
site in the Bighorn Canyon area of Montana and Wyoming, which
would, before the decade ended, become a National Park Service-
administered national recreation area. Among other site visits,
Udall and Kennedy attended and spoke at the formal dedication
ceremony for Whiskeytown Dam in California and then traveled
sixty miles east for an overnight stay in northeastern California's
spectacular Lassen Volcanic National Park.[22]

One of the reasons dam building was a common practice in the
mid–twentieth century was that there was a real fear among many
sectors of society that the nation would run out of water if additional sources were not secured. Population, agricultural production, and energy use were on upward trajectories. Furthermore, the
entire Eastern Seaboard endured a major drought in the early and
mid-1960s. For these reasons, the nation's politicians put policies in
place that would enable the country to have ample water and electricity well into the future.

The Columbia River Treaty and
Pacific Northwest–Pacific Southwest Intertie

In order to obtain additional electricity, stamp out the probability of electricity shortages for citizenry of the far-western United States, ensure energy efficiency, and enable agricultural expansion in eastern Washington and Oregon, the interior secretary as well as several other individuals, most notably Senator Henry "Scoop" Jackson (D-WA), Bonneville Power Administration administrator Charles Luce, and Bureau of Reclamation director Floyd Dominy, pushed for the passage of two major electric power generation and transfer projects in the 1960s. These ventures involved securing electricity rights for a series of dams in construction along the US-Canada border as well as the development of one of the largest, longest power lines in the world.

Proposed as early as the 1930s but somewhat formalized during the last days of the Eisenhower administration as a way for the United States to gain some of the Canadian section of the river's power supply, the Columbia River Treaty was planned out and approved only after Udall, Jackson, Luce, and others worked out all of the logistics and controversies with their British Columbian provincial and Canadian federal government counterparts. Udall in particular became heavily involved in the push to pass the treaty due to, in his words, the "monkey wrenching" done by British Columbia premier (governor) William Bennett, who understandably wanted his province, not just the US Pacific Northwest and Canadian federal government, to benefit from the project. Udall attended several Canadian government negotiation and planning meetings in Ottawa.[23]

Details were eventually fleshed out, and in 1964 the Columbia River Treaty was signed by LBJ and the Canadian prime minister. Four dams along the upper Columbia—three in British Columbia and one in northern Washington—were constructed as part of the treaty, while half of Canadian power generation from the dams was then given to the United States on an ongoing basis. The United States paid Canada sixty-five million dollars for dam construction and also paid yearly thereafter for its electricity supply. Canadian historian and public policy analyst Richard Kyle Paisley notes that "as a result of the treaty, the Columbia River is now the most dammed river in North America and the continent's biggest hydro-electricity producer. It is also perhaps the classic example in the world of the successful and equitable sharing of downstream benefits between two countries."[24]

For the same reasons as those claimed for ratifying the Columbia River Treaty, the same US politicians and bureaucrats pushed to pass the Pacific Northwest–Pacific Southwest Intertie. In lobbying for the intertie, the interior secretary described the project as the "truest" measure of conservation because "it will conserve energy, capital, manpower, and materials—the ingredients of a strong healthy economy."[25]

The massive project involved several private electric utility companies working with the Bonneville Power Administration, a power-transfer and infrastructure agency within the Department of the Interior at the time, on a system of four large power lines running from the Pacific Northwest to the Pacific Southwest. Each line was to be one thousand miles long. The intertie bill passed Congress, was signed by LBJ, and then was implemented in order to maximize the use of and minimize the waste of hydroelectric power.[26]

Described as an extra-high-voltage transmission system, the Pacific Northwest–Pacific Southwest Intertie benefited both the southwestern and the northwestern corners of the country. Immediately upon its completion, during the summer months populations in the US Southwest, including in Southern California, began using excess electricity from the Columbia and Snake River hydroelectric dams in order to keep their air conditioners and other appliances running. The northwestern rivers were swollen with snowmelt in summer, and thus hydroelectric power peaked during this time of year, yet not all of the electric power generation was being utilized until the intertie was built. Reversing the electricity sources and supply areas, during the winter months the intertie began benefiting Seattle, Portland, and other northwestern cities by taking excess electricity from the Southwest. With well-below-freezing

temperatures in the northern Rockies, Canadian Rockies, and Cascade Range, the Columbia and Snake River water flow was minimal
in winter and couldn't provide as much electricity as during the
summer months. But in the Southwest, with less air conditioning in
use during the winter, Colorado River hydropower was not used to
its capacity. Its excess was therefore transferred northward. Thus,
the intertie was seen as a win-win for both the Southwest and the
Northwest, as it maximized use of preexisting hydropower plants.[27]

According to a 1980 Bonneville Power Administration report,
the Pacific Southwest gained a net flow of more than 111 billion
kilowatt-hours of secondary energy from the Northwest, thus
saving the country from eventually having to build forty additional
500-megawatt coal-fired power plants. Between 1968 and 1976,
this energy flow conserved approximately 186 million barrels of
oil, worth about two and a half billion dollars. Bureau historians
Andrew Gahan and William Rowley note that "later in their lives
both Udall and Dominy remarked that the intertie was one of their
greatest accomplishments in government service."[28]

At a Portland, Oregon, dignitary breakfast celebrating the intertie legislation in late 1964, speaking to a crowd that included President Johnson and many others, Udall praised Charles Luce, the
Bonneville Power administrator, for his work on behalf of the intertie. "I know of no one that I have served with the last three and a
half years in the highest offices of government who is a better public
servant," the interior secretary claimed.[29]

Water Desalinization and Conservation

Besides dams, associated storage reservoirs, and water and electricity transfer infrastructure, an additional way of securing water is
desalinization, and there was emphasis on this in the 1960s. "Much
of the progress that has been made toward cheaper desalting is due
to a relatively small government agency called the Office of Saline
Water, which was established in the Department of the Interior in
1952," Udall wrote in an early 1960s newspaper article. He continued, noting that the Office of Saline Water was unique: "It does no
research itself. All the work it undertakes is conducted by contracts

with universities, private research organizations, industrial firms or other Federal agencies. Thus it is able to take advantage of the best brains across the country and apply that talent to desalting problems."[30]

Regarding research and development, back in 1958 Congress had authorized the construction of four desalinization plants, each one using different technologies to turn saltwater into freshwater. Udall was the interior secretary who oversaw the completion and resulting operation of these plants. They were located in Freeport, Texas; San Diego, California; Roswell, New Mexico; and Webster, South Dakota. While the Freeport and San Diego desalinization plants took water directly out of the ocean, the ones in New Mexico and South Dakota converted brackish water from underground aquifers.[31]

The San Diego plant in particular proved invaluable when Fidel Castro, just a few years after the Cuban Revolution and shortly after US-backed Cuban exiles tried to dispose of him in the failed Bay of Pigs incident, cut off the water supply to Guantánamo Naval Base. The solution to providing the isolated US military complex on the island with freshwater was for the Department of the Interior to offer up the San Diego desalinization plant, which was then moved lock, stock, and barrel to Guantánamo.[32]

Saline water research and development appropriations reached more than $11 million during the eight years of the Eisenhower administration, but during Kennedy's only three years as president, this amount was nearly doubled. The Johnson administration then skyrocketed appropriations for desalinization to $125 million over its five-year tenure. As a result, in the 1960s, saline water costs decreased from $1.75 per one thousand gallons in 1960 to $0.65 in 1968. And since the 1960s, the number of desalinization plants in the United States has grown from four experimental plants to almost four hundred.[33]

In addition to dam and desalinization development, Udall also emphasized the need to simply conserve water in each and every household and business. "We are a nation of water wasters," the interior secretary lamented.[34] Conserving water came naturally to Udall, due to his childhood growing up on arid land. President

Johnson, having been born and raised on a rural Texas farm and sharing some conservation convictions with Udall, put it succinctly when he said that "a civilization of faucet turners can regard water supply indifferently. The generations of bucket-carriers and cloud-watchers cannot. As one myself, I know."[35]

In regard to water conservation, one thing in particular that Udall did was lobby for New York City to make its citizens pay for their water; it was free for residents of the Big Apple until the 1960s. By charging households for water, Udall believed that families would be more inclined to watch and conserve their water usage rather than waste it. This was especially important, as the period from roughly 1960 to 1965 witnessed a drought up and down the Eastern Seaboard. Other cities were already charging for water, and New York City residents eventually did, too. Today, of course, almost every household in the United States pays for its water.[36]

Conservation Diplomacy and the Visit with Nikita Khrushchev

Udall emphasized and believed that American know-how in terms of water reclamation, desalinization, and conservation should be shared with other nations because it would "contribute, not only to world prosperity and to the war against hunger, but also to world peace."[37] As a result of this belief, and as a result of the Kennedy and then Johnson administrations wanting to promote the US version of democracy and capitalism worldwide, Udall and water engineers from the Interior Department went on several diplomatic trips abroad.

The interior secretary headed delegations to several arid countries in the eastern Mediterranean and Middle East, including Iran, Greece, Turkey, Jordan, Saudi Arabia, and Kuwait. Udall and his entourage talked to foreign officials about the benefits that desalinization plants would bring to their countries. He visited dam sites and discussed reclamation with heads of state.

Udall also enjoyed a two-week trip to East Africa to look at dam sites, national parks, and mines in Uganda, Tanzania (then known as Tanganyika), and Kenya. While the trip culminated in a world conference on national parks, perhaps the interior secretary's favorite part of it involved climbing Mount Kilimanjaro for fun, exercise, and the cause of conservation.

The climb was completed with a *Life* magazine photographer-journalist as well as members of the Tanganyika Rifles. Udall wrote that, on top of the 19,341-foot mountain, he was "elated by the stunning view of vast glaciers only miles from the equator." "Unlike any mountain in the world" were the words he used to describe Kilimanjaro. The interior secretary also noted that the hike had been a grueling one due to the shortness of breath and fatigue brought on by the high elevation. And while most of the climb was not too steep, the last four miles involved enduring a steady incline of forty-five degrees on a slope similar in consistency to deep sand.[38] "The most ambitiously vigorous member of the vigorous new Frontier" were the words *Life* used to describe the interior secretary.[39]

While Tanzania was a rather exotic locale for a US secretary of the interior to visit, perhaps the most surprising of Udall's international conservation trips was to the Soviet Union. The two-week trip focusing on USSR reclamation projects and electric power generation was capped by Udall's visit with Nikita Khrushchev. Ironically, it was not Secretary of Defense Robert McNamara or Secretary of State Dean Rusk but rather the secretary of the interior who became the first Kennedy administration cabinet member to meet with the Soviet premier in his home country.

In September 1962, Udall traveled to the Soviet Union with officials and advisers from the Department of the Interior's dam-building agency, the Bureau of Reclamation, as well as its electric power marketing and transfer bureaus, the Bonneville Power Administration, Southwestern Power Administration, and Southeastern Power Administration. Also along on the trip were administrators and engineers from the US Army Corps of Engineers, Tennessee Valley Authority, and Federal Power Commission. With the goal of seeing what they could learn from Soviet Union reclamation projects and engineers, the US delegation, headed by Udall, visited hydroelectric plants and electric power transfer and generation stations in Irkutsk, Bratsk, Saratov, Volgograd, and Moscow. They were given technical Soviet government documents related to dams and were overall received quite well throughout the adventure.[40]

Toward the end of the trip, while Interior Undersecretary John Carver led most of the group to northern Europe, Udall flew to Pitsunda, Georgia, to meet with the Soviet premier. At his mansion on the Black Sea, Chairman Khrushchev and the interior secretary talked for a couple of hours by Khrushchev's swimming pool, had a swim in the Black Sea, and then ate lunch. Khrushchev was quick to show off to Udall his sliding-glass doors, state of the art for the time. The conversation was most likely a bit tense for Udall, though.[41]

An expert on conservation rather than international politics and the Cold War, Udall must have been briefed significantly by the State Department before his meeting, for he handled the conversation with the USSR chairman extremely well, even with Khrushchev's critical remarks toward the United States. The premier told Udall that the United States was growing "old and impotent" and that "both of your [political] parties represent the interest of big capital." The Soviet premier would actually be removed a few months after Udall's visit, in large part due to his controversial rhetoric.[42]

On a more diplomatic note, however, when the two began discussing conservation and electricity generation and efficiency, Khrushchev told Udall that "the power field is a good one for competition [between the United States and the Soviet Union].... America has great potential in the field, and that's precisely why we want to compete with America. America is far ahead of us at present, and that makes the competition more interesting. Because when you catch up from so far behind, you have much more to be proud of. And in this competition, no one loses. This is not a competition to accumulate armaments—it's a competition for stockpiling wealth."[43]

Udall, with a thoughtfully executed Cold War joke, then succeeded in making Khrushchev laugh heartily. "I would agree with that, Mr. Chairman. You were very much behind, and you started to catch up with us," Udall told Khrushchev. "From what I have seen your people are doing very well in the power field. The most important thing is what a country does in the long run with its resources, and our two countries are both richly endowed with resources.

Where our engineers are ahead, we teach your technicians—and where Soviet engineers are ahead, we borrow their knowledge. Frankly, I am here to find out some of your secrets!"[44]

The Water Quality Act of 1965 and Its Aftermath

Besides emphasis on dam building and desalting plants, great stress was placed on water-pollution mitigation by Udall and the Department of the Interior, especially beginning in the mid-1960s. The major factor that pushed this emphasis on cleaner water was the increasing contamination of America's rivers and lakes.

As industries boomed in post–World War II America, there were very few laws regarding air- and water-pollution control. This resulted in unprecedented filth. Pesticides used in agriculture eventually washed into rivers, and factory refuse often did the same. And in urban areas, ample sewage from households and businesses was dumped straight into riverways due to antiquated sewer systems and the massive costs and engineering challenges of renovating them correctly.

Udall was given a firsthand example of water-pollution problems during a tour of the Lake Erie shoreline as well as the Cuyahoga River outside Cleveland. "I've seen rivers all over this country and this is one of the dirtiest," he told the Ohio crowd. He described the connection between the Cuyahoga, adjacent industries, and the river's pollution as "the 19th Century approach. It's outdated. It's barbaric."[45] The Cuyahoga River in particular ended up being a national symbol of pollution, its waters several times catching on fire due to the significant amounts of industrial-released oil in it.

Udall's major push on water-pollution mitigation began in earnest a year after the Water Quality Act of 1965, which passed Congress unanimously. The act increased federal funds for sewage-treatment plants, called for states to set and implement water-quality standards, and established the Federal Water Pollution Control Administration within the Department of Health, Education, and Welfare. However, due to Udall's push for pollution control, success on conservation and environmental measures, and strong relationships with the president and first lady, as well as

Udall, with Representative Tip O'Neill (*left*) and
Senator Ted Kennedy (*right*) observing a dirty river
in the late 1960s. Courtesy of the White House.

the fact that a geological and water-system study agency—the
US Geological Survey—was already operating within the Interior
Department, convinced Johnson to transfer the new bureau to the
Department of the Interior in 1966. With this move, Udall and com-
pany hit the ground running with water-pollution control.[46]

In order to decide and define water-quality standards, the first
thing that Udall did after gaining control of the FWPCA was to organize a group of eighty-six scientists, engineers, and water experts
to come up with the criteria. Next, Udall went to each state governor and asked them to provide the FWPCA with their state's proposals for water-quality standards.[47] In setting the standards, Udall

emphasized that "the water in rivers should be as clean as possible, not as unclean as admissible."[48]

The standards were critical in that they represented the keystone to the nation's massive water-cleanup program, providing it with a set of objectives. Therefore, it was important that the standards be stringent rather than lax. Congress, in passing the act, required that standards "protect the public health or welfare" and "enhance the quality of water." These principles guided the Interior Department in its work with the states and in its review of state standards, and Udall emphasized repeatedly to states that his Interior Department would not approve their standards unless they "provided for upgrading waters now polluted and protecting waters already clean." Udall's policy was that if states sent in their standards and they were too lax, the Department of the Interior would send the standards back to them and tell them where they needed to be improved. If the state did not then revise their standards, the federal government would move in to set the standards according to its rights and responsibilities under the Water Quality Act.[49]

By the end of 1968, state water-quality standards had all been submitted and reviewed and were in the process of negotiation, revision, and approval by the Interior Department. Unfortunately, however, several pieces of legislation regarding water-pollution mitigation were hotly debated in both houses of Congress. Bills passed the House but not the Senate, and vice versa, in both 1967 and 1968. Thus, it wasn't until the early 1970s and the Nixon administration that water-pollution mitigation legislation and implementation were really front and center. During this era, unprecedented funding was given to increasing the capacity of and creating new sewage-treatment plants.[50]

⌒

WITHIN THE ADMINISTRATIONS of LBJ and JFK, environmental historian Martin Melosi believes that "no one wielded more influence over conservation policy than Udall." And as an environmental protection cheerleader, Udall was heavily involved in 1960s water policies. He supported both the designation of wild rivers and traditional reclamation projects, pushed for an increase in water-pollution mitigation projects, and believed in wasting as little water and hydroelectric energy as possible. Water programs in the 1960s were not cohesive, in part because pollution-mitigation laws were so new and so complex, but much was initiated and accomplished in the decade.[51]

Notes

1. Tim Palmer, *Endangered Rivers and the Conservation Movement* (New York: Rowman & Littlefield, 2004), 89–91. While Floyd Dominy seemingly always supported dam projects, the powerful head of the Bureau of Reclamation actually opposed Rampart Dam, like Udall. To Dominy, the dam would be a waste, as very few people inhabited Alaska in general and the area near the dam in particular. The water and hydroelectric power would go largely unused, he believed, if the dam were to be built.

2. Roddy Scheer and Doug Moss, "The Downside of Dams: Is the Environmental Price of Hydroelectric Power Too High?," *Scientific American*, September 8, 2012.

3. Palmer, *Endangered Rivers*, 160–61.

4. Udall interview, ibid., 160.

5. Ibid., 161. Udall had the utmost respect for Muskie. See Dean B. Bennett, *The Wilderness from Chamberlain Farm: A Story of Hope for the American Wild* (Washington, DC: Island Press, 2001).

6. Ibid.

7. Ibid.

8. "Frank Craighead History: Writing the Wild and Scenic River Act," Craighead Institute, craigheadresearch.org/frank-craighead-legacy.html; Smith, *Green Republican*, 208.

9. US Department of the Interior, Office of the Secretary, news release, "Secretary Udall Sends Draft Bill to Congress to Establish National Wild Rivers System," box 162, folder 7, Udall Papers.

10. US Fish and Wildlife Service, "A National System," rivers.gov/national-system.php.

11. Palmer, *Endangered Rivers*, 164.

12. Zaslowsky and Watkins, *These American Lands*, 245–46.

13. "Secretary Udall Sends Draft Bill to Congress."

14. "Frank Craighead History."

15. Lyndon B. Johnson, "Remarks upon Signing Four Bills Relating to Conservation and Outdoor Recreation," October 2, 1968, presidency.ucsb.edu/ws/index.php?pid=29150#axzz1xE2odobr.

16. "Frank Craighead History."

17. Andrew H. Gahan and William D. Rowley, *The Bureau of Reclamation: From Developing to Managing Water, 1945–2000*, 800.

18. US Department of the Interior, "Water Resources Development (Bureau of Reclamation) General Summery," in vol. 1 of *The Department of the Interior During the Administration of President Lyndon B. Johnson, November 1963–January 1969*, administrative history, pt. 2, box 151, Udall Papers.

19. Gahan and Rowley, *Bureau of Reclamation*, xi, vi.

20. On pages 310–11 of his well-written *American Canopy: Trees, Forests, and the Making of a Nation* (New York: Scribner, 2012), Eric Rutkow notes that Senator Gaylord Nelson (D-WI) was also a key player in getting Kennedy to take the conservation trips.

21. "Kennedy Conservation Trip," box 103, folders 12–13, Udall Papers. Jerry Brown, the current as well as former California governor, is the son of Pat Brown. Regarding the Oahe Dam, it's actually a US Army Corps of Engineers–administered dam, not one administered by the Bureau of Reclamation.

22. Box 112, folder 1, Udall Papers.

23. Transcript, Stewart Udall oral history interview III, by Joe B. Frantz, April 18, 1969, LBJ Library, lbjlibrary.net/assets/documents/archives/oral_histories /udall/UDALL03.PDF. See also Thomas A. Blinkhorn, "Columbia Treaty Deadlock Involves High Power Feud," *Milwaukee Journal*, December 17, 1961, news.google.com /newspapers?nid=1499&dat=19611217&id=aVEAAAAAIBAJ&sjid=6yYEAAAAIBAJ&pg =3451,3106704&hl=en.

24. Richard Kyle Paisley, "A River Runs Through Us: The Columbia River Treaty Is a Model of International Cooperation but It Could Soon Expire," Canada's History, February 2013, internationalwatersgovernance.com/uploads/1/3/5/2 /13524076/columbia_river_history_of_canada.pdf. The treaty also provided flood control for downriver communities and infrastructure along the Columbia River.

25. Udall quoted in Gahan and Rowley, *Bureau of Reclamation*, 817. See also Joshua D. Binus, "Bonneville Power Administration and the Creation of the Pacific Intertie, 1958–1964" (master's thesis, Portland State University, 2008), pdxscholar .library.pdx.edu/cgi/viewcontent.cgi?article=2723&context=open_access_etds.

26. Bonneville Power Administration, *U.S. Columbia River Power System, 1964 Report*, 3–7, bpa.gov/Finance/FinancialInformation/AnnualReports/Documents /BPA408_1964AnnualReport.pdf. See also Joshua Binus, "History of the Pacific Northwest–Pacific Southwest Intertie," Oregon Historical Society, 2004, ohs.org /education/oregonhistory/historical_records/dspDocument.cfm?doc_ID=66FE 472D-BE34-65A7-CC58314273CCFDCB.

27. Ibid.

28. Gahan and Rowley, *Bureau of Reclamation*, 819.

29. "Transcript of Secretary Udall's Introductory Remarks and President Johnson's Speech at the Intertie Victory Breakfast at the Sheraton Hotel," Oregon Historical Society, September 17, 1964, ohs.org/education/oregonhistory /upload/18122_1.pdf. Just upriver from Portland, Oregon, in 1966, Udall designated a Bonneville Power Administration electricity substation at Hood River as the Woodie Guthrie Substation. The folk singer was dying at the time, and since he

had done so much through his music to promote Columbia River power and development during the 1930s ("Your power is turning darkness to light," he sang in "Roll On, Columbia, Roll On"), Udall felt it right to honor him.

30. Stewart L. Udall, "Is Our Country Running Out of Water?," *Coronet*, October 1964, box 207, folder 3, Udall Papers.

31. Charles F. MacGowen, "History, Function, and Program of the Office of Saline Water," US Department of the Interior, Office of Saline Water, 1963, usbr .gov/research/AWT/OSW/MacGowan.pdf.

32. Udall, "Is Our Country Running Out of Water?"

33. US Department of the Interior, *Department of the Interior During the Administration of Johnson*; Rachel Leven, "U.S. Desalination Industry Grows Since 2000; Seen as Essential to Meeting Supply Needs," Bloomberg BNA, August 21, 2013, bna.com/us-desalination-industry-n17179876105/.

34. Udall, "Is Our Country Running Out of Water?"

35. Ibid.

36. Ibid.

37. Ibid.

38. Udall, "The Secretary Writes Story of His Climb," *Life*, October 11, 1963. Udall's two-week stint in eastern Africa occurred at the same time as the September 15, 1963, bombing of Birmingham, Alabama's Sixteenth Street Baptist Church, in which four African American girls were killed and twenty-two others were injured by racist white males. This sad episode led to sobering informal discussions between Udall and East African officials on the state of civil rights in the United States. Unrelated to the church bombing and Udall's September 1963 visit to East Africa, just a couple of months later Udall led the US delegation to Kenya's independence celebration. With John Johnson, the editor and owner of the African American cultural magazine *Ebony*, Udall shook hands with Kenyan prime minister Jomo Kenyatta.

39. "Secretary Udall Assaults Kilimanjaro: Stu (Whew!) Makes It to the Top," *Life*, October 11, 1963. Udall also climbed Japan's Mount Fuji while serving as interior secretary. For a short video clip of this, see youtube.com/watch?v=P1BV1 VQPJHW.

40. US Department of the Interior, *Recent Electric Power Developments in the U.S.S.R.: Report of the United States Delegation Tour to Soviet Russia, August 28–September 9, 1962, Under U.S.-U.S.S.R. Exchange Agreement*, books.google.com. See also box 111, folder 1, Udall Papers.

41. US Department of State, "Transcripts and Notes from Meeting Between Nikita Khrushchev and Stewart Udall," September 6, 1962, box 105, folder 2, Udall Papers.

42. Ibid.

43. Ibid.

44. Ibid.

45. Leunes, "Conservation Philosophy of Udall," 128, 143.

46. Sirgo, *Establishment of Environmentalism*, 63. See also Melosi, "Johnson and Environmental Policy," 130–37.

47. US Department of the Interior, "Water Pollution Control," in *Department of the Interior During the Administration of Johnson*.

48. US Department of the Interior, Office of the Secretary, news release, May 10, 1966.

49. US Department of the Interior, "Water Pollution Control." See also "1967 Oversight Hearings," in *cq Almanac, 1967*, 23rd ed. (Washington, DC: CQ, 1968), 1007–9, library.cqpress.com/cqalmanac/cqal67-1313310.

50. US Department of the Interior, "Water Pollution Control." See also David J. Eaton, "The Past and Future of the Johnson Administration's Water Quality Policies," in *LBJ's Neglected Legacy: How Lyndon Johnson Reshaped Domestic Policy and Government*, edited by Robert H. Wilson et al. (Austin: University of Texas Press, 2015).

51. Melosi, "Johnson and Environmental Policy," 130.

9 | Exercising Caution with Oil, Coal, and Mineral Development

I'm for oil shale development —
over the course of a thousand years!

IN THE 1960S, many Department of the Interior agencies worked closely together and were charged with overseeing energy development and mineral extraction within the United States and its coastal waters. These bureaus and divisions included the Bureau of Land Management; the offices of Oil and Gas, Coal Research, and Minerals and Solid Fuels; the Oil Import Administration; the Bureau of Mines; and the US Geological Survey. Specifically, the DOI was responsible for all leasing of public lands for both onshore and offshore energy development; providing geological data on fuel resources, production, utilization, and conversions; administering the oil-import program; and acting as liaison with the petroleum industry. As the Department of Energy was not created until 1977 under the Carter administration, the DOI was the primary agency responsible for America's energy supply during this time—and Udall was the de facto secretary of energy.[1]

Oil Shale, Oil Imports, and Outer Continental-Shelf Oil Drilling

While oil today is seen as controversial in light of anthropogenic climate change as well as the fact that the United States obtains some of its oil from extremely undemocratic nations like Saudi Arabia, oil has actually been a touchy political issue for decades.

President Johnson knew this, as did Stewart Udall. Born and raised in oil-rich Texas and knowing full well the power and influence that oil tycoons wielded as a result of his many years in Congress, LBJ, soon after assuming the presidency from Kennedy, made Udall the administration's point man on "all things oil" in order to protect and distance himself from it. Udall himself knew full well the potential controversies surrounding oil and their implications, as a 1920s secretary of the interior and resident of Texas and New Mexico had actually gone to prison over the Teapot Dome (oil field) Scandal. As such, Udall proceeded cautiously with oil extraction in the 1960s. In general, he emphasized research over development and efficiency over waste.[2]

With America's booming economy based largely on petroleum, the 1960s witnessed the oil industry's increasing interest in the development of oil shale on public lands, particularly in Wyoming and Utah. President Hoover had closed oil-shale lands in the public domain back in 1930. A geologist himself, he wanted more information on the extractive process for oil shale before he approved or disallowed its being developed as an energy source. By 1963 oil industries were again putting pressure on the federal government—this time the interior secretary—to open up the public domain to oil-shale exploration.[3]

Udall, wanting to study all of the potential problems and side effects associated with oil-shale development prior to giving industry the green light for extraction, in 1964 created a study and advisory board on the subject. The Oil Shale Advisory Board consisted of mining experts, two economists, two lawyers, and the president of Resources for the Future. The board was tasked with identifying and evaluating the major public policy questions involved in oil-shale development.[4]

While the group ultimately ended up, to quote Udall, being "seven experts with seven different [final] reports" and opinions, the reports nevertheless proved valuable. Per the group's recommendations, the Department of the Interior developed a strict leasing program that Udall believed protected the public interest and promoted natural resource conservation. The oil industry by and large rejected this leasing plan because they wanted more power and less governmental oversight, but Udall did not cave in. Due to this, oil-shale development was essentially at a standstill upon the interior secretary's leaving office in early 1969. "I had to administer this [oil-shale program] very carefully because if we moved too fast, gave too many concessions, it would be regarded quite rightly as a giveaway," Udall recalled in 1969. "On the other hand, there was a feeling of some of the congressional people, particularly the ones from these mountain states and from some people in industry that if you'd open up a leasing program the thing would move forward and so on. [But] I think this [oil-shale land] is a great reserve for the nation. Probably ultimately the federal government ought to do more research and development work itself and not just leave it up to industry under a leasing program."[5]

Regarding oil imports, in the 1960s only about 4 percent of the oil used in the United States came from the Middle East. European nations were much more reliant on Middle Eastern oil than the United States during this time period, as America obtained most of its oil from domestic sources, Canada, and Mexico (the three major sources today), and also Venezuela. Still, Udall was handed a heavy responsibility when he was tasked with overseeing oil-import policy. At practically every press conference, questions were raised about specific oil-import proposals received from the oil industry as well as departmental regulations.[6]

The oil-import program was a touchy topic. On one side, domestic oil companies, their lobbyists, and politicians representing the states where these companies were found argued for increasing domestic supplies of oil and decreasing foreign imports in order to benefit their states' economies. Representative Bob Dole (R-KS), later a US senator and presidential candidate, lobbied Udall for exactly this reason.[7] On the other side, multinational oil firms lobbied the Interior Department for increasing oil imports. "I'll probably end up right in the middle with both sides shooting at me. That's usually how it works," Udall told the press once. Interior Department lawyers were also busy in the 1960s, because in *Pancoastal Petroleum Limited v. Udall* and other court cases, the US-based multinational oil firms and their lobbyists challenged established conservation laws in order to increase company profits.[8]

Offshore and outer continental-shelf oil development actually increased in the 1960s, primarily in the Gulf of Mexico and off the coast of central California. Twelve to fourteen thousand offshore oil wells were built in the 1960s, though law professor Sam Kalen notes that this was minuscule compared to the sector's development in the 1970s and more recently.[9] Offshore development in general was based on the Submerged Lands Act and Outer Continental Lands Act, both of which passed Congress in 1953. All this said, due to an event off the coast of England in early 1967, oil-pollution mitigation evolved.[10]

The SS *Torrey Canyon*, an oil supertanker, ran aground in that year, causing the largest oil spill in United Kingdom history and indeed the biggest ever in the world at that time. An estimated fifteen thousand birds and countless marine creatures perished when the *Torrey Canyon* spilled its almost 120,000 tons of oil into the Atlantic. As a result of the oil spill, the Johnson administration, through Udall and the Interior Department, began an extensive study on how to mitigate oil spills should they happen in the Gulf of Mexico or elsewhere in US waters. The US Senate then passed a bill dealing with the subject the same year as the spill as well as another in 1968. However, due to delays in the US House of Representatives and other factors, historian Martin Melosi notes, the LBJ administration has been unfairly accused of neglecting to act on the topic.[11]

While the Land and Water Conservation Fund was created in 1964 in order to have offshore drilling provide benefits to the public other than oil, Udall and Representative John Saylor worked to augment LWCF funds through the utilization of mineral-lease receipts from outer continental-shelf oil drilling. "Udall believed this to be a new concept for the management of American resources in which the values of non-renewable resources, the oil and mineral resources of the vast continental shelf, were used to build a permanent land estate for future generations," notes one historian. Over the years, the LWCF has partially funded more than forty thousand park and recreation projects at the local, state, and national levels.[12]

The Battle to Regulate Surface Mining

Part of Udall's constituent base when he was a US representative from Arizona in the 1950s were southern Arizona's copper miners, and the interior secretary knew the importance of mining to the local as well as the national economies. At the same time, he understood the growing environmental and health concerns associated with open-pit mining and strip mining. For these reasons, just after becoming interior secretary, Udall began calling for federal regulation—stricter regulation—of surface-mining operations on both private and public lands.[13]

Opposition to strip mining, particularly regarding mountaintop coal mining in Appalachia, grew significantly in the middle of the twentieth century as the environmental consequences of the extractive practice became more widespread and detrimental. The problems stemmed from the fact that after mining companies dug hundreds of thousands of tons of soil and coal deposits out of the earth, they didn't then resoil and replant the land. They weren't required to do so under the law, and since ample mining occurred on mountaintops and steep slopes, the practice affected downstream properties. "Stripping [strip mining] denuded millions of acres of steep slopes and rolling hills in the coalfields, and this loss of vegetation caused soil erosion as well as increased surface runoff. Increased surface runoff caused heavier flooding and floods where there had been none before," notes historian Chad Montrie.

> The bare hills also deprived numerous animal and plant species of habitat. Acid mine drainage, produced when sulfur-containing compounds such as pyrite and marcasite are exposed to air and water, polluted streams and groundwater. Even when limestone was present to neutralize some of this acidity, the drainage and acid-laden soil made revegetation and post-mining crop production nearly impossible. In areas where surface mines perched above homes, schools, and whole towns, the lack of revegetation and the abandon with which operators dumped "spoil" down steep slopes led to disastrous landslides. Some of these slides were fatal.[14]

Udall in a West Virginia coal mine. As the US Department
of Energy was not created until the late 1970s, Udall as 1960s
interior secretary was the de facto energy secretary.
Courtesy of the US Department of the Interior.

Opposition to strip mining spread with the formation of groups
like West Virginia's Citizens Task Force on Surface Mining, southwestern Pennsylvania's Allegheny County Sportsmen's League,
the Kentucky Civil Liberties Union, Tennessee's Save Our Cum-
berland Mountains, and so on. Interestingly, Montie noted that,
unlike most other environmental activists of the time, who were
primarily urban and suburban, middle-class, white Americans,
the anti-surface-mining forces were primarily composed of lower-
class, rural-dwelling, non-college-educated citizens. These people
simply wanted to protect their farmland and property from destruction they had not asked for. Unfortunately, however, groups
like the Central Pennsylvania Open Pit Mining Association, West
Virginia Surface Mining Association, and other mining representatives proved to be powerful forces in keeping the status quo, as from

an economic standpoint, to reclaim mined lands would cost mining firms extra money and reduce their total profits. Thus, a long battle ensued.[15]

Senator Frank Lausche (D-OH) introduced several bills in Congress in the late 1950s and '60s that called for the regulation of strip mining, mainly requiring mining firms to reclaim the land before leaving it and moving on to the next terrain.[16] In 1965 Lausche's Appalachian Regional Development Act was passed, a small component of which required the secretary of the interior to study the problems and then complete a report providing solutions to the strip-mining dilemma. Udall in turn organized a task force on the matter. Under the direction of an assistant interior secretary as well as officials from the Bureau of Mines, the task force worked with several Interior Department agency representatives, surveying more than eighteen thousand mine operators; meeting with state officials, mine industry representatives, and conservation groups; and visiting almost seven hundred randomly selected surface-mining locations throughout the lower forty-eight states.[17]

"A lack of concern has accompanied much of the mining for the minerals that have such an important role in the development of the economy," Udall wrote in the opening pages of the surface-mining task force's concluding report. He might well have said, "A lack of concern for the environment and for future generations," as putting emphasis on the need to manage natural resources for the long-term good was a recurring theme of Udall's.

> It was and still is accepted to mine as cheaply as possible the deposits that are most accessible and provide the greatest profit to the producer. This preoccupation with short term gain too frequently has ignored long term social costs involved— the silted streams, the acid laden waters, and the wasteland left by surface mining. Thus valuable mineral resources have already been lost and several million acres of productive land and waters have been left derelict.
>
> When such actions are viewed against the backdrop of time—the desperate need of a lusty young country to feed and

develop itself and the earlier limitations of knowledge and technology—some tolerance may be justified. Indeed, it might even be said truly that without such an approach the United States probably would not have reached its present economic levels. Today, however, our national sense of values and attitudes is changing; so are our knowledge and technical skills. We are an affluent society; but we can no longer tolerate (or afford) either prodigal waste of natural resources or cumulative degradation of our environment.[18]

As the interior secretary's words suggest, the departmental report confirmed and reiterated the importance of reclaiming mined lands after soil and mineral removal. In addition, the report recommended the creation of a central government bureau tasked with administering all surface-mining activities. At the same time, it noted that since widespread diversity of opinions regarding the role of the federal governmental existed in Appalachia, imposing a uniform set of federal standards across the region would be a real challenge.[19]

In light of this, Udall and his Interior Department legal team wrote a new bill, which the interior secretary handed to Senator Scoop Jackson, the chairman of the Senate Committee on Interior and Insular Affairs beginning in 1964, who then introduced it to the legislature. The bill called for states to create their own strip-mining standards and to be helped out in the process by a federal advisory committee if they wanted the assistance. If the states didn't act in a reasonable amount of time, however, then the bill allowed the federal government to step in and impose regulations.[20]

Udall pushed hard for the bill, lobbying for it during congressional hearings and even after he left office. "Coal strip mining is, I think, one of the worst forms of man's activity," the interior secretary said. "By using big machines and everything to really strip and gut an area… [t]hey go so deep you see, and they tear the top soil off, that even these areas will remain scarred permanently, because they've just stripped right down to rock." Udall also came to believe that the absolute worst form of water pollution was acid mine drainage from coal mines, as it destroyed hundreds of miles of stream habitat throughout Appalachia.[21]

It took eight years after Udall left office for a strip-mining bill to be signed into law. Udall's like-minded brother on the subject, Representative Morris Udall, who won Stewart's seat after he left to become interior secretary and served in Congress from 1961 to 1991, was a major supporter of the bill. Yet mining company executives and their lobbyists provided a formidable opposition, and it certainly didn't help that Wayne Aspinall, chairman of the House Interior and Insular Affairs Committee, was one of the people these lobbyists persuaded with their views. A primary argument used in batting down strip-mining regulations for so long was the classic jobs-versus-environment one. "Industry is properly concerned over the dangers in all efforts at regulation or study by any governmental agency," an official from the Kentucky Coal Association stated. "There is always the danger that such efforts, however well-meaning, may result in ill-considered action which *could impose economic hardships on industries* which, due to the limitations of their number and size, have only a limited ability to defend themselves."[22]

Yet Montrie as well as law professor Patrick McGinley note that strip mining was (and is) so technologically advanced compared to other types of mining that it does not require nearly as many miners for each ton of coal mined, and thus it doesn't provide that much in the form of local jobs—it is machine based, and not so much worker based. Furthermore, mining firms have often dragged their feet in giving back to the community they extracted from; because they often refused to pay severance taxes, local school and hospital infrastructure suffered.[23]

Though the surface-mining regulations didn't get approved during Udall's time in office, the interior secretary was a strong proponent of them. In part because of his education on the problems associated with surface mining, and in part because of the abuses he observed in Arizona's national forest lands as a congressman, Udall became a staunch advocate of completely revising the country's mining laws, not just those related to strip mining.

One of Udall's very last pieces of business as interior secretary involved scribing a letter to powerful members of Congress—including Aspinall—that had influence over public lands and mineral management. In the letter, he called for a new mining law to replace the outdated Mining Law of 1872, which served as a key reason strip miners could leave a mined site on public lands without cleaning and restoring it.[24]

Air-Pollution Mitigation and
Sounding the Alarm on Global Warming

While extracting coal and oil from the earth can denude mountainsides if the area is left bare, on the other end of the spectrum, our use of oil and coal during the 1960s led to massive amounts of air pollution. Air-pollution control was primarily a responsibility of the Department of Health, Education, and Welfare during the time, which was led for three years by Udall's friend and fellow cabinet member John Gardner, a Republican. Nevertheless, Udall and the Department of the Interior did have some involvement in the growing issue.

Similar to water pollution during the mid-twentieth century, air pollution witnessed a drastic increase during this time period. The increase in the number of automobiles used as well as miles driven by Americans led to growing sulfur dioxide emissions from tailpipes and smokestacks. Thus, cities like New York, Chicago, and especially Los Angeles became smog cities. In the Los Angeles metropolitan area alone, historian John McNeill notes, smog negatively impacted ten million residents and significantly decreased tree growth in the 1960s.[25]

To partially combat this sickening air, Udall and Interior Department advisers worked out some slight changes to oil-import regulations, thus allowing additional low-sulfur fuel oil into the country in order to curb the use of high-sulfur fuel oil. Udall noted that the new regulations would "accomplish no miracles in air pollution abatement," but they would "make a substantial contribution toward alleviating a serious problem."[26] Outside of the Oil Import Administration's involvement in air-pollution mitigation, the

Department of the Interior's Bureau of Mines increased research and development on antipollution technologies.[27]

Udall saw that more and more Americans were calling for a decrease in air pollution, and he warned extractive industries of coming changes. During a keynote address to the National Petroleum Council in 1967, Udall told the crowd that "America of the late Sixties and Seventies is not going to put up with the smoke, the soot, and the noxious and corrosive gases that have blighted our countryside for these many years gone by."[28]

Outside of sulfur dioxide emissions, the secretary of the interior foresaw another problem associated with the country's increasing use of fossil fuels: global warming and climate change. Udall may have been introduced to the science of global warming by Roger Revelle, the science adviser to the secretary of the interior, a position created by Udall. Revelle was a highly regarded cutting-edge scientist at the time. "We have ignored the vital fact that we are utterly dependent on natural cycles of a thin and fragile layer of living plants and animals which exist where conditions of air, water, and solid earth combine to favor life, and which our scientists call the biosphere," noted the interior secretary in 1967, almost forty years prior to Al Gore's documentary *An Inconvenient Truth*. "These cycles can, of course, be seriously disrupted by our industrial and agricultural activities. Combustion in the furnaces and engines that power our industrial system produces such vast quantities of carbon dioxide that the foliage of the earth and the plankton of the sea may not be able to convert it back to carbon and oxygen. In turn, this may alter the heat-absorption capacity of the atmosphere and cause the earth's climate to grow warmer, melting the polar ice and raising the level of the seas."[29]

Against a Nuclear Power Facility
at Bodega Head

One other Udall involvement in 1960s energy policy deserves a brief examination. The powerful Atomic Energy Commission, created in 1946 to develop nuclear energy, bombs, and "peacetime use of the atom," increasingly came under attack in the 1960s and early '70s for its perceived disregard for air and water pollution. As such, when the private energy firm Pacific Gas and Electric (PG&E), with support from the AEC, began pushing for the nation's first nongovernmental nuclear power plant at Bodega Head, California, local environmentalists knew exactly whom to contact to get on their side.

The proposed site was a coastal landmark just north of Bodega Bay and Point Reyes, and after area residents asked for Udall's support against the nuclear plant, the interior secretary, wanting to have his scientific facts straight before saying yes or no, asked the US Geological Survey to study the landmass and its geology and provide a safety assessment—essentially an environmental impact statement. After their analysis, the USGS concluded that developing an atomic energy facility so near the San Andreas Fault was dangerous. The fault, a geologic feature causing numerous earthquakes per year, combined with a nuclear power plant equaled potential environmental and human catastrophe. Due to this recommendation, Udall came out against the Bodega Head nuclear facility, and PG&E and the AEC scrapped their plans for the plant in 1964.[30]

$\sim$

THOUGH HIS ENERGY POLICIES and beliefs were not perfect, Udall's approach to surface coal mining, oil-shale development, oil imports, and even nuclear power development paralleled in many ways his approach to wildlife protection, National Park System expansion, and outdoor recreation expansion. He believed in using and developing energy resources in ways that protected the land and its people and provided for the long term.

Notes

1. US Department of the Interior, "History of Petroleum and Oil Shale Activities," in *The Department of the Interior During the Administration of President Lyndon B. Johnson, November 1963–January 1969,* administrative history, pt. 1, box 151, Udall Papers.

2. Ibid.

3. Ibid.

4. Ibid.

5. Transcript, Stewart Udall oral history interview V, by Joe Frantz, December 16, 1969, LBJ Library, lbjlibrary.net/assets/documents/archives/oral_histories /udall/UDALL05.PDF.

6. US Department of the Interior, "History of Petroleum." In large part to maintain good ties with Venezuela due to its oil supply, LBJ had Udall head the US delegation for the inauguration ceremony of President Raúl Leoni, Venezuela's head of state from 1964 to 1969—the United States had much better diplomatic relations with Venezuela back then!

7. Bob Dole to Stewart Udall, October 17, 1966, Robert J. Dole Archives and Special Collections, University of Kansas, Lawrence, dolearchivecollections.ku .edu/collections/press_releases/661020con.pdf.

8. F.2d 805 (DC Cir. 1965). See also Skelly Oil Company v. Udall, Civ. A. No. 297-68, US District Court, D. Columbia, July 31, 1968.

9. US Department of the Interior, "History of Petroleum"; Sam Kalen, "Cruise Control and Speed Bumps: Energy Policy and Limits for Outer Continental Shelf Leasing," Environmental and Energy Law Policy (2013): 161, law.uh.edu/eelpj /publications/7-2/02KalenFinal.pdf.

10. Transcript, Stewart L. Udall oral history interview III, by Joe B. Frantz, April 18, 1969, LBJ Library, lbjlibrary.net/assets/documents/archives/oral _histories/udall/UDALL03.PDF.

11. Melosi, "Johnson and Environmental Policy," 138; Patrick Barkham, "Oil Spills: Legacy of Torrey Canyon," Guardian, June 24, 2010, theguardian.com /environment/2010/jun/24/torrey-canyon-oil-spill-deepwater-bp; National Oceanic and Atmospheric Administration, "Torrey Canyon," incidentnews.noaa .gov/incident/6201.

12. "Stuart [sic] L. Udall," American Academy for Parks and Recreation Admin- istration, aapra.org/pugsley-bios/stuart-l-udall.

13. Chad Montrie, To Save the Land and People: A History of Opposition to Surface Coal Mining in Appalachia, 131.

14. Ibid., 3. For more on the environmental effects of coal strip mining, see M. A. Palmer et al., "Mountaintop Mining Consequences," Science 327 (January 2010), filonverde.org/images/Mountaintop_Mining_Consequences_Science1[1].pdf.

15. Montrie, To Save the Land and People, 81, 46, 47.

16. Ibid., 132–34.

17. US Department of the Interior, Surface Mining and Our Environment: A Special Report to the Nation, 1966, 8–9, books.google.com.

18. Ibid., 3–4.

19. Ibid.

20. Ibid., 132–35.

21. Transcript, Udall oral history interview V, 3.

22. Patrick C. McGinley, "From Pick and Shovel to Mountaintop Removal: Environmental Injustice in the Appalachian Coalfields," Environmental Law 34, no. 1 (2004): 21 (emphasis added); Montrie, To Save the Land and People, 131.

23. Montrie, *To Save the Land and People*, 2–3.

24. Stewart Udall to Public Land Law Review Commission, January 15, 1969, box 181, folder 7, Udall Papers.

25. J. R. McNeil, *Something New Under the Sun: An Environmental History of the Twentieth Century World* (New York: W. W. Norton, 2000), 72–73.

26. Quoted in "Congress Strengthens Air Pollution Control Powers," CQ *Almanac, 1967*, 23rd ed. (Washington, DC: CQ Quarterly, 1968), library.cqpress.com /cqalmanac/document.php?id=cqal67-1313061.

27. US Department of the Interior, "Mineral Resources," in *Department of the Interior during the Administration of Johnson*, pt. 2.

28. US Department of the Interior, Office of the Secretary, news release, "Remarks of Secretary of the Interior Stewart L. Udall before the National Petroleum Council, Washington, D.C.," January 31, 1967, Udall Papers.

29. Udall, *1976: Agenda for Tomorrow*, 104.

30. Brian Balogh, *Chain Reaction: Expert Debate and Public Participation in American Commercial Nuclear Power, 1945–1975* (Cambridge: Cambridge University Press, 1991), 246; Thomas Raymond Wellock, *Critical Masses: Opposition to Nuclear Power in California, 1958–1978* (Madison: University of Wisconsin Press, 1998), 17–67; Carl-Henry Geschwind, *California Earthquakes: Science, Risk, and the Politics of Hazard Mitigation* (Baltimore: Johns Hopkins University Press, 2001).

10 | Advocating for the Wilderness Act

*Plans to protect air and water, wilderness
and wildlife are in fact plans to protect man.*

IN THE SPRINGTIME OF 1962, three prominent conservationists and a famous poet met for an informal gathering and ceremony in the secluded woods of Washington, DC's Dumbarton Oaks Park. Among the blooming daffodils and bluebells in one of the park's miniature meadows sat Howard Zahniser, executive director of the Wilderness Society; William O. Douglas, the longest-serving Supreme Court justice in US history; poet Robert Frost, who had written about the American land in many of his signature poems; Secretary of Interior Stewart Udall; and other dignitaries and invited guests. The secretary was friends with Douglas, having hiked the Chesapeake and Ohio Canal Towpath several times with him in order to exercise and escape the office for an afternoon and also to call attention to the need for preserving the long, linear canal. Udall was also friends with the eighty-eight-year-old Frost, as Frost had gone to dinner at the Udall home several times. Udall had respect for Zahniser, though he was not on such intimate terms with him.[1]

The point of the gathering in Dumbarton Oaks Park, which was arranged and planned by Udall, was to honor the legacy of Henry David Thoreau on the one hundredth anniversary of his death and to promote the pending Wilderness Act. Thoreau, seeking solitude and simplicity in and around his miniature cabin on the shore of Massachusetts's Walden Pond, had once written, "In wildness is the preservation of the world." Thoreau's words were what united

Zahniser, Udall, and Douglas: each of them believed in the value of wildlands, and each lobbied, in his own way, for the establishment of the National Wilderness Preservation System.[2]

Wilderness areas, as envisioned by their proponents since the 1920s and '30s, were to be congressionally designated areas set up to protect specific tracts of land in their highly natural state. Federally designated wilderness was seen by its proponents as an antidote to increasing roadway and highway development and automobile usage. Furthermore, while national parks protected flora, fauna, and landscapes, wilderness bill advocates took the concept a large step further by excluding practically all forms of recreation and human development in these areas. Therefore, unlike Yosemite Valley with its lodges, restaurants, roadways, visitor centers, ranger stations, and auto campgrounds, wilderness areas, by design, were to have no permanent structures; with the exception of trails for hiking, backpacking, and horseback riding, not a single house or even a dirt road was to be built in them.[3]

Since the history of the Wilderness Act has been well documented by environmental historians, only a brief overview need be given here. The battle to set aside an official system of federal wilderness areas began decades before the group met in Dumbarton Oaks Park, but the formal battle began in 1956 when Zahniser introduced into Congress a bill to establish a national system of wilderness areas. Pushed for by Senators Hubert Humphrey (D-MN), Frank Church (D-ID), and Thomas Kuchel (R-CA) and Representatives John Saylor (R-PA), Clinton Anderson (D-NM), and others, the Wilderness Act was debated and rewritten dozens of times before its final bipartisan passage in 1964.

The bill received substantial opposition from the American Pulpwood Association, American National Cattlemen's Association, and the American Mining Association, as well as from Wayne Aspinall. The organizations and "special interest congressman," whom Udall referred to under his breath sometimes as the "Aspinall Blockade," felt that the wilderness legislation would either exclude these industries entirely from wilderness areas or at minimum significantly restrict them. The bill was also opposed by both the National Park

Service and the US Forest Service at first, as the government agencies saw it as an attempt by Congress to limit their control and authority over their land systems.[4]

The bill was helped along, though, when Kennedy and his interior secretary announced administration support for the bill. Udall himself, with Douglas and David Brower, also pushed for the wilderness act's passage at special events such as the 1961 Wilderness Conference.[5] In addition, compromises were fleshed out to appease the natural resource interest groups, including the setting aside of wilderness areas generally only in roadless, rugged locales that were usually almost impossible for the logging, cattle, and mining industries to reach—economically useless lands, in the eyes of the special interests. Also, regarding mineral leasing in wilderness areas, the final bill called for a phaseout period spanning almost two decades rather than a termination of the policy immediately upon signing of the bill.[6]

In a 1962 article in the *New York Times* promoting the passage of the legislation and trying to spell out exactly what the act would and would not do, Udall explained, "Basically, the Wilderness Bill is a tool which will enable us permanently to preserve selected areas of our federally owned lands as untouched, primeval country." The interior secretary continued:

> Those areas designated as part of the Wilderness System would contain no roads, no buildings or commercial development—in short, the hand of man would be nowhere in evidence. Under the present terms of the bill, it is likely that about 35 to 45 million acres—a scant 2 percent of our nation's land area—would be encompassed in the system.
>
> None of these acres would be taken away from private owners or state, or from public lands now used primarily for commercial purposes; all of the wilderness areas would be designated within the boundaries of National Parks; National Forest wilderness, wild and primitive areas; and the game ranges and wildlife refuges administered by the Fish and Wildlife Service [later, wilderness areas would be permitted on BLM land].[7]

President Johnson hands Udall a commemorative pen
after the signing of the Wilderness Act in 1964.
Courtesy of the Lyndon Baines Johnson Library and Museum.

After a long battle, including Udall's lobbying on the floors of
Congress for the final two days of debate, the National Wilderness
Preservation System Act, commonly referred to as the Wilderness
Act, was passed and then signed into law by President Johnson in
September 1964, the exact same day that Udall's Land and Water
Conservation Fund was enacted. In the signing ceremony, John-
son handed symbolic pens to a few different individuals heavily
involved with the legislation, Udall among them. Alice Zahniser
received another pen; her husband Howard died just a couple of
months before passage of the bill he so championed.[8]

With the passage of the Wilderness Act, more than nine million
acres of public lands were immediately designated as wilderness,
primarily in the northern Rockies of Idaho, Montana, and Wyoming;
the Cascade Range of Oregon and Washington; the Sierra Nevada of
California; and Minnesota's Boundary Waters Canoe Area. Perhaps
more important than these initial wilderness areas, though, was
that the act set up a formal method for establishing wilderness areas
in the future. As such, today the National Wilderness Preservation
System has grown, especially in the Southwest, Appalachia, New
England, and Alaska.[9]

Black Elk Wilderness, located within the Black Hills National
Forest of South Dakota. Passed with the help of Udall in 1964, the
Wilderness Act created the National Wilderness Preservation System,
a system of primitive federal lands that has grown exponentially
over the years. Photo by author.

Most important, perhaps, these primitive, roadless, minimal-use areas federally designated as wilderness are probably the most pristine and natural landscapes in all of the United States—they are the areas that have been least affected by humans. As a result, in the future wilderness areas will be of increasing importance to native animal and plant protection as well as to scientific study.

Notes

1. US Department of the Interior, "Commemoration of Hundredth Anniversary of Henry David Thoreau," Dumbarton Oaks Park, Washington, DC, May 11, 1963, box 102, folder 7, Udall Papers.

2. Ibid. According to Michael Frome in *Regreening the National Parks*, 27, a photo of Udall, Frost, Warren, Douglas, and Zahniser, together at the Dumbarton Oaks Park event, was a favorite photo of Udall's during his later years; he proudly hung it above his desk in his Phoenix law office in the 1980s.

3. Regarding wilderness-area designation as a backlash against highway development and the rise of the automobile, see Paul S. Sutter, *Driven Wild: How the Fight Against Automobiles Launched the Modern Wilderness Movement* (Seattle: University of Washington Press, 2009).

4. Schulte, *Aspinall and the Shaping of the American West*, 145; Dee V. Benson, "The Wilderness Act of 1964: Where Do We Go from Here?," *Brigham Young University Law Review* 1975, no. 3 (1975), digitalcommons.law.byu.edu/lawreview/vol1975/iss3/6; Richard A. Baker, "The Conservation Congress of Anderson and Aspinall, 1953-64," *Journal of Forest History* 29, no. 3 (1985): 104-19.

5. David Brower, *For Earth's Sake: The Life and Times of David Brower* (Salt Lake City: Peregrine Smith Books, 1990), 233.

6. Benson, "Wilderness Act of 1964"; Mark Harvey, *Wilderness Forever: Howard Zahniser and the Path to the Wilderness Act* (Seattle: University of Washington Press, 2005), 245; Benson, "Wilderness Act of 1964."

7. "To Save the Wonder of the Wilderness," May 27, 1962, box 207, folder 1, Udall Papers.

8. Harvey, *Wilderness Forever*, 245.

9. Ibid.

11 | Revitalizing the Urban Environment and Stabilizing Human Population

Is there an optimum population, an ideal land-people ratio, for our continent?

In order by topic, the past several chapters have discussed Udall's environmental trials and tribulations as US secretary of the interior. One specific event, though, after Kennedy had been in office for just under three years, had a profound impact on Udall and the nation. A brief look at the event provides an intimate look into Udall's thoughts and feelings. It also serves as a segue into the topic of urban environmentalism and Udall's involvement in it.

The Kennedy Assassination and LBJ Moves into the Presidency

While John F. Kennedy was not as close with his cabinet members as his secretary of the interior would have liked, Udall and Kennedy were on relatively good terms during JFK's time in office, and Udall had a lot of respect for his boss at the time. Of course, Kennedy's time in office was cut short. On November 22, 1963, while Udall and several other cabinet members were en route to Japan for a meeting on economic relations, the president was assassinated while sitting in the back seat of his open-top convertible in Dallas, Texas.

When news of the tragedy arrived aboard the specially chartered plane to Japan, it did a 180-degree turn and headed back toward the nation's capital. All were in shock. Udall, while flying toward Washington, DC, wrote down his initial thoughts on the JFK assassination

Mr. and Mrs. Stewart Udall, Mr. and Mrs. Harry Belafonte, Mr. and Mrs. Robert Kennedy, enjoying each other's company at Carter Barron Amphitheatre in Washington, DC's Rock Creek Park, ca. 1961. Both JFK's and RFK's assassinations in the 1960s hit Udall hard as one was his boss and the other was a friend. Courtesy of the National Park Service.

in his private notebook. "Why should one so young, so gallant, who had so much to give mankind, who had such a large role to play for peace, be struck down violently in full daylight? Why does so much history end so wrongly?" Udall questioned. "He had the mind of a president none of his predecessors have.... The larger tragedy is that he was denied the opportunity to make his full, eight-year contribution to the common cause of all man."[1]

Vice President Lyndon Baines Johnson was quickly sworn in as the new president. Several weeks of mourning for Kennedy as well as confusion as to who shot him and how ensued. In the executive branch of the federal government, there was also some confusion, as none of the cabinet members knew exactly what Johnson would do. Would policies they were working on under Kennedy be continued, or would LBJ take a new direction? And for Stewart Udall, would he be kept on as interior secretary or asked to resign?

Indeed, Johnson had a good memory, and he certainly remembered that it was Udall who swung Arizona's votes for Kennedy instead of him in the 1960 Democratic primary. Yet Udall was a popular cabinet member and had already gained a reputation as a highly successful and efficient interior secretary. Furthermore, he had just written his first book, *The Quiet Crisis*, which was well received. As a result of these factors, the president, who met with all of his cabinet members in December, chose to meet with Udall last.

One can perhaps imagine LBJ glaring at Udall while watching the interior secretary speak to his conservation accomplishments during the meeting. Yet LBJ had likely made his decision to allow Udall to continue on as secretary of the interior before the meeting. The president was perhaps pushed in the direction due to the fact that he received many letters asking him or telling him to keep Udall. Ansel Adams, the famous nature photographer and longtime associate of the Sierra Club, wrote one of these letters:

> Rumor has it that our distinguished Secretary of the Interior, Stewart L. Udall, is to leave your Cabinet following the forthcoming Election. If this rumor is true it is of great concern to conservationists throughout the country, and I hope that you will use every persuasion to retain him.
>
> Seldom has any Secretary shown such devotion to the cause of conservation, and expanded such energy and intelligence in that domain. His accomplishments were all the more difficult because of hostility in Congress and the concerted efforts of pressure groups in the exploiting of timber, mining, and industrial world.
>
> He is a *great* Secretary of the Interior, and it will be difficult indeed to find anyone to match him in these times.[2]

Horace Albright, the second director of the National Park Service and a highly regarded conservationist himself, also addressed a letter to 1600 Pennsylvania Avenue. "Secretary Udall is, in my opinion, one of the ablest men ever to serve as the head of this Department. He is very highly regarded by conservationists in all parts of our country; and I am sure that all who know of his work want him to stay," Albright wrote Johnson. "He is young, highly intelligent, widely-travelled, well-read, energetic, intimately familiar with the many agencies of his Department, and a hard worker."[3]

And so Udall gained another five years as interior secretary, resulting in his becoming just one of three heads of the Interior Department, in its almost 175-year history, with eight years or more in service. Harold Ickes, FDR's one and only interior secretary, served the longest, while Ethan Allen Hitchcock served from February 1898 to March 1907, technically two weeks longer than Udall. President Clinton's interior secretary, Bruce Babbitt, also from Arizona, served three weeks less than eight years.

Agenda for Tomorrow:
Problems in Urban America, 1976

While Udall's staying on as the Department of the Interior's chief was a great personal accomplishment, all was not well in the decade. In these years of the mid- and late 1960s, as urban blight and pollution became more widespread; as African American protests against racism and discrimination gained momentum; and as an extremely popular presidential candidate as well as two civil rights icons were gunned down just like John Kennedy, the secretary of the interior began seeing how environmental problems were interrelated with the social problems of the time. More importantly, he foresaw solutions to the problems and began pushing for them.

As the decade wore on, Udall came to understand that conservation and environmental protection were needed in more areas than just public lands. As he saw it and lived it, the two chief failures that America confronted as it closed in on its 200-year anniversary in 1976 were "a failure to build livable cities and a failure to eradicate racism." The progressive Udall, with personal long-standing beliefs in conservation of natural resources as well as equality for all, came to believe that urban blight and racism could be solved by cleaning up cities, putting more emphasis on urban planning, and creating life-giving environments in them. As a personal friend of civil rights crusader Robert F. Kennedy, and as a member of Washington "society" due to his serving in the cabinet, the interior secretary undoubtedly must have had discussions with influential people about these topics, thus strengthening his convictions. This is all to say that Udall came to believe that conservation and environmental protection needed to enter main-street America: the city and suburbs.[4]

Udall put these thoughts succinctly during a fact-finding mission to West Germany to study environmental conservation. When asked by a reporter why he had brought an urban-affairs expert along on the trip, the interior secretary responded, "The resources now are all interrelated, and the old fashioned idea of conservation as saving bits and pieces of land here and there is outdated." Udall noted that "since 75 percent of our people live in urban areas, since they must have water and air in order to exist, we had better address ourselves to the total problem, the problem of the overall environment."[5]

Udall's specific thoughts and philosophies on improving cities and city life culminated in his second book, *1976: Agenda for Tomorrow*. Part discussion of how urban problems came to be and part discussion of how to fix the issues moving forward into America's third century (which began in 1976), the book, published in 1968, continued the tradition of powerful and poetic Udall prose. After seven years in the cabinet, and with President Johnson deciding not to seek another term, Udall probably understood in 1968 that his tenure as interior secretary would end with the close of LBJ's presidency in early 1969. As such, this was essentially a "lame-duck session" for Udall, and he perhaps felt more at liberty to write candidly.

In discussing how American cities got to such a dirty, impoverished state, Udall lamented that "the bulldozer, the billboard, and the belching smokestack were the authentic emblems of postwar progress.... The last three generations of Americans have exploited the cities as surely as our nineteenth-century ancestors stripped and raided the forestlands of this continent," the interior secretary wrote. "More often than not local officials paved the way for the developers who gradually dehumanized the cities. 'Take,' not 'give'; 'hasten,' not 'consider'—these were the cardinal rules."[6]

Udall went on to observe that "our auto obsession made road-building the main handmaiden of 'development.'" He also questioned why the nation spent billions of dollars to put a man on the moon yet largely ignored the "inner space" of cities where most of its people lived. "Feats of technology confused our purpose and produced a massive diversion of energy and resources toward the over-achievement of military and industrial goals and away from what might have been the more creative pursuits of civilized society," he said. Regarding foreign policy, Udall even questioned the merit of increasing US involvement in Vietnam—a dangerous thing for a sitting cabinet member to do.[7]

An additional threat to cities as well as natural resources, Udall believed, was increasing human population. Individuals like Stanford University's Paul Ehrlich, whose widely read *The Population Bomb* was published the same year as Udall's book, helped make the country and world think about population in a critical light. Udall, an avid reader and student who researched the issue thoroughly, also placed a major emphasis on population pressures. While the topic of increasing human population as an environmental problem is a complex one, the 1960s witnessed about a 2 percent annual increase in human population worldwide, the highest rate of increase to this day. "The ancient and once essential admonition 'Be Fruitful and multiply' is a disastrous doctrine," he wrote in *1976: Agenda for Tomorrow*. "Unwise, uncontrolled human increase is deplenishing, not replenishing, the earth. The tyranny of overpopulation is cheapening life, lessening the importance of the individual, and aiding the forces that erode the human soul."[8]

Udall wrote that it was impossible to match infinite population growth with finite natural resources. He despised the fact that planners were saying that it was inevitable that the population of the United States would continue to increase drastically, hitting three hundred million inhabitants in 2020 and one billion in 2080. Actions could be taken now, Udall believed, that could significantly decrease this projection and thus protect overburdened natural resources. Again one to promote planning ahead, Udall proposed that the nation decide on its ideal population: "Is there an optimum population, an ideal land-people ratio, for our continent?...We have long since perfected the concept of the land's carrying capacity for animals, and we practice the principle of sustained yield in the management of trees and plants. Yet strangely, we forget the law of a natural balance when we come to man. We must now identify the carrying capacity of continents, and evolve an ecology for man in harmony with the unfolding ecology of other living things."[9]

Agenda for Tomorrow:
Solutions to the Urban Problems, 1976

With all these problems of the inner city and of increasing human population, Udall was still an optimist, believing that the mistakes of the past and present could be fixed. Therefore, he proposed Project 76, a massive program to "make all our cities fair, and all our human relations amicable." The first phase of this plan, Udall suggested, involved every community drafting "a master plan to achieve the redesign and renovation of its entire environment." Then, Udall suggested, "each mayor could convene a 'Council to Recreate the City' whose dynamic, representative, revolving membership would educate the community, review all individual [building and engineering] projects, and gear future plans to aims of excellence." Udall believed that "this would initiate a continuing and creative dialogue between artists, designers, leaders of labor, business, and the professionals, politicians, and the people."[10]

In addition to this first step, Udall believed that the widespread implementation and construction of mass-transit systems—subways—could decrease automobile usage in the inner city, thus decreasing noise, air pollution, traffic, and ugliness. Cities could also be made more walkable and bicycle-friendly with ample open space, parks, bicycle lanes, and trails. How to pay for this? "I would propose as part of Project 76 that upon completion of the interstate highway system at least half of the Highway Trust Fund monies be employed for at least two decades to make our nation's urban transportation systems more humane."[11]

"Once by the Pacific"

Urban pollution in terms of dirty water and air moved front and center as a focus in the 1960s, but Udall also expressed concern over noise pollution. An amateur poet at times, Udall wrote eloquently about this issue after an early-morning stroll he took during a San Diego work trip.

> At sunrise near a city on a beach
> I heard the wash of surf
> The call of birds
> The chiming of church bells
> A fog horn's far-off song
> A dog's cry and a boy's.
>
> Tender noise like this
> Has salved the waking mind
> Since Homer; but sullen morning came
> And engines ripped the urban air
> Annulling all the subtle sounds.
>
> Must all the soft chords go,
> Torn by a savage celerity,
> To caress us only at dawn and dusk?
> Or must we curse the sonic time
> And brace our ears against the din?

Source: *Saturday Review*, May 11, 1968, quoted in *Legacies of Camelot: Stewart and Lee Udall, American Culture, and the Arts*, by L. Boyd Finch, 103.

Regarding population stabilization, Udall obviously did not call for drastic solutions such as waging warfare or adopting national quotas for family sizes, but he did call for an increase in sex education in schools, family planning services, and birth control distribution. "If we are wise," Udall noted in regard to family planning, "we will memorize and incorporate into our action plans for our third century these quality-of-life maxims: Bigger is not better. Slower is faster. Less is more." The maxim "Bigger is not better" referred to Udall's belief that society shouldn't push for large families. If some couples didn't want to have kids, then fine. "Let us cease our thoughtless disapproval of childless marriages and lend moral support to those who perhaps rightly shun the complex and demanding task of child nurture," he said. "We must recognize that the talent for child care is a gift not all possess." In "Slower is faster," Udall believed that due to the high divorce rate among the young, a powerful argument for late marriage (and child rearing) could be made. Finally, with "Less is more," Udall was expressing the idea that by having a two-child family become the norm, parents could focus more on their children's well-being and education.[12]

To be fair, with Udall being the father of six children, his beliefs on the need to stabilize human population can be seen as hypocritical. One can only say that Udall's views on environmental protection, human life protection, and population stabilization evolved from the late 1940s and '50s—when Lee gave birth to their six children—to the 1960s.

At any rate, Udall was not the secretary of health and human services and therefore could not push for a population planning program as much as he might have wanted to. He did, however, make a bold step in this direction in 1965. Early in the year, he became the first federal official to take effective action on the issue of birth control when he directed the Bureau of Indian Affairs and the Office of Territories to make family planning services available as part of the Department of the Interior's social service program. "This is not an effort arbitrarily to control the growth of particular groups of citizens," he said. "Nor is it aimed at arbitrarily limiting the size of the Indian or the territorial populations. It is aimed at opening the door of free choice, thereby enlarging the measure of human freedom available."[13]

Mitigating Urban Problems Through the Youth Conservation Corps (YCC) and LWCF

Outside of his call to make population control a focus in 1976: *Agenda for Tomorrow*, Udall argued for urban improvements in a number of other ways. These included his lobbying for the Youth Conservation Corps, pushing for additional park and green spaces throughout urban America, and working to end racism.

Udall argued for the YCC throughout his years as interior secretary. The corps, Udall believed, would enable inner-city youth to gain meaningful work skills while working to conserve natural resources and public lands. Udall associated some of the 1960s city riots and protests with the fact that urban young people were out of work and didn't have anything constructive to do. The YCC, he believed, would combat this problem. "A Youth Conservation Corps would conserve and develop the capacities of our two most precious national assets—our youth and our natural resources," the interior secretary told Congress shortly after arriving at the Department of the Interior.[14]

Udall's proposed YCC program was based largely on FDR's highly successful Civilian Conservation Corps of the 1930s, which involved tens of thousands of young men living in temporary work camps on public lands, taking educational classes by night and working on conservation projects for the greater good by day. Work projects that Udall proposed for this modern-day CCC were not in short supply and included soil conservation, invasive plant eradication, wildlife preservation and management, grounds maintenance, dune stabilization, reforestation, rangeland rehabilitation, historical preservation, and trail, road, campground, and picnic ground construction.[15]

Udall's YCC proposal, which he lobbied for before the House Labor Committee, called for a workforce including large numbers of American Indians, in addition to urban African American youth. "A properly functioning Youth Conservation Corps would be of unique significance to the Bureau of Indian Affairs, and would bring far-reaching and beneficial results for the Indians of the United States," the interior secretary noted. "Here, the program would have a threefold purpose—the employment of Indian youth, the training of Indians in leadership and management, and the highly important work in the development of conservation of natural resources on Indian lands." With American Indians being pushed onto reservation lands in the 1800s that were not of their choosing and generally had extremely poor soil, natural resource conservation work on the reservations would be a huge step forward, Udall believed. "Neglect of the Indians' resources is one of the major obstacles to a fuller life for Indians," he said.[16]

Unfortunately, it took many years for the YCC to get established, and by this point Udall was no longer a cabinet member. According to Udall, the long delay was largely due to differing opinions between Udall and his Department of the Interior and Sargent Shriver and his Department of Labor. Shriver, who served as the first director of the Peace Corps and also as director of the Office of Economic Opportunity in the 1960s, clashed with Udall on the topic of youth labor. While Shriver's idea for a youth employment program was geared more toward training youth in various trades, crafts, and technical education skills, Udall leaned much more toward natural resource conservation projects for youth. While Udall came to be highly respected by LBJ and was on good terms with him, Udall lost to Shriver in the end when Shriver's Job Corps was established under Johnson.[17]

The YCC was established a few years later, largely due to the efforts of Senator Scoop Jackson (D-WA). Though the Nixon administration opposed it and ten years later Ronald Reagan severely cut its funding, the YCC has completed conservation projects over the years since. However, as far as can be discerned, it has never offered a major role to American Indian youth, as Udall once suggested. Nor has YCC involved work camps and classes, like Udall suggested and as was commonplace with the CCC.[18]

In addition to his pushing for the YCC in part to resolve youth unemployment in the inner city and on the reservations, the interior secretary oversaw an unprecedented increase in urban green spaces and recreation centers via the Land and Water Conservation Fund. A recent study released by the University of Washington's College of the Environment shows that neighborhoods with green spaces and ample trees and shrubbery have significantly less crime—including assault, vandalism, theft, and graffiti—than neighborhoods without.[19] Udall perhaps read similar studies in the 1960s. He also learned about the benefits of green spaces and recreation areas through personal experiences and discussions with staff.

At Udall's urging, Congress approved the LWCF in 1964. Thanks to this fund, which filled its coffers from recreational and extraction-based user fees on public lands, numerous new national park units were purchased from private property owners and numerous new outdoor recreation areas and parks were set up on federal, state, county, and city lands. Approximately $241 million went to forty-two hundred outdoor recreation and park projects in the 1960s thanks to the LWCF, and the largest percentage of these projects occurred in metropolitan areas.[20]

The following are some specific urban LWCF projects of the 1960s: Ten public swimming pools were constructed in Birmingham, Alabama, a city that served as an epicenter at the time for civil rights campaigns as well as murderous attacks on African Americans by white supremacists. A system of parks in Anchorage, the largest city of the largest state, was created, and $455,000 in assistance to New York for creating a park on the Bronx side of the Harlem River was issued. And on the other side of the Potomac River from Washington, DC, the metropolitan area received its Four Mile Run, a paved multiuse trail. Connecting the Mount Vernon Trail to the Washington and Old Dominion Trail, the Four Mile Run Trail welcomes tens of thousands of bicyclists per year.[21]

One additional urban LWCF project example involved the preservation of 324 acres of open space in the middle of the Phoenix-Scottsdale metropolitan area in Udall's native state. The open space, consisting of the rugged Camelback Mountain, was private property until the late 1960s. Not wanting the mountain to be developed and instead wishing to secure the scenic natural backdrop of the city for all time, a conservation group composed primarily of the Phoenix business and political elite formed in order to raise funds to purchase the mountain. Among these elites was the politician dubbed "Mr. Conservative," Senator Barry Goldwater (R-AZ); Goldwater and his wife donated $25,000 to the cause.[22]

After about half of the funds had been raised, in 1968 the Bureau of Outdoor Recreation (the DOI agency responsible for overseeing the LWCF) and Udall made plans with Goldwater to match the local group's fund-raising efforts with a $200,000 save-the-mountain grant from the LWCF. The interior secretary and first lady then traveled to Arizona to attend a purchasing ceremony for Camelback Mountain. "I'm sure, Mrs. Johnson...that if you find me and Barry Goldwater in intimate collaboration on some cause, it has to be a good one," Udall told the first lady, who was in the audience. Thanks to these 1960s preservation efforts, Camelback Mountain today remains largely in its natural state, with hikers loving the view from the top. Goldwater, a staunch conservative, and Udall, a staunch liberal, found common ground in protecting the landscape.[23]

An Example of Urban Renewal in Action:
Stewart Udall, Lady Bird Johnson, and Washington, DC

As noted above, the 1960s was a time of civil and societal unrest due in large part to ingrained racism and the struggle for equal rights for African Americans. The assassinations of two very well-known and well-liked Kennedys, not to mention an increasingly unpopular war in Vietnam, also spurred unrest. Udall believed that much of this unrest could be resolved by cleaning and greening the cities as well as by stamping out racism. Reviewing the interior secretary's work in the national capital area as a case study, one can see how involved Stewart Udall was in pushing for these two causes.

The exodus of middle-class white Americans to the suburbs in the middle of the twentieth century was instigated in part by the increasing ugliness and unhealthiness of cities—increasing air pollution, congestion, and more. Left behind to continue living in these deteriorating cities were generally the poorer classes of society, those who couldn't afford to move. And due in large part to several decades of discriminatory practices in the workplace, in real estate, and elsewhere, a disproportionate number of those that remained in the cities were African Americans. This was the case in Washington, DC, circa 1961, the first large city in America with a majority black population. Historian Robert Winks notes that it was a "blighted and shameful national capital" at the time, and even JFK during his inaugural parade down Pennsylvania Avenue noticed downtown DC's dilapidated buildings and general unattractiveness.[24]

Kennedy set up the President's Advisory Council on Pennsylvania Avenue to combat the unsightliness of the major thoroughfare and its environs, running through downtown Washington. After JFK's death, LBJ formed a similar working group with additional members, including Udall. Thus, the President's Temporary Committee on Pennsylvania Avenue was formed, enabling the interior secretary to work with one of the preeminent landscape architects of the mid-twentieth century, Nathaniel Owings, on the regreening of the National Mall and downtown area. Owings, the 1936 founder of Skidmore, Owings, and Merrill, one of the largest and most influential architectural, interior design, engineering, and urban planning firms in the world, was forward-thinking and progressive. Udall was, too, in addition to being open and receptive to Owings's ideas, and the duo developed a strong working relationship.[25]

Udall helped spearhead a similar working group in the Committee for a More Beautiful Capital, of which the interior secretary and Owings were both a part. Lady Bird Johnson, perhaps best known for her highway and national capital beautification work by way of wildflower and tree plantings, has traditionally received credit for the beautification committee work by historians and her biographers. Less known is the fact that Stewart Udall was the one most responsible for helping channel her conservation interests into the beautification committee in the first place. It began when Udall discovered Lady Bird's interest in natural beauty and conservation while he was at the LBJ Ranch, or the "Texas White House," as the president referred to it, during the 1964 holiday season. There, during a series of cabinet meetings in which the first lady was present, Udall found her very knowledgeable about conservation matters. As a result, Udall organized a meeting with Lady Bird and Liz Carpenter, the first lady's press secretary and good friend, back in the nation's capital. "Stewart Udall, the Secretary of the Interior, who was a great salesman, came to see me hoping to interest me in the field of conservation," the president's wife remembered years later.[26] She was interested, and during the meeting the trio brainstormed about how the first lady could promote conservation to the nation. The result of the discussion was the initiation of the Committee for a More Beautiful Capital.[27]

With Udall serving, according to Lady Bird, as the committee's "captain and leader," the group came to include, among others, Walter Washington, then director of DC's public housing program and later the first African American mayor in the capital's history; philanthropists Mary Lasker and Laurance Rockefeller, who were keys to funding the committee's projects; Nathaniel Owings; the chairwoman for the National Capital Planning Commission; the chairman for the US Commission of Fine Arts; and the National Park Service's regional director. The Committee for a More Beautiful Capital met almost twenty times and, thanks in large part to Rockefeller and Lasker, purchased and helped plant thousands upon thousands of azaleas, flowering dogwoods, cherry trees, pink magnolias, daffodils, and other plant species throughout the District of Columbia. Specific planting sites included but were not limited to the Pennsylvania Avenue corridor, the National Mall, the Tidal Basin, the Rock Creek and Potomac Parkway area, and Hains Point in East Potomac Park, where a children's playground was dedicated. The group also completed planting projects in rundown inner-city neighborhoods such as Bryce Park; Greenleaf Gardens, a public housing apartment complex; and Watt's Branch Park, to which Rockefeller donated seventy-five thousand dollars for development.[28]

Lady Bird and others took a particular interest in developing a planting plan and park in an area along the Potomac River in Washington, DC, known as Columbia Island. In the mid- and late 1960s, around one million daffodils were planted here, probably the largest planting of daffodils in a public space in the world. Thousands of pink and white flowering dogwoods were also planted.[29]

As a result of the first lady's conservation and beautification efforts, Udall officially named a section of the island Lady Bird Johnson Park in her honor in late 1968. The interior secretary had kept the renaming plans a surprise until his announcement during a small gathering on the island, the result being Lady Bird's probable blushing but also no doubt feelings of honor, happiness, and appreciation for Udall.[30]

After LBJ's death, the Lyndon Baines Johnson Memorial Grove was established in the middle of Lady Bird Johnson Park, distinct from but in the midst of it. While most if not all of the original daffodils are now long gone, the park and grove remain picturesque and well landscaped.

Udall, Lady Bird, and many other committee members shared the conviction that planting trees as well as creating and beautifying green spaces in the nation's capital would decrease pollution and crime rates, increase recreational opportunities for the urban masses, and improve mental health. Lady Bird's work on the committee blossomed afterward into other conservation efforts.[31]

As significant as these activities were, the Pennsylvania Avenue and DC beautification committees did more than just plant trees, shrubs, and flowers. Udall set up subcommittees at one of the very first Committee for a More Beautiful Capital meetings and tasked them with brainstorming about how to not only regreen but also revitalize the entire downtown area. Having completed his homework, Owings attended the next meeting equipped with a grand plan for downtown DC.

Aside from densely planting trees in formal areas bordering both sides of Pennsylvania Avenue, Constitution Avenue, and the long, linear National Mall, the landscape architect called for the busy roadways dissecting and bordering the National Mall to be closed off to vehicular traffic. Keeping automobile congestion off of "America's front yard" and limiting autos within the downtown area was a more environmentally and recreationally friendly plan, he believed. Owings called for diverting the National Mall traffic through underground tunnels and then constructing massive subterranean parking garages accommodating up to twenty-five

Udall with Lady Bird Johnson and Laurance Rockefeller at the
White House, studying an architectural model proposal of the
National Mall area in Washington, DC. The trio spearheaded the
planting of thousands of trees in the nation's capital, among
other beautification and conservation projects. Courtesy of the
Lyndon Baines Johnson Library and Museum.

thousand automobiles underneath downtown DC. Minibuses could
then shuttle tourists around the National Mall and downtown area,
in addition to using "your own feet for transportation."[32]

That wasn't all. Similar to the long reflection pool in front of
the Lincoln Memorial, Owings proposed a Capitol Reflecting Pool
on the other end of the long, linear National Mall. He also drew
up the design and layout for the Hirshhorn Museum and Sculpture Garden, as well as an additional sculpture garden and outdoor

restaurant in the large empty square between the Smithsonian In-
stitution's Museum of Natural History and the private National Gal-
lery of Art. Additionally, Owings called for the creation of National
Square, a formal yet open public gathering place, where Pennsylvania Avenue intersected the White House grounds, as well as for the
construction of specific new architecturally impressive buildings.
Udall loved Owings's plan, as did Lady Bird, though she wrote in
her private diary that it would take at least ten years to complete
the projects and that, in the meantime, she hoped flowers and trees
would be planted![33]

Part of Owings's plan benefited from one of Udall's secretarial
orders, which the two worked on together. Pennsylvania Avenue,
the ceremonial thoroughfare leading from the Capitol to the White
House, which served as the historic route for numerous presidential
inauguration parades and protest marches over the years, had been
originally developed by the capital city's designer, Pierre-Charles
L'Enfant, in the 1790s. In order to protect downtown, raise awareness of the avenue's history, and also revitalize the area, Udall established the Pennsylvania Avenue National Historic Site in 1968,
comprising a roughly ten-block-by-three-block area between the
president's house and the Capitol, with Pennsylvania Avenue running down the midsection.[34] The Historic Sites Act of 1935 enabled
the interior secretary to create this unique National Park System
unit. In the legislation, he directed the historic site to be overseen
by a twenty-one-member presidential commission in charge of
approving private development plans. "That Pennsylvania Avenue
will be redeveloped is inevitable. We must be sure that this development will be of a character worthy of this historic axis," noted LBJ in
words that Udall might well have echoed.[35]

At least in part due to Udall's support of Owings's work, the
National Mall and downtown DC area witnessed some significant
improvements in the middle and late 1960s and afterward. Pennsylvania Avenue and Constitution Avenue received major tree
corridors, and the Capitol Reflecting Pool and Hirshhorn Museum
building were constructed using Owings's design, as was the
sculpture garden adjacent to the Museum of Natural History.[36] In

addition, thousands of parking spaces can be found underneath downtown DC, as can sections of a few major road corridors.[37]

Though others were involved and though the downtown area today is by no means in perfect aesthetic and historic preservation shape, Udall's work in revitalizing and regreening this area of Washington, DC, enhanced the residential and tourist experience.

Udall, DC Public Lands, and Integration

Udall also improved the city in another way, by promoting civil rights in the nation's capital. Three examples are briefly highlighted below. They involve changing a policy of a professional sports team, helping to establish one of the first units of the National Park System dedicated to an African American, and corresponding with none other than Martin Luther King Jr. regarding the civil rights leader's most famous march.

Ironically, DC, a predominantly African American city, had an exclusively white professional football team at the time Udall became interior secretary. In the early 1960s, the Redskins remained the only team in the National Football League (NFL) without a single black player. Udall had some "coaching power" due to the fact that the Redskins' stadium was on official federal government—National Park Service—property. Indeed, after discussing the situation with his departmental lawyers, Udall realized that he could have the owner of the Redskins, George Marshall, sign a lease for the stadium that required him to hire at least one African American player. If Marshall chose not to sign the lease, then Udall could force the team to find somewhere else to play. Udall did just this and, in doing so, became "Coach of the Year," according to an Arizona newspaper:

> The time has come after only a pair of league games to close the books on selection of the professional football coach of the year. The winner is a politician named Stewart L. Udall, presently employed full time as Interior Secretary in the Kennedy cabinet. As a coach, Udall is unique. He has not appeared at any practice sessions of his team, the Washington Redskins....

It could only happen in Washington, of course, that a politician, merely by a commitment to civil rights, could turn a
losing football team into a winner....

The article then went on to describe how Udall integrated the team:

Marshall's Redskins were notable in pro football as the squad
that had no Negro players. Redskins games were widely tele-
vised in Dixie and it may have been that chief Redskin Marshall believed the Southerners would prefer an all-white team
as its very own.

There was quite a hassle when Udall told Marshall to inte-
grate, or else. Udall was backed by a Supreme Court decision
which in general terms, held that what the government sub-
sidizes, it can also control. So Udall said he would cancel
Marshall's stadium contract if the Redskin color bar were
maintained.

Marshall was given a season of grace—last season—with
the understanding that there would be a Negro on the Redskin
squad this year. Marshall made a winter trade.[38]

Bobby Mitchel, as well as a couple of others, became the first African American players to regularly start for the Redskins, in 1962.
That season, with fitting symbolisn, Mitchel led the National Football League with eleven touchdowns, seventy-two catches, and 1,384
yards, and he went to the Pro Bowl. Marshall, though he said Udall
had nothing to do with the team's integration, invited the interior
secretary to the team's home opener. Udall accepted and watched
from the stands as Mitchell caught two touchdowns. More than fifty
year later, the Washington Redskins have a predominantly African
American team, but it all started with a secretary of the interior
who had a moral compass.[39]

In addition to integrating the District of Columbia's professional
football team, Udall personally accepted the deed to the Frederick
Douglass House from the National Association of Colored Women's
Club and the Frederick Douglass Memorial and Historical Association. Authorized in 1962 as the Frederick Douglass National Historic

Site, the park was one of the first national park units in the nation dedicated to commemorating and promoting African American history and culture. The hilltop home and grounds were restored by the National Park Service before being opened to the public.[40]

The same year that Udall accepted the deed to the historic home, the interior secretary corresponded with Dr. Martin Luther King Jr. The cordial letters involved a request from Dr. King and other civil rights activists to host their March on Washington for Jobs and Freedom, the peaceful protest that concluded with MLK's famous "I Have a Dream" speech. The event was to take place on the one hundredth anniversary of President Lincoln's Emancipation Proclamation, and since the march was taking place on the National Mall—NPS property—the civil rights icon needed to first get an official permit. Usually special-use permits were processed through the NPS, but since the march involved so many people and was such a big deal, Udall and his office took over the permitting process.[41]

Notes

1. Stewart Udall, personal note upon hearing news of the Kennedy assassination, November 22, 1963, special exhibition, September 2014, University of Arizona Special Collections Department.

2. Ansel Adams to Lyndon B. Johnson, September 4, 1964, box 190, folder 1, Udall Papers (emphasis in the original).

3. Horace Albright to Johnson, December 8, 1963, box 190, folder 2, Udall Papers.

4. Udall, *1976: Agenda for Tomorrow*, 77.

5. Stewart Udall, "The New Urban Conservation," *Nation's Cities*, June 1966, box 207, folder 5, Udall Papers.

6. Udall, *1976: Agenda for Tomorrow*, 13, 31, 32.

7. Ibid., 15, 16. Health, Education, and Welfare Secretary John W. Gardner (1965–68), a Republican Party member, wrote the foreword to Udall's book. Gardner actually resigned from the LBJ cabinet in protest over the president's policy in Vietnam.

8. US Census, "World Population," census.gov/population/international/data/worldpop/table_population.php; Udall, *1976: Agenda for Tomorrow*, 41, 42, 45.

9. Ibid., 47, 59.

10. Ibid., 83–85.

11. Ibid., 86, 92.

12. Ibid., 61, 125–26.

13. US Department of the Interior, Office of the Secretary, news release, "Secretary Udall Announces Family Planning Services Policy in Indian and Territorial Areas," June 20, 1965, box 158, folder 11, Udall Papers. See also Leunes, "Conservation Philosophy of Udall," 173.

14. US Department of the Interior, "Statement by Secretary of the Interior Stewart L. Udall on S. 404 and S. 2036 Before the Senate Subcommittee on Employment and Manpower of the Committee on Labor and Welfare," June 20, 1961, box 162, folder 14, Udall Papers.

15. Ibid.

16. Ibid.

17. Transcript, Stewart L. Udall oral history interview III, by Joe B. Frantz, April 18, 1969, LBJ Library, lbjlibrary.net/assets/documents/archives/oral _histories/udall/UDALL03.PDF.

18. US Department of the Interior, "History of the Service and Conservation Corps Movement," doi.gov/21csc/history/upload/21CSCBackground.pdf.

19. K. L. Wolf, "Crime and Fear: A Literature Review," in *Green Cities: Good Health* (Seattle: College of the Environment, University of Washington, 2010), depts.washington.edu/hhwb/Thm_Crime.html.

20. Fitch and Shanklin, *Bureau of Outdoor Recreation*, 140–44; Phyllis Myers, *State Grants for Parklands, 1965–1984* (Washington, DC: Conservation Foundation, 1987), 6.

21. Fitch and Shanklin, *Bureau of Outdoor Recreation*, 140–44.

22. Ibid.; Brian Allen Drake, *Loving Nature, Fearing the State: Environmentalism and Antigovernment Politics Before Reagan* (Seattle: University of Washington Press, 2013), 50.

23. Josh Protas, "The Straw That Broke the Camel's Back: Preservation of an Urban Mountain Landscape," *Journal of the Southwest* 43, no. 3 (2001): 379–421.

24. Robin W. Winks, *Laurance S. Rockefeller: Catalyst for Conservation*, 145.

25. See box 38, all folders, Nathaniel Owings Papers, Library of Congress.

26. Michael L. Gillette, *Lady Bird Johnson: An Oral History* (Oxford: Oxford University Press, 2012), 357.

27. Isaac D. Kremer, "NHPA at 50: The Growing Partnership Between Stewart Udall and Lady Bird Johnson," July 12, 2013, placepromotion.blogspot.com/2013/07 /nhpaat50-growing-partnership-between.html.

28. Lady Bird Johnson, *A White House Diary*, 240–42, 248–49, 254. See also Winks, *Laurance S. Rockefeller*, 141–60; National Park Service, *National Capital Region Administrative History* (Washington, DC: National Park Service, 2008), 99–103; and PBS, *Lady Bird Johnson*, pbs.org/ladybird/shattereddreams/shattereddreams _report.html.

29. National Park Service, *Lady Bird Johnson Park Cultural Landscapes Inventory* (Washington, DC: National Park Service, 2005), 19, 24–25, 48–52.

30. Ibid.

31. Kremer, "NHPA at 50"; PBS, *Lady Bird Johnson*. Outside of their joint work on the DC committees, Udall and the first lady took several conservation trips

together, similar to Udall and Kennedy's two conservation trips. In order to increase interest in conservation nationwide, Udall and Lady Bird visited several sites in Vermont, including what is currently known as Marsh-Billings-Rockefeller National Historical Park. They also visited Grand Tetons National Park twice and completed a five-day tour of western Texas, where they explored, rafted, and hiked Big Bend National Park; visited the San Antonio Riverwalk; and dedicated Fort Davis National Historic Site. They visited other areas as well in order to spread the gospel of conservation.

32. Johnson, *A White House Diary*, 248–49. See also Nathaniel Alexander Owings, *The Spaces in Between: An Architect's Journey* (Boston: Houghton Mifflin, 1973), 229–45; and box 38, Owings Papers.

33. Ibid.

34. US Department of the Interior, Office of the Secretary, *Pennsylvania Avenue National Historic Site Order of Designation*, September 30, 1965.

35. Ibid.; US House of Representatives, *Communication from the President of the United States Transmitting a Proposed Joint Resolution to Provide for the Administration and Development of Pennsylvania Avenue as a National Historic Site*, 89th Cong., 1st Sess., Doc. No. 296, September 30, 1965.

36. Joseph Judge, "New Grandeur for Flowering Washington," *National Geographic*, April 1967, 500–539; box 38, Owings Papers; Office of the US President, *Pennsylvania Avenue: Report of the President's Temporary Commission on Pennsylvania Avenue*, January 1969, box 38, Owings Papers.

37. National Park Service, *National Capital Region Administrative History*, 53–54.

38. Lyle C. Wilson, "Udall 'Coach of Year'?," *Mesa (AZ) Tribune*, September 27, 1962, box 90, folder 8, Udall Papers. See also Thomas G. Smith, *Showdown: JFK and the Integration of the Washington Redskins*. Smith's book is strangely titled, as the author writes practically nothing about JFK. Kennedy had almost nothing to do with the integration of the Washington Redskins; it was the initiative of Stewart Udall. Smith writes about Udall at length in the book.

39. Ryan Basen, "Fifty Years Ago, Last Outpost of Segregation in N.F.L. Fell," *New York Times*, October 6, 2012, nytimes.com/2012/10/07/sports/football/50-years -ago-redskins-were-last-nfl-team-to-integrate.html?_r=0; Thomas G. Smith, "1962: The Year That Changed the Redskins," *Washingtonian*, October 10, 2011, washingtonian.com/blogs/capitalcomment/1962-the-year-that-changed-the-red skins.php. One of the last acts Udall signed as US secretary of the interior was redesignating District of Columbia Stadium, the home of the Redskins, as RFK Stadium. He did this to honor his slain friend. Udall was able to rename the stadium due to the fact that it was on National Park Service land; he also worked with the NPS's concessioner in charge of the stadium. See Dan Steinberg, "William Geoghegan, Who Gave RFK Stadium Its Name, Dies at 90," *Washington Post*, January 26, 2015, washingtonpost.com/nws/dc-sports-blog/wp/2015/01/26/william -geoghegan-who-gave-rfk-stadium-its-name-dies-at-90/; and Dan Steinberg,

"RFK Stadium Was Almost LBJ Stadium," *Washington Post*, March 25, 2010, voices
.washingtonpost.com/dcsportsblog/2010/10/03/rfk_stadium_was_almost_lbj_sta
.html.

40. National Park Service, *National Capital Region Administrative History*, 112–13.

41. See correspondence between Martin Luther King Jr. and Stewart Udall,
King Center, Library and Archives, thekingcenter.org/archive/list?keys=stewart
+udall&=Apply. Udall, in one other push for civil rights, wrote an open letter to his
church. He wrote the president and other high-ranking members of the Church of
Jesus Christ of Latter-day Saints, requesting that they terminate the ban on black
men receiving the priesthood. Udall's letter received mixed reviews, but it was a
significant letter, as he was the highest-ranking Mormon in the federal government at the time. For more on this, see "The Stewart Udall Sequence," a series of
six thoughtful articles written on thoughtsonthingsandstuff.com/stewat-udall
-sequence-i-the-conscience-of-a-jack-mormon/.

12 | Controversies of the Interior Secretary

But I kept telling him [LBJ] this is the one instance as you go out the door, you shouldn't care whether Congressmen like it or not. The issue is what's good for the country.

IN TERMS OF CONSERVATION of natural resources and environmental protection, it can easily be argued that Stewart Udall was the most successful US secretary of the interior in history. He added more acres to the National Park System and National Wildlife Refuge System in the continental United States than any other interior secretary and pushed for the greening and cleaning of urban America by way of downtown revitalization efforts in the nation's capital, providing unique employment opportunities for city youth, and so on. Yet no one is perfect. Everyone makes mistakes, and everyone makes decisions that they later regret. Undoubtedly, the most controversial aspect of Udall's eight years as interior secretary involved his support of a dam whose backwater would have entered Grand Canyon National Park. This chapter begins by analyzing this topic and continues by reviewing some of Udall's unsuccessful attempts at national park unit establishment. Finally, it ends with a discussion of Udall's failure to get LBJ to create numerous new national monuments during the president's lame-duck term.

Grand Canyon Dam Controversy

Water planning and water security are critical in the Intermountain West due to the area's general aridity and lack of significant rainfall. At midcentury, with Arizona's population and agricultural lands increasing as well as Tucson and Phoenix growing and likely to continue to do so, securing steady and reliable sources of water for the future was a high priority for planners and politicians.

Beginning in the 1940s, the US Bureau of Reclamation and long-time Arizona senator Carl Hayden pushed for the Central Arizona Project (CAP), a 250-mile aqueduct transporting Colorado River water to Phoenix, Tucson, and vicinities. Hayden's bill reached and passed the Senate in 1950, but was stalled in the House of Representatives due to California's congressional delegation. With California wanting to make sure it was not left out of the Colorado River "pie," the two states were involved in a long-standing dispute regarding each other's claim to the lower Colorado River water supply. The contest went all the way to the Supreme Court of the United States. In the early 1960s, in *Arizona v. California*, the High Court essentially ruled that Arizona could proceed with its project but that Congress had to approve it first. Thus, the court sent the project back to congressional deadlock.[1]

Like all of Arizona's congressional delegation, Stewart Udall as a congressman voted in favor of reclamation projects on the Colorado Plateau. It was no different with the CAP. After the Supreme Court case, the Arizona delegation, including Hayden, Goldwater, Morris Udall, and John Rhodes, again pitched the Central Arizona Project to Congress. Stewart, though, now not solely representing the state of Arizona but rather the entire country as well as the executive branch of the government, decided to push a regional, multistate approach to Colorado River water. Udall was asked to do so by Colorado's Wayne Aspinall, the conservative Democrat and powerful and controversial chairman of the House Interior and Insular Affairs Committee.[2]

As a result, Udall, Bureau of Reclamation director Floyd Dominy, and other staff worked on and then submitted the Pacific Southwest Water Plan to all parties in August 1963, which was designed to please California and other southwestern states enough to get the bill to pass. The PSWP was "an ambitious, multistate project" involving seventeen different water projects in total, including the Central Arizona Project. Historian Stephen Sturgeon notes that

Udall's strategy with the PSWP was to gain approval of CAP by offer-ing possible opponents their own projects as well.[3]

While Arizona's delegation was not sure about Udall's plan at first, they eventually came around. So too did California and other states after some amendments were made to the bill. However, a faction of environmentalists, led by David Brower, executive direc-tor of the Sierra Club, did not. To Brower, it was a problem of reser-voir location.

As part of the Pacific Southwest Water Plan, the Central Arizona Project called for an aqueduct to be run overland from Lake Havasu on the California-Arizona border. But the plans also called for two dams to be built along the Colorado River in northern Arizona in order to supply electricity for the project. The problem was that the Colorado River in northern Arizona flows through one of the most scenic areas on earth: the Grand Canyon, specifically Grand Canyon National Park and Grand Canyon National Monument (Con-gress merged the national monument into the national park at a later date).[4]

The plans called for a dam upstream of the national park at Marble Canyon, but also downstream of the park. The dam up-stream was not a grave concern to most environmentalists, because it didn't intrude on national park lands. However, the bridge down-stream, called Bridge Canyon Dam, would have backed up water ninety-three miles upstream. Dominy's assessment determined that the first fifty-three miles of backwater would be within the Lake Mead National Recreation Area. The basis for national recreation areas was often reservoirs, so there was no real controversy with this action. However, the next twenty-seven miles of Bridge Canyon Dam reservoir water would border or be within Grand Canyon Na-tional Monument. And finally, thirteen miles would border Grand Canyon National Park, while a one-mile section would be within the national park proper.[5] Historian Tim Palmer noted that the dam would have put Lava Falls, a Colorado River cascade "regarded by some people as the most exciting rapid in the country," 214 feet under water, while "Havasu Creek—a paradise to many—would be 85 feet under."[6]

Udall knew that Brower and certain environmentalists would not like the fact that parts of the national monument and national park would be, in their minds, violated. Still, Udall was surprised, furious in fact, when he saw the *New York Times* one morning. Taking up an entire page was a Sierra Club advertisement lobbying against the dams. Written by Brower and company, part of the page included cutout mail-in notes addressed to LBJ, Udall, and Scoop Jackson, requesting that they terminate the Grand Canyon dams plan and seek other options. In humongous bold typescript, the ad also proclaimed, "Dinosaur and Big Bend, Glacier and Grand Teton, Kings Canyon, Redwoods, Mammoth, even Yellowstone and Yosemite. And the Wild Rivers, and Wilderness. How can you guarantee these, Mr. Udall, if Grand Canyon is dammed for profit?"[7]

Soon after the newspaper published the ad, Brower followed up with a personal letter to Udall, in 1966, stating his strong convictions against the dams: "Nothing you have done, and nothing else you are hoping to do for conservation, can offset the damage that will ensue if you let Grand Canyon go down the drain, and with it everything that has meaning in the National Park idea.... It will do this administration no good to attempt to complete the National Park System if Grand Canyon's integrity, and the Park System's with it, is destroyed."[8]

This was not good publicity for Stewart Udall, especially the newspaper advertisement. Yet the interior secretary found himself in a difficult situation. Historian Barbara Leunes notes that on one side, he was deeply interested and committed to conservation. He loved the National Park System, natural wonders, and open space. Yet on the other side, "he knew that Arizona's underground water was being used up at an alarming rate and that traditional policy required a hydro dam to provide the electric power needed for pumping water into arid valleys." Udall himself said of the situation, "We are trying to conserve these places for beauty on one hand, and trying to develop our areas and solve our economic problems on the other." In the instance of Grand Canyon National Monument and Grand Canyon National Park, Udall sided with reclamation—at first.[9]

Whether the reader is in shock right now about Udall supporting the dam or does not see the issue as as big a controversy as Brower saw it, there are a few reasons why Udall's recommendation to flood a small portion of the Grand Canyon might be seen as not simply a black-and-white matter. First, the 1919 legislation establishing Grand Canyon National Park, put forth by a much younger Carl Hayden, had a clause in it permitting future water and reservoir development.[10]

Second, Brower and the environmentalists with him, not to mention most historians writing about the Bridge Canyon Dam controversy ever since, essentially ignored a key landowning faction involved in the fight: the Hualapai, an American Indian group that owned half the land in which the dam and reservoir would be located. The tribe, which was largely supportive of the dam, believed that a reservoir could lead to public recreation based on their reservation, which in turn would significantly benefit their economy and bring them out of poverty. The Udall brothers and Wayne Aspinall argued in favor of the dam, which they referred to as the Hualapai Dam, not the Bridge Canyon Dam, in part because it would help the Hualapai.[11]

Third, the result of not constructing the dams was the building of a coal-fired power plant. Hydropower provided by the Bridge Canyon Dam would have been clean, efficient, and renewable, while the coal-fired power plant has created significant air pollution over the years (ironically, some of this air pollution impairs the views within Grand Canyon National Park) and has increased the amount of carbon dioxide in the atmosphere.

Fourth, the Colorado River would not have been inundated by the reservoir up to the top of the Grand Canyon, as Brower and the Sierra Club argued in their lobbying. Rather, the dam's backwater would have been only a few hundred feet deep. Relatedly, the reservoir water would have been much too far away to have seen from almost all of the park's roads, visitor centers, hotels, and even trails, meaning only a tiny portion of park visitors would have been aware of the man-made intrusion.[12]

Despite these facts that may or may not make the controversy seem more like a shade of gray, Udall did end up having a change of heart regarding the dam proposal. Certainly, some of this was brought about by the Sierra Club's very effective antidam campaign, as Udall and other departmental officials received mass quantities of mail from the public asking them to stop the dam from being built.[13] Brower himself hammered Udall in the interior secretary's office on the subject on multiple occasions. But due to the controversy, even before Brower's advertisements, the DOI completed a study concluding that a no-dam solution to the Grand Canyon–Central Arizona Project controversy was possible. Perhaps as a result of all these conflicting thoughts, Udall, in the thick of the controversy, decided to take a float trip down the Grand Canyon to see the proposed dam area for himself.

"The Secretary of the Interior should never make armchair judgments on national conservation issues," he said in a 1967 *Life* feature article after the two-week float trip with his family down the Colorado River. Instead of "armchair judgments," Udall noted that it was much better to see an area under debate firsthand before making up one's mind. "I confess now that I approached this problem with a less-than-open mind in early 1963, when we began our planning at Interior for the Lower Colorado Project," Udall wrote. "This was all changed in January of 1966, when Interior experts, after a four-month study, produced a no-dam solution to Arizona's water problem that won the support of the White House. Under the new plan, electricity to pump water over the hill to the central valley would come from a coal-fired steam plant, not a hydro dam. The cost of the project would be drastically reduced, and so would the controversy."[14]

Despite these words, perhaps in part to save face or in part because he really thought silt was a potential problem, Udall was unable to declare his full support for the no-dam solution. At the end of the same article, the interior secretary, arguing that the Bridge Canyon Dam might have a shortened life span due to the significant amounts of topsoil that could fill it up with silt, was unable to buckle down and fully support dam or no dam. "If hydropower prevails and the national interest dictates that a dam be built, a high dam, not a half dam, should be constructed. On the other hand," Udall wrote, "if a hydro dam is not really needed, the boundaries of the Grand Canyon National Park should be changed [and expanded to include the dam site]."[15]

By the next year, though, Udall's change of heart was complete, as he fully advocated for national park unit expansion in Grand Canyon and no dam. And ultimately, with Carl Hayden retiring at the end of his term, and his expertise from forty-two years in the Senate and more than fifty-five years in combined House-Senate service leaving with him, and with Udall leaving with Johnson's outgoing administration, and with a new presidential administration coming in, the Arizona congressional delegation and Aspinall decided to let the Grand Canyon dams plan wither.[16]

The bill for the Colorado River Basin Project—essentially a scaled-down version of Udall's Pacific Southwest Water Plan—passed Congress and was signed by the president into law in 1968. After a long period of construction, Arizona gained an additional water supply for its farmers and city dwellers in Phoenix and Tucson, and the power for the project came from the Navajo (coal-fired) Generating Station instead of dams within the Grand Canyon. The Central Arizona Project component of the Colorado River Basin Project involved the construction of three hundred miles of aqueduct, with the main portion of this man-made waterway deeper than a two-story building and wider than an eight-lane highway. Also, 547,000 kilowatts of energy were created from the Navajo power plant.[17]

Stewart Udall later acknowledged that he had been on the wrong side of history in his support of Bridge Canyon Dam as well as some other dam projects in the 1950s and '60s. He also gave ample credit to Brower for putting up a fight—and winning. And despite Brower's attack ads directed at Udall, the Sierra Club leader still remembered Udall as the most "environmentally conscious" interior secretary in US history. The two men had significant respect for each other.[18]

Failed 1960s National Parks: Great Basin National Park and Prairie National Park

While it might be impossible for a public official to escape all controversy, it's also practically impossible for a politician to get everything he asks and lobbies for. That said, Udall arguably achieved more as interior secretary than any other head of the Interior Department. But some of the bills he strongly pushed for did not pass. He created dozens of new national wildlife refuges and national park units, but there could have even been more. While the biggest disappointment for Udall in his push for parks and wildlife sanctuaries was caused by Lyndon Johnson (as discussed in the next section), there were other examples of national parks not getting established in the 1960s. In the cases of Great Basin National Park in Nevada and the proposed Prairie National Park in Kansas, Udall probably came to realize that if there is *some* local opposition to a park, then it can probably become a park, but if there is *major* local opposition, it's nearly impossible to establish it.

Great Basin National Park, which fortunately was ultimately established in 1986 thanks in part to the efforts of then US representative Harry Reid (D-NV), is a case in point. The national park, comprising some of the highest peaks in Nevada as well as the oldest trees on earth, was first suggested by the National Park Service in the early 1960s, before the agency's park-planning duties were transferred to the Bureau of Outdoor Recreation. Udall argued for the establishment of the national park throughout his time as interior secretary, but was lambasted on his visit to the area as well as nearby Ely, Nevada, in 1965.[19]

A meeting with Ely citizens about the proposed park proved to be an opposition festival. While the town's mayor endorsed the park due to its tourism potential, the vast majority of area cattlemen did not. As a newspaper article reporting on the meeting put it, "George Swallow, vice chairman of the Central Committee of Nevada State Grazing Boards, said the loss to the livestock industry because of a park would be overwhelming." Swallow also said, in a convoluted and ironic argument, that "creation of a park would increase fire hazards and losses to predators such as wolves and mountain lion and damage the watersheds on which some ranches rely."[20]

It was true, however, that about a thousand cattle and a thousand sheep were grazed in the proposed national park area each summer. The cattle were owned by just six ranchers. Yet these ranchers were politically connected and apparently powerful, and they would stand to lose much of their seven-million-dollar businesses were the park to be established. Eventually, when the park was established a couple of decades later, a compromise was arranged whereby grazing continued to be legal in certain areas.[21]

East of Great Basin, Kansas's Prairie National Park was proposed repetitively in the late 1950s and '60s as a fifty-seven-thousand-acre national park, which would include a loop road, viewpoints, hiking trails, a campground, and a visitor center, and which would focus on the unique biodiversity and ecology of prairie ecosystems. It eventually became the much smaller eleven-thousand-acre Tallgrass Prairie National Preserve, established in 1996 with a partial emphasis on ranching. Udall lobbied unsuccessfully for the establishment of this larger national park through the 1960s, and as a private citizen in the '70s.[22]

National Park Service reports and some local support led Kansas's fully Republican congressional delegation to support the park idea, and they repeatedly introduced legislation for the national park.[23] Udall, seeing the park as serving to protect a unique ecosystem of grasslands and also recognizing that it would be the only national park for miles around, jumped on board with the proposal wholeheartedly upon becoming interior secretary.[24]

Before his first year as interior secretary was up, Udall had even met with President Kennedy to pitch the park idea to him. "Kansas? Why do you want a national park in Kansas? What the hell have they ever done for us?" was the president's initial response, as Kansas had voted for Nixon instead of him in 1960. But after Udall pushed the subject and even sent Kennedy a specially made NPS booklet on the proposed park, JFK loosely endorsed the Prairie National Park legislation. There was loud and vocal local opposition, however.[25]

On an inspection and testing-the-waters trip to the proposed Kansas parkland, Udall hopped out of a helicopter to study the terrain only to be apprehended by the rancher who owned the land. While different versions of the story were reported by the media (one including a shotgun being pointed at the interior secretary), the rancher told Udall something to the effect of "Get off my land. You're on private property." Udall and entourage quickly headed skyward, the trip not beginning on a good note. At a meeting later that day, Udall lamented, "It's too bad when a member of the president's cabinet tries to take a walk on a hill and is told to get off.... But the national park will remedy that."[26]

But the full national park was never established. The meeting site was a packed house of opposition. One of the ranchers who opposed the park told Udall to take a drive: "I suggest that Mr. Udall take a trip from here to Oklahoma and look at the bluestem grass which paves the way. How do you expect tourists to drive through 12 million acres of the same grass to look at 60,000 acres of the same grass which you say would be unique?"[27]

LBJ's Lame-Duck Session and the Antiquities Act: "My Biggest Disappointment as Interior Secretary"

In addition to the 1960s failures to establish national parks in Kansas and Nevada, probably Udall's biggest disappointment as interior secretary played out over the final few months of his eight-year tenure. Udall and President Johnson and even Udall and Lady Bird had established great relationships in terms of conservation. Part of this stemmed from the fact that LBJ and Udall both grew up in rural western landscapes and were deeply connected to the land from a young age. Sadly, though, their relationship ended on a negative note at the very end of Johnson's presidency. The controversy involved LBJ and his failure to establish and enlarge several national monuments. In the final months and days of the administration, Udall and his staff worked incredibly hard on getting the president to sign the interior secretary's proposal for unprecedented new additions to the National Park System that would have increased the system's total acreage by one-fourth. Unfortunately, Johnson, wanting to make sure he remained on good terms with Congress, ended up only minimally following the proposal.

By the power vested in them by the 1906 Antiquities Act, presidents have the authority to establish national monuments on pre-existing federal lands so long as the monuments protect something scientifically or historically significant. The Antiquities Act has been used by many presidents over the years, especially during their final weeks in office when they perhaps no longer need to worry as much about congressional opposition. Presidents can act more on their convictions and morals during their lame-duck term and also establish land legacies for themselves. Not known as the greatest president by any means, Herbert Hoover nonetheless set aside four million acres of national monuments just prior to FDR's taking office. These national monuments included Death Valley in California, Great Sand Dunes in Colorado (both of which were later reclassified as national parks), and White Sands in New Mexico, among others. Theodore Roosevelt established numerous national monuments, including Devils Tower in Wyoming and several monuments based on ancient American Indian archaeological sites in the Southwest.

Wanting the president and himself to leave office with a conservation grand finale, Udall drew up big national monument plans for LBJ. "Mr. President," Udall told Johnson in a formal meeting on the proposal, "if four million acres is right for Herbert Hoover, seven million acres is about right for Lyndon Johnson."[28]

Udall's national monument proposals, developed in tandem with high-up officials of the NPS and the BOR, included creating a massive Gates of the Arctic National Monument in the Brooks Range of northern Alaska, as well as additional protection for the greater Denali ecosystem by way of a Mount McKinley National Monument bordering Mount McKinley National Park. In the US Southwest, the interior secretary's plan called for the establishment of Sonoran Desert National Monument south and west of Tucson. The Udall brothers had been pushing for a Sonoran Desert National Park for a few years in Congress, which would have included Organ Pipe Cactus National Monument as well as the adjacent Cabeza Prieta National Wildlife Refuge, which protected critical habitat for the endangered Sonoran pronghorn antelope. With the bills stalling in the halls of Congress, though, Stewart proposed it as a national monument. Finally, on the Colorado Plateau, just above the Grand Canyon, Udall proposed a Marble Canyon National Monument as well as expansions to Arches National Monument and Capitol Reef

National Monument, the latter to protect a unique geological feature known as the Waterpocket Fold.[29]

Johnson told Udall to get the projects cleared and approved by the key congressional stakeholders. LBJ, having a deep respect for Congress and also having worked in Congress for some years prior to his vice presidency and presidency, did not want to do anything controversial to stir up negative sentiments during his final days in office. Yet Udall was somewhat reluctant to go to Congress. "There's a normal protocol that President Johnson was a master of, of always touching the Congressional base," Udall said in an interview just a few months after he had left the Interior Department. "But I kept telling him this is the one instance as you go out the door, you shouldn't care whether Congressmen like it or not. The issue is what's good for the country, and that they will accept it."[30] Udall also knew that some of the congressmen LBJ wanted him to consult would not approve of the national monument proclamations. Finally, with his experiences of the past decade to back him up, the interior secretary knew that there was not enough time or energy left in the administration to undertake the long-drawn-out compromises necessary to get the parks passed by Congress. One major obstacle to Udall's working with Congress under the time limit was, once again, Wayne Aspinall, who wanted the power and decisions to come from the legislature, not the executive branch.[31]

At the same time, Udall knew that many of the congressmen he had worked with over the past fifteen years—primarily the ones on the House Interior and Insular Affairs Committee and its US Senate counterpart, or the "'Saylors' and the 'Jacksons,'" as he called them, referring to John Saylor and Henry "Scoop" Jackson—would approve of the new additions.[32]

To make matters more dramatic, as the final weeks of the Johnson administration played out, a series of "excruciating coincidences" occurred, the first being that Alaska governor Walter Hickel was offered the job of interior secretary by president-elect Nixon. According to bureau historian and future NPS director William C. Everhart, Johnson's announcement about the new national monuments was supposed to come out over Christmas as a "conservation Christmas present" to the nation. But because Hickel was from Alaska, LBJ stalled on it, asking Udall to check in with the incoming interior secretary to make sure he approved of the national monument additions to his home state. LBJ wanted to make sure that the national monument proposals would not cause complaints from Hickel or Nixon. Yet Udall knew Hickel and knew that he would disapprove of the national monuments. Hickel, a strange politician who would become a populist during his brief stint as interior secretary before being fired, was in fact enraging conservationists and environmentalists throughout the nation at the time by criticizing conservation before he even became interior secretary. This led to his long-drawn-out confirmation hearings and his nomination almost being withdrawn.[33]

Udall kept making the same arguments to Johnson, saying that the president should proclaim the national monuments even if some politicians didn't approve because it was ultimately for the greater good. Johnson, on the other hand, kept telling Udall to talk about the national monument plans with these select individuals. It seemed to be a stalemate. The final weeks of the administration turned into the final days.[34]

Another drama came about due to a sentence LBJ added during his final State of the Union address. Just five days before the official end of the Johnson administration, during the president's speech, he turned to the topic of conservation. After stating that much land had been set aside for conservation during his five years as president, he said, "There is more going to be set aside before this administration ends." With this statement, Johnson "let the cat out of the bag," according to Udall, which led the interior secretary to believe that the president was going to approve all of his proposals.[35]

Yet Wednesday came, and LBJ did not sign the new national monument proclamations Udall and staff had written up and sent to the White House. Thursday and Friday came without the president signing. Saturday, in Udall's mind, was the very last day that Johnson could make the announcement, as Sunday was the traditional day of rest and Monday was Nixon's inauguration.[36]

Udall, believing and hoping that his boss would approve the 7 million acres of new national monuments, on Friday night gave a copy of the prewritten press release, which announced that Johnson had signed the proclamations, to some members of the media. Whether Udall hoped the newspaper articles of the next morning would force Johnson's hand, and whether he gave the reporters a green light to report or told them to hold off on publishing until they had the "go-ahead" from the administration, we will never know for sure. What is known is that when LBJ saw the articles prematurely stating that he had created the national monuments, he called Udall by phone. A heated argument between the president of the United States and the US secretary of the interior ensued.[37]

"You let the cat out of the bag yourself, Mr. President, in your speech," Udall yelled. When LBJ ordered his interior secretary to terminate the press release, Udall offered his resignation in disgust and protest. Johnson denied Udall's request, but then snapped at his interior secretary, "Hell of a way to run a department." LBJ then hung up the phone, and these were the last words ever spoken between Udall and Johnson.[38]

In his final minutes in office that following Monday, LBJ did sign a proclamation, but it created only Marble Canyon National Monument at a meager 32,665 acres and expanded Arches and Capitol Reef. Udall had asked Johnson to expand the National Park System by 7 million acres, but LBJ expanded it by less than 300,000 in the end. Fortunately for conservationists and lovers of outdoor recreation and scenic grandeur, many of Udall's proposed national monuments, including Gates of the Arctic and Mount McKinley, would be established by President Carter and Interior Secretary Cecil Andrus in 1978 and then expanded and reclassified with the 1980 Alaska National Interest Lands Conservation Act. Stewart Udall's brother Morris would be a major player in and endorser of the latter act. But in early 1969, this piece of legislation was far in the future, and Stewart feared the chance for protecting the areas had been lost.[39]

Notes

1. Smith, *Green Republican*, 181–83.

2. Ibid. See also US Department of the Interior, Bureau of Reclamation, *Pacific Southwest Water Plan Report* (Washington, DC: Bureau of Reclamation, 1964).

3. Sturgeon, *Politics of Western Water*, 71.

4. *Pacific Southwest Water Plan Report*.

5. Ibid.

6. Tim Palmer, *Endangered Rivers and the Conservation Movement* (New York: Rowman & Littlefield, 2004), 84.

7. Special advertisement, *New York Times*, July 25, 1966, online copy. The Sierra Club actually created a series of bold advertisements like this that they then published in national newspapers.

8. David Brower to Stewart Udall, April 29, 1966, box 190, folder 4, Udall Papers.

9. Leunes, "Conservation Philosophy of Udall," 37.

10. *Pacific Southwest Water Plan Report*. In fact, perhaps contrary to popular belief, many national park units have been established with such clauses in their legislative language.

11. Bailey, "Politics of Dunes, Redwoods, and Dams."

12. Ibid.

13. See Byron E. Pearson, "Salvation for the Grand Canyon: Congress, the Sierra Club, and the Dam Controversy of 1966–1968," *Journal of the Southwest* 36, no. 2 (1994): 159–95; Mark Kitchell, *A Fierce Green Fire* (DVD, First Run Features, 2013); and Rachel Whitted, "The Sacred and the Profane: An Analysis of the Rhetoric in David Brower's Campaign to Save the Grand Canyon," *Young Scholars in Writing* 11 (2014), cas.umkc.edu/english/publications/youngscholarsinwriting /documents/11/10-The-Sacred-and-the-Profane.pdf.

14. Stewart Udall, "Shooting the Wild Colorado," *Venture*, February 1968, box 249, Udall Papers.

15. Ibid.

16. Sturgeon, *Politics of Western Water*, 118–22.

17. Smith, *Green Republican*, 202–5; Frank Walsh, *How to Create a Water Crisis* (Boulder, CO: Johnson Books, 1985).

18. David Brower, *For Earth's Sake: The Life and Times of David Brower* (Salt Lake City: Peregrine Smith Books, 1990), 233. Much more has been written about the Grand Canyon dam controversy. See Charles Coate, "'The Biggest Water Fight in American History': Stewart Udall and the Central Arizona Project," 79–101; M. Udall, Neuman, and Udall, *Too Funny to Be President*, 46–64; Byron E. Pearson, *Still the Wild River Runs: Congress, the Sierra Club, and the Fight to Save the Grand Canyon* (Tucson: University of Arizona Press, 2002); and Schulte, *Aspinall and the Shaping of the American West*, 177–227. Another controversy involving Udall, albeit a much smaller one, involved his 1968 move that changed the official logo of the Department of the Interior. Udall changed the symbol from that of the bison,

a classic symbol of the American West, to a logo involving a "stylized pair of hands embracing symbols of the sun, mountains, and water." While he believed the new logo was more representative of the department's myriad responsibilities, many criticized the symbol and it was short-lived—the logo represented "the Good Hands of Allstate," some joked. Udall's successor, Walter Hickel, swiftly changed the departmental logo back to the bison, which it has remained ever since. See US Department of the Interior, "Cultural Resources and the Interior Department: An Overview," no. 4 (1999): 7.

19. For the general story of how Great Basin National Park came to fruition, see National Park Service, "Lehman Caves Becomes a National Park," nps.gov/grba /historyculture/lehman-caves-becomes-a-national-park.htm.

20. "Udall Hit by Nevadan over Park," *Idaho Daily Statesman*, June 4, 1965, box 156, folder 8, Udall Papers.

21. Ibid.

22. See Stewart L. Udall, foreword to *Tallgrass Prairie: The Inland Sea*, by Patricia D. Duncan; and Udall, keynote speech for the Second Annual Tallgrass Prairie Conference, Elmdale, KS, September 28, 1974, box 186, folder 12, Udall Papers.

23. National Park Service, *Tallgrass Prairie National Preserve Legislative History, 1920–1996* (Washington, DC: National Park Service, 1998).

24. Udall, foreword to *Tallgrass Prairie*, by Duncan.

25. See box 156, folder 7, Udall Papers.

26. "Udall's Park Plan Stirs Kansas Storm; Rancher Orders Him Off Land," *Daily Oklahoman*, December 5, 1961, box 156, folder 7, Udall Papers.

27. Ibid.

28. Transcript, Stewart L. Udall oral history interview IV, by Joe B. Frantz, October 31, 1969, LBJ Library, lbjlibrary.net/assets/documents/archives/oral _histories/udall/UDALL04.PDF.

29. Ibid. In specific regard to the Sonoran Desert National Park proposal, see oral history interview transcript, "Stewart Udall Sonoran Desert National Park," *Journal of the Southwest* 39, no. 3 (1997). In 1978 and 1980, Mount McKinley National Park was expanded and reclassified as Denali National Park and Preserve. Capitol Reef and Arches were later upgraded from national monuments to official national parks.

30. Transcript, Udall oral history interview IV.

31. Ibid.; Everhart, *The National Park Service*, 177. Aspinall was very much against presidential use of the Antiquities Act. When President Eisenhower and his interior secretary, in the final days of their administration, proclaimed a small Chesapeake and Ohio Canal National Monument north of the District of Columbia, Aspinall was so offended that he practically single-handedly denied the NPS any start-up funds or appropriations for the new national monument for years.

32. Transcript, Udall oral history interview IV.

33. Ibid.; Everhart, *The National Park Service*, 174–79. The story of Walter Hickel is a story of odd politics. Essentially, Hickel was a conservative governor of Alaska,

then an extremely liberal secretary of the interior, and then a conservative again
in his later years. Hickel surprised environmentalists as interior secretary by
largely being on their side. His cabinet post was short-lived, however, as he was
fired by President Nixon during Nixon's first term because of a leaked story to the
press involving Hickel's adamant stance against the administration's involvement
in the Vietnam War. Interestingly, back-to-back interior secretaries Udall and
Hickel, after long lives, passed away within weeks of each other in the late winter
and spring of 2010.

34. Ibid. According to Wayne Aspinall's version of the story, Udall actually
told President Johnson that he and Aspinall had talked about the new national
monuments and that Aspinall was supportive of LBJ's creating them. When Johnson then went to confirm this with Aspinall, the Colorado congressman notified
LBJ that this was the first he had heard of the proposals and that Udall had never
brought the topic up with him. See Schulte, *Aspinall and the Shaping of the American
West*, 232–33.

35. Transcript, Udall, oral history interview IV; Everhart, *The National Park
Service*.

36. Ibid.

37. Ibid.

38. Ibid.

39. Ibid.

13 | Final Days in Office

From the bottom of my heart,
thanks for your help and your friendship.

EVEN WITH ALL the last-minute drama between LBJ and the interior secretary, and even though Udall was surely disappointed in the president not establishing the series of new national monuments that he had so recommended, the final weeks of Udall's tenure at the Department of the Interior had some nice moments and closures.

One of these endings involved the interior secretary writing a heartfelt letter to the members of the US Senate and House of Representatives with whom he had worked most closely. Many of these congressmen Udall had been working with since he was elected to Congress himself back in 1955. John Saylor, Henry "Scoop" Jackson, Wayne Aspinall, Frank Church, Thomas Kuchel, and a few dozen others received Udall's letter. "I believe our children and grandchildren will take pride and satisfaction that men and women of diverse views from all parts of our nation could work together so well to accomplish so much," Udall wrote. "From the bottom of my heart, thanks for your help and your friendship."[1]

Scoop Jackson, chairman of the Senate Committee on Interior and Insular Affairs, wrote back to Udall. "Stewart," he wrote, "There is no question in my mind that you have done more in the field of conservation than any Secretary in the history of our country. Your contributions in this and other areas under your jurisdiction are legion."[2]

Udall also began receiving fan mail in his final days and weeks. Hundreds of letters, both printed and handwritten, poured into the interior secretary's office, thanking Udall for his work on behalf of conservation and protecting the American environment. Thank-you letters came in from Tanzanian national park officials and California state legislators, regional park departments and business executives, conservation organizations and private citizens, field-workers within the Department of the Interior and even religious leaders. Perhaps the most sincere letter of all was written by, of all people, an executive producer for the network ABC:

> Dear Mr. Secretary,
> Just a short note in the middle of a busy day…
>
> While looking over the news wires here at ABC and noticing especially the Walter Hickel stories, it suddenly occurred to me that I've long considered you the best damned Secretary of the Interior in the history of this nation. And it also occurred to me that I have seldom taken the time to let superior public officials know my appreciation for their work. It's an unfortunate characteristic of most Americans where government officials are involved, that we readily criticize but are reluctant to praise.
>
> So I'll repeat, I think you're the best Secretary of the Interior America has had and I want you to know that I sincerely and deeply appreciate all that you've done.
>
> As a sportsman and conservationist and as one who produced and hosted outdoor shows on radio and TV for ten years, I think I know whereof I speak.
>
> At your age, I'm positive those of us in the news business will be hearing about Stewart Udall again. So, the best of luck to you and again, thanks.
>
> Cordially,
> Bob Hoyt
> Executive Producer/News[3]

Udall's boss also wrote a thank-you letter to the interior secretary. Just before the national monuments debacle escalated, on January 7, 1969, Lyndon Johnson wrote some very kind words to Udall: "I have no doubt that you have been one of the most active, colorful and productive Interior Secretaries in history. In your eight years of Cabinet service, you have not only been a supporter of the New Conservation—you have become its symbol. To your fellow citizens, you leave millions of acres of new parks, wilderness and recreation areas, a new awareness of the importance of the environment, and some important first steps toward clean air and waterways. This is a rich, even priceless, legacy."[4]

With the exception of Johnson not going all the way with him on the national monuments proposals, it had indeed been a good eight-year run for Stewart Udall. That is why on that final day, the outgoing interior secretary had good reason to stand in his office with key staff, sip a glass of celebratory champagne, and uncharacteristically smoke a cigar with them. Then in came Nixon and new interior secretary Walter Hickel, and overseas went Stewart and wife Lee for a well-deserved one-month vacation to Italy and France. Though out of political office, Udall was certainly not done with promoting conservation and environmental protection, however.

Notes

1. Stewart Udall to US Senate Interior Committee, US House Interior Committee, and US Senate Public Works Committee, box 181, Udall Papers.

2. Henry M. Jackson to Udall, March 4, 1969, box 181, folder 3, Udall Papers.

3. Hoyt to Udall, January 16, 1969, box 181, folder 5, Udall Papers.

4. Johnson to Udall, January 7, 1969, box 207, Udall Papers.

PART THREE

Udall's Life After Politics, 1970–2010

14 | Lobbying for Energy Conservation

Discouraging private automobile usage while promoting more energy-efficient means of transportation, such as buses and trains and subways, offers the single best hope.

AFTER SERVING SIX YEARS in the US House of Representatives and eight years as US secretary of the interior, Stewart Udall was still just forty-nine years old in 1969. He was not about to slow or quiet down on the national conservation and environmental front. From the moment he left the Department of the Interior and continuing to when he moved back out west with his wife around 1980, Udall lectured on numerous college campuses, discussing environmental and energy issues and solutions with young people. He also practiced environmental law and served on the board of a half-dozen nonprofit organizations, including the Environmental Defense Fund and National Wildlife Federation, in addition to creating a short-lived environmental planning consulting firm named Overview. To a lesser degree, the outside-of-government Udall played an active role in campaigning for Democratic presidential candidates George McGovern in 1972 and his brother Morris during the primaries in 1976.

Perhaps the primary activity Udall was involved in during the 1970s, though, was lobbying for environmental protection and conservation, primarily through writing and speaking. Eloquent in the 1960s, the former interior secretary became even more outspoken in the 1970s. Indeed, soon after leaving the Department of the Interior, Udall began a regular syndicated column for *Newsday* titled "Udall on the Environment." His series of articles broadly interpreted and spotlighted both the environmental problems and solutions of the time. Topics included but were not limited to the benefits of sewage irrigation; a discussion of Joan Hayes, "Hawaii's quiet crusader," who helped repeal the state's abortion statute; the *Whole Earth Catalog*; and a defense of Udall friend and former work associate Rogers C. B. Morton, Nixon's second interior secretary, who had significant portions of the department transferred out from under him during his tenure.

Udall wrote on an array of topics for the column and elsewhere in the 1970s, but a major environmental happening involving oil took up more and more of his time.[1]

The Arab Oil Embargo of
1973, 1970s Oil Issues, and Solutions

Udall's foresight with regard to environmental protection and conservation is particularly evident when we look at his proposals for overhauling the nation's energy practices and policies in the 1970s. It is interesting to note that many of the energy conservation and weaning-off-of-oil measures that Udall called for during this decade are what environmentalists continue to advocate for today, especially in light of climate change mitigation and energy independence. As energy issues came to be front and center in the 1970s, oil came to be seen as more and more connected to all the other environmental problems of the time, and the former interior secretary put major emphasis in his writings on how to resolve the problems associated with "black gold."

In the mid-twentieth century continuing into the early 1970s, the fact that oil was a nonrenewable resource was simply not pondered by the vast majority of Americans. Though there were several reasons for this, foremost was the fact that oil engineers and oil company executives uniformly stated that there was enough oil in the United States to last for centuries. Maybe the only scientist to say that this was not true was M. King Hubbert, a senior research geophysicist for the Department of the Interior's US Geological Survey who predicted, after substantial analysis, that around

1970, US oil supplies would peak and then go into a steady decline. US oil production did peak and go into a decline for a time right when Hubbert predicted, but then new forms of oil extraction increased productivity, and the country also began importing more from other nations. Thus, no energy shortages developed. However, this all changed in 1973 with the first widely felt oil scare in modern US history.

As historian Mark Fiege explains, "In the early 1970s, at the very moment that U.S. oil consumption dramatically increased, the rate of extraction from the nation's domestic reserves peaked and went into decline. To make up for the deficit, the United States drew from overseas sources as never before. This reliance on imported oil left the nation vulnerable to manipulation by foreign governments. In October 1973, after the United States supported Israel in a war with Egypt and Syria, a group of Middle East countries retaliated against the nation with an oil embargo."[2] Thus, the amount of oil available to the United States suddenly drastically shrank. Millions of US citizens experienced the Arab oil embargo of 1973 firsthand, by waiting in line at gas stations for hours on end, by being forced to significantly decrease their automobile usage and gasoline consumption, and by paying much more money for gas.

Fiege notes that many citizens couldn't see, or chose not to see, past the immediate concerns to the underlying causes of the oil shortage: "They were too invested in oil to do otherwise." He continues, "Yet there is another side to the story.... Not all Americans were helpless, mindless, self-absorbed victims willing to debase themselves for a few gallons of gas. In response to the crisis, many questioned their presumptions about the world and their place in it. A few tried to understand the environmental basis of what was happening to them, and some attempted alternative courses of action."[3]

Stewart Udall was one of the ones who attempted to understand the environmental basis, and he also pushed for alternative courses of action for America. He had been doing this since before the embargo, as he was well aware of the problems associated with oil, namely, America's obsession with the automobile, the resulting air pollution and pavement "pollution" of cities, and domestic oil-supply depletion. This is why, one and a half years before the embargo, Udall found himself arguing in favor of oil conservation before the Senate Public Works Subcommittee on Roads. Standing before former congressional colleagues, Udall represented the Highway Action Coalition, an "amalgam of 17 national environmental, civil rights, consumer, professional, and conservation organizations," including the Sierra Club and Environmental Action. "Discouraging private automobile usage while promoting more energy-efficient means of transportation, such as buses and trains and subways, offers the single best hope for conserving the nation's rapidly diminishing energy resources," Udall told the committee.

> In fact, the disproportionate importance of the automobile in the nation's transportation system presents immediate opportunities for significant savings in future fuel consumption. If, for example, by 1980, we could effect a shift of one-fourth of urban travel away from private automobiles to public transport, the savings in petroleum consumption would exceed one million barrels per day. Making revenues in the multi-billion dollar Highway Trust Fund available to improve often decrepit public transportation systems and to build them where they do not exist, is, therefore, a critically important first step in solving the nation's increasingly serious energy crisis.[4]

For Udall personally, the energy crisis had begun not in 1973 but in 1971, when he read a National Petroleum Council report shedding light on diminishing domestic oil supplies. Udall, who as interior secretary had actually chaired the council, which was composed mainly of the nation's biggest oilmen, remembered their "uniformly expansive oil outlook" in the 1960s. To see this view take a 180-degree turn two years after leaving the Department of the Interior must have come as a profound shock to Udall.[5]

In a series of one-on-one lunch meetings with Hubbert, the engineer who had correctly predicted the peak and then decline of American oil, Udall realized that the National Petroleum Council's most recent report was true. And then, perhaps feeling guilty for not having seen this coming in the 1960s when he could have done more about it while serving in government, Udall began speaking and writing on the issue immediately. He thought that he perhaps owed it to society to do so. "The period of cheap energy has ended. The sooner we begin adjusting to leaner lifestyles, smaller cars, industrial efficiency, and improved forms of public transportation the better for everyone involved," he wrote in a newspaper column soon afterward. In order to "walk his talk" himself, Udall bought a smaller car with higher gas mileage.[6]

Unfortunately, during this time, the highest-ranking national political and corporate leaders did not share Udall's views. Oil industry executives as well as President Nixon and, after his resignation, President Ford pushed for a short-term increase in foreign oil imports while additional US reserves were being developed. Then, after the widespread development of oil-shale lands and the widespread development of outer continental-shelf oil reserves and the Prudhoe Bay oil field in Alaska, there would be no energy problem anymore, they believed. In addition, President Ford believed in decontrolling oil and giving all the power to industry executives. Udall criticized this approach adamantly. "Let's cut our consumption a little bit and give the industry fresh incentives and big profits and the energy industries will solve the problem. That's a nice neat conclusion for a politician. It just happens to be 100 percent wrong," the former interior secretary complained.[7]

A Blueprint for Conserving Oil and Utilizing Renewable Energy

In the early 1970s, Udall became increasingly disturbed by the oil industry, as well as by some of Nixon's and Ford's proposed solutions to the energy crisis. He believed that their solutions would lead to more environmentally damaging oil spills, more pollution, and more deplenishing of energy resources, thus ensuring less oil in store for future generations. As a result, the former interior secretary began writing articles promoting and educating the populace on his oil and energy convictions.[8] His interest in the subject deepened, and before long Udall decided to write another book. With the hopes of bringing more attention to what he perceived as the

correct ways to decrease American oil dependency, in 1974 Udall co-
authored *The Energy Balloon* with associates Charles Conconi, a journalist and lecturer, and David Osterhout, a writer and legislative
specialist. The 288-page book offered a comprehensive history of
how the country's energy crisis came to be as well as, more important, blueprints for getting out of and staying out of the oil shortages
forever.

"The American pageant of waste" was one reason for the energy
crisis, according to the trio. Large, heavy cars built by Detroit that
sometimes got only seven miles to the gallon, a "throwaway society"
that ran counter to the natural law of recycling, and sealed glass
buildings requiring round-the-clock air conditioning or heating
were all part of this waste.[9]

The oil industry, specifically its executives and stockholders,
were also to blame for their shortsightedness and secrecy. "This is
the richest, most powerful, most secretive industry in this country.
It touches the lives of almost everyone, it is crucial to the success of
our economy.... Yet it is not regulated in the public interest," the
authors pointed out.[10]

In solving the energy crisis, one thing Udall was highly critical of
was the belief shared by many that science and technology could get
America out of the predicament. In his first book, Udall had referred
to this as the Myth of Scientific Supremacy. As interior secretary
and even earlier, as a congressman, Udall had seen this myth play
out with the incredible political power of the Atomic Energy Commission, as the vast majority of federal funds for energy research
and development went to the AEC in the 1950s and '60s, in part to
develop the "Atoms for Peace" nuclear energy program. While high-
tech nuclear energy did not pollute the air, and while it did provide ample electricity to areas around nuclear plants, it had proven
dangerous due to the risk of reactor meltdowns. Scientific optimists
believed that once oil wells ran dry, nuclear energy could solve all
of America's energy needs, but Udall knew it couldn't and wouldn't.

For these reasons and more, Udall, Conconi, and Osterhout recommended a two-pronged approach to overhauling the country's
energy policies and overcoming the energy crisis. It involved the

While Udall (*right*) spent significant time in the 1970s focusing on getting the country on to a sustainable energy pathway, he took a short break in the middle of the decade for his official portrait unveiling at the US Department of the Interior building. The painting was by Allan Houser, a Chiricahua Apache artist. Also in the photo are Senator Henry "Scoop" Jackson (*second from right*) and Morris Udall (*far left*). Courtesy of the US Department of the Interior.

widespread implementation of energy conservation measures across all sectors of society and a diversification of energy sources, with an emphasis on clean, renewable forms, specifically solar.

In the vast sector of transportation, energy conservation measures could be made to decrease US oil usage by billions of gallons per year, the authors believed. De-emphasizing the automobile and bringing public transportation back into the mainstream was central to the plan, as buses, subways, and passenger trains all used much less energy per person than the automobile. "First-rate systems of mass transit must be built.... The railroad must have a renaissance." Looking to European high-speed passenger trains as a model, the trio wrote that "Amtrak should be given whatever subsidies are needed to modernize U.S. rail service."[11]

Bicycling and walking in the inner cities also needed a renaissance. These forms of commuting and travel were not only more healthful for people than driving but also did not pollute. "Pedestrian malls within cities, the blocking off of some streets to traffic, and the creation of well-traveled pathways should take precedence over the laying down of more concrete roadways and parking areas," wrote the authors. Funds for developing urban bikeways and walkways—what the authors referred to as "shoe-leather routes"—could come from using just 5 percent of Highway Trust Fund revenues. An increase in biking and walking with a decrease in automobile usage would help purify urban air, cut down on noise pollution, and make cities more community based and livable.[12]

Regarding automobiles themselves, government requirements could force automobile companies to make more fuel-efficient vehicles, and a fifty-five-mile-per-hour maximum speed limit could conserve significant gasoline as well, the authors wrote. In the thirty years following 1945, Udall, Conconi, and Osterhout pointed out that autos had actually decreased in fuel efficiency, from twenty miles per gallon to around eleven. Why not reverse this trend?[13]

Outside of the transportation sector, the built environment could be reformed to cut down on energy usage, as more than one-third of all energy consumed in the country was allocated to air conditioning, heating, ventilation, and lighting of residential and commercial buildings. Why couldn't office appliances be turned off at five o'clock when workers left for the day? Why couldn't walls be more thickly insulated to conserve the amount of energy needed for artificial air control? And why not learn to take advantage of the natural environment and develop building styles that utilized regional climatic characteristics? Udall and company used the example of Santa Fe and its beautiful adobe architecture to spotlight this.[14]

Other proposals called for building-design methods that took advantage of the illumination of natural light while at the same time blocking heat: shading features and awnings could be constructed, and trees could serve as natural air conditioners by shading homes and businesses in the summer. "Then, in the fall, when the warming rays of the sun are welcome, there is a natural thermostat which

sheds the leafy cover in a colorful display which man cannot dupli-
cate by turning a switch."[15]

Regarding the industrial sector, the authors called for a massive
shift to the recycling of resources. They noted that making steel
from recycled steel took 75 percent less energy than making steel
from scratch with iron ore, and that 70 percent less energy was used
in making paper from recycled paper than by using virgin pulp and
wood. The authors acknowledged, however, that large-scale industrial change would occur only "when the laws of economics and the
laws enacted by governments combine to make full-scale resource
recovery and recycling a reality."[16]

Energy conservation measures in the industrial, transportation,
commercial, and residential sectors of American society would do
more than just conserve oil and other energy sources and cut back
on pollution; they would increase the country's standing in world
affairs, the authors believed. Indeed, in thinking about why certain
terrorist organizations and foreign countries despise the United
States and how much of the earth's resources and food are consumed by America in contemporary times, it's perhaps interesting
to note the view of Udall, Conconi, and Osterhout on the relationship between these matters more than forty years ago: "In a time
of catastrophic shortages, a nation that owns half of the world's
motor vehicles, eats one-third of its beef, and uses one-third of its
raw materials cannot possibly maintain a reputation as a magnani-
mous 'helper.' If unbridled U.S. consumption continues, our claims
to moral leadership will inevitably be forfeited.... The generous
image that the U.S. has enjoyed is fading fast. Our new image is that
of the corpulent diner demanding a third dessert as a hungry world
watches at the window."[17]

In regard to diversifying energy resources and promoting the
use of clean forms of energy, Udall believed that a lesson of the
past couple of decades was the need to never again rely on a single
energy source: "Balanced research and development of all energy
options is probably the best investment for the future." That said,
Udall, Conconi, and Osterhout then analyzed the potential for increasing usage of nuclear energy, oil shale, coal, and so on. Though

they discussed the benefits of these forms of energy, the authors also shed light on the environmental problems and dangers associated with each one. For instance, the strip mining needed to increase coal reserves to provide even a small portion of the country's oil needs "would entail an earth-moving operation comparable to digging a Panama Canal every day."[18]

For these reasons, they believed that more promising forms of energy could be found in geothermal and hydrogen technologies and, most of all, solar and wind power. Due to the fact that solar and wind were nonpolluting sources of energy and thus worked with nature, the authors believed that these technologies should and could be developed and implemented on a large-scale basis in ten to fifteen years, "if we would only accord them the priority they deserve." Noted by the authors were two different kinds of solar energy applications under consideration; one was still in need of large-scale research and development, but small-scale infrastructure changes on each and every building could begin immediately:

> The first would use big technology to power industrial furnaces or generate electric power which could be fed into conventional electric grid systems for distribution along normal utility lines. Such big dreams of solar application envision "solar ranching" installations in desert areas, giant solar furnaces using parabolic mirrors, or huge satellites in outer space beaming power to earth via microwaves. Research should be started on these big-technology alternatives, but economic and environmental constraints make it unlikely that any meaningful contributions will come from them until well into the twenty-first century.
>
> On the other hand, if we give a big push to small-scale solar-wind installations, they might provide most of the energy needs for our homes and commercial buildings, say, twenty years from now. Given the necessary encouragement, solar-wind combinations could supply a significant segment of our energy needs this century. The basic technologies are already available and do not depend upon massive engineering efforts

of hook-ups with large utilities. Sophisticated new windmills, solar panels, and batteries can be mass produced if the government provides the initial subsidies and policies which are needed to achieve a takeoff in this area.[19]

To Udall, Conconi, and Osterhout, the reasons for the widespread implementation of small-scale solar installations were numerous. They were "renewable indefinitely, have a zero net impact upon the environment," and entailed relatively modest investments of capital by the owners of homes and other buildings, especially after government incentives were put in place. Furthermore, they required minimal energy to operate for space heating and cooling and could be "exploited by using small, easily maintained technologies within the reach of all nations."[20]

It wasn't just the authors saying this, as a joint panel of energy experts at the National Aeronautics and Space Administration (NASA) and the National Science Foundation estimated just before the book was published that within ten years, small-scale solar energy could save $180 million in energy costs and supply more than one-third of space cooling and heating in the country. It could also provide the nation with about one-fifth of its total electricity.[21]

To summarize *The Energy Balloon*, Udall, as he had done six years before in *1976: Agenda for Tomorrow*, offered clear paths for how the country could get out of its current and worsening predicament. In the case of *The Energy Balloon*, Udall and his coauthors focused on the energy crisis that was caused by an American obsession with oil. To decrease domestic oil usage, decrease the need to import oil from problematic nations in the Middle East, purify America's air and atmosphere, and increase the livability of cities, Udall recommended a broad program of energy conservation as well as major development of solar and wind energy. To be clear, Udall was not the first or the only person to recommend such actions, but he was one of the first and also one of the most outspoken to recommend them.

Did these ideas of solar and wind power and energy conservation get implemented? The answer is complicated, but, essentially, it is in part yes, in part no. In the mid- and late 1970s, some of the

Highway Trust Fund was used to develop better public transportation within cities. Congress and President Ford also created Corporate Average Fuel Economy standards in 1975, requiring that by 1985, automakers would design cars that averaged 27.5 miles to the gallon or more. A national highway speed limit of fifty-five miles per hour was also instituted, fifty-five miles per hour being the speed at which automobiles obtain the highest gas mileage.[22]

But oil industry executives, their lobbyists, and their politicians proved too influential to make Udall's dreams full realities. President Carter, in 1977, proposed a national energy policy that had numerous similarities to Udall's proposals, emphasizing energy conservation and a focus on renewable energy development. The bill passed the House but never passed the Senate. Carter then implemented as much of it as he could by using his executive power, but when Ronald Reagan came to power, almost all energy conservation measures and alternative energy research and development programs were severely cut. To Reagan, energy conservation was essentially un-American. And before Reagan, President Ford had also vetoed several major environmental bills, including the Electric Vehicle Research, Development, and Demonstration Act; Automobile Transport Research and Development Act; TVA Pollution Control Act; Surface Mining Control and Reclamation Act; and Rural Environmental Assistance Act.[23]

End of the 1970s, End of Udall in DC

As historian Henry Sirgo notes, Ford's vetoes actually "provided major rationale for Morris K. Udall's presidential candidacy" for the 1976 presidential election. With the Udall brothers sharing the same general views on environmental protection and energy conservation, and with Morris having served as a popular congressman for a decade and a half, the younger brother threw his hat in the ring, and Stewart jumped in to lead Morris's campaign. Unfortunately, however, the campaign ended after Morris placed second in a string of states in the Democratic primaries, and it became clear that Carter was the front-runner. It "ended up in a heap, with me at the bottom," Stewart said.

Indeed, Stewart Udall felt bad about the campaign's failure, and during the mid- and late 1970s, he also became more disillusioned with politics in general by observing the energy battles and debates in Congress and seeing not enough action being taken, in his mind. These setbacks, as well as the fact that, though Stewart enjoyed writing, it didn't pay as well as he had hoped, forced the Udalls to think about some life changes.

Notes

1. "Mankind Faces a Very Tall Order," *Newsday*, June 1970, box 210, folder 2, Udall Papers; "Alaska's Wildlands: Secretary Morton's Biggest Test," *Newsday*, January 29, 1972, and "Joan Hayes: Hawaii's Quiet Crusader," *Newsday*, May 1, 1972, box 207, folder 10, Udall Papers. During the early '70s, Udall also wrote about his convictions for international pollution-mitigation efforts, calling for an international tax on airplanes and boats. For more on this, see "Some Second Thoughts on Stockholm," *American University Law Review* 22 (1973).

2. Mark Fiege, *The Republic of Nature: An Environmental History of the United States*, 361. For more on 1970s US energy policy, see Robert Lifset, ed., *American Energy Policy in the 1970s*.

3. Fiege, *Republic of Nature*, 361–62.

4. *Testimony Before Senate Public Works Subcommittee on Roads*, May 26, 1972, box 185, folder 5, Udall Papers.

5. Stewart L. Udall, Charles Conconi, and David Osterhout, *The Energy Balloon*, 7.

6. Transcript, "Former Secretary of the Interior Stewart Udall on M. King Hubbert and Peak Oil," Global Public Media, old.globalpublicmedia.com/transcripts/675; Udall, "Oil: A Year of Self-Deception," October 1, 1974, box 210, folder 2, Udall Papers.

7. "The Energy Crisis: Three Perspectives. There Are No Technological Solutions: An Interview with Stewart L. Udall," Udall Papers, library.arizona.edu/exhibits/sludall/articleretrievals/threeperspx.html; Udall, Conconi, and Osterhout, *The Energy Balloon*, 99.

8. See "Monday Guest: Stewart Udall, U.S. Secretary of the Interior, 1961–1969," *Grand Rapids (MI) Press*, April 11, 1972, Udall Papers, library.arizona.edu/exhibits/sludall/articleretrievals/mondayguestx.html; Udall, "Solar Power: New Job for NASA?," *Newsday*, October 24, 1970, box 210, folder 2, Udall Papers; Udall, "The Brownout Crisis," *Newsday*, August 2, 1970, ibid.; Udall, "The Uncommon Dr. Commoner," *Newsday*, December 4, 1971, ibid.; Udall, "The Energy Crisis: A Radical Solution," *World Magazine*, May 1973, box 208, folder 8, ibid.; Udall, "The ABC's of Energy Reform," *New York Times*, July 12, 1973, box 208, folder 7, ibid.; Udall, "Oil: A Year of Self-Deception"; Udall, "How Families Can Fight Inflation," September 1974, box 208, folder 10, ibid.; Udall, "The Energy Illusions," *New York*

Times, November 21, 1973, box 208, folder 7, ibid.; Udall and Charles N. Conconi, "The Energy Crisis: The Script for the 1970s Is Written," *Washington Evening Star News*, December 1973, box 210, folder 2, ibid.; Udall, "Put the Spring into Energy," *Arizona Daily Star* (Tucson), April 8, 1977, ibid.; Udall, "The Roots of the Energy Crisis," ibid.; and Udall, "Supertechnology: Another God That Failed," *New Mexico Alumnus* 49, no. 8 (1977), library.arizona.edu/exhibits/sludall/articleretrievals/supertechnologyx.html.

9. Udall, Conconi, and Osterhout, *The Energy Balloon*, 21–55.

10. Ibid., 14.

11. Ibid., 140, 166, 183, 185.

12. Ibid., 177–78.

13. Ibid., 170.

14. Ibid., 190–91.

15. Ibid., 215–16.

16. Ibid., 232, 243.

17. Ibid., 252, 264.

18. Ibid., 103–24.

19. Ibid., 125–26.

20. Ibid., 126.

21. Ibid.

22. Fiege, *Republic of Nature*, 358–402.

23. Jimmy Carter, "The President's Proposed Energy Policy," transcript, April 18, 1977, *American Experience*, pbs.org/wgbh/americanexperience/features/primary-resources/carter-energy/; US Congress, "H.R. 8444: National Energy Act, 95th Congress (1977–1978)," congress.gov/bill/95th-congress/house-bill/8444/.

15 | Defending Navajo Uranium Miners

*The only victims of U.S. nuclear arms
since World War II have been our own people.*

IN 1976, BEING FINANCIALLY strapped and having exhausted his writings on the energy crisis and how to fix it, Udall joined the Washington, DC, law firm of Duncan, Weinberg, Miller & Pembroke. However, things apparently did not click for Udall at the firm. As a result, three years later, feeling like he had perhaps outlived his welcome in the national capital, wanting to find a cheaper location to move to, seeking to return to his native Southwest, and already having legal case leads, Stewart Udall and his wife, Lee, moved to Phoenix. Here he opened up a law office, as he had done almost thirty years earlier in Tucson.[1]

Defending Navajo Uranium Miners

It was as a lawyer again, in the late 1970s, that Udall delved into his longest, saddest, and most thought-provoking series of cases. With an introduction to the issue thanks to distant family members and others who had served as "downwinders" during atomic bomb testing in the 1940s and '50s, the former interior secretary and law office associates whom he recruited began detecting a pattern of governmental wrongdoing in the atomic bomb era, specifically but not exclusively related to the extremely powerful and secretive Atomic Energy Commission and government contractors managing uranium mining operations. And so, having worked for the government in the 1950s and '60s, Udall filed suit against the federal government in 1979 on behalf of hundreds of Mormon and Navajo plaintiffs. His involvement in the cases challenged many of Udall's beliefs about his beloved federal government. Though the multiyear endeavor demoralized him, his work and the work of others led to the Radiation Exposure Compensation Act, passed by Congress in 1992 and since amended, updated, and improved.

In the numerous radiation court cases, Udall came to represent three types of clients who were negatively affected by midcentury atomic bomb development and testing. First were residents living downwind of Nevada's atomic bomb test sites, known as the "downwinders." Government documents at the time of the test bombs claimed the area around the testing zones was "substantially uninhabited," yet there were in fact twenty-five thousand rural residents scattered throughout the areas of southern Nevada and Utah. These residents were never warned of the dangers of being downwind of the massive explosions. As Udall told a group of law students, "One woman, a Nevada hell-raiser, angered by the situation, used a variation of a biblical saying to describe this situation—'Woe be unto those who live in a "substantially uninhibited zone,"' she said."[2]

The second set of cases involved Udall's defense of a series of construction workers employed by government contractors. The workers had specifically been tasked with going into recent test areas to set up for the next atomic bomb test. In some cases, the workers set up new towers and other infrastructure at the exact location where less than a week earlier, bombs had been tested and exploded that were more powerful than those dropped by the US military on the Japanese cities of Hiroshima and Nagasaki in 1945. The workers were not notified of the long-term dangers associated with working around soilborne and airborne radioactive particles.[3]

Udall's third set of cases, and the ones he worked the longest on, involved Navajo uranium miners, their widows, sons, and daughters. Like the downwinders and construction workers, the Navajo men employed in the mines during the late 1940s and '50s had not been warned of the dangers of doing so. Furthermore, the Navajo had a language barrier in that they spoke their own unique language; most couldn't speak, write, or understand English. Also, they were, by and large, uneducated and unemployed due to years of government neglect. These factors apparently made the American Indian group incredibly ripe for being taken advantage of.[4]

The cost of working near uranium sources for all three sets of victims was cancer and death. Specifically for the Navajo, many of the former miners had died or were dying from lung cancer during the time of the trials.[5]

Udall came to directly represent more than two hundred Navajo plaintiffs in total (and indirectly hundreds more), most living within the Red Valley Chapter of the Navajo Nation, in northwestern New Mexico. He and his legal team spent countless hours in the late 1970s and early '80s researching the history of uranium mining, atomic bomb development, and the AEC; listening to stories of affected peoples; interviewing former and current medical doctors and governmental nuclear scientists; reading congressional hearings on the downwinders; and reviewing more than thirty thousand declassified documents related to the radiation lawsuits. The behind-the-scenes work became a family affair, as Stewart's daughter Lori and sons Denis, James, and Tom—Tom Udall being the future New Mexico attorney general and current US senator—worked hard on the case, serving as reservation investigators. Stewart's wife, Lee, was also heavily involved, creating a nonprofit organization designed to raise funds for financing the long-drawnout legal battle. Bill Mahoney, an Arizona attorney and longtime friend of Udall's, worked closely with the former interior secretary on the case as well.[6]

The extensive research conclusively confirmed for Udall and his team that in the Atomic Energy Commission's quest to create nuclear bombs on an unprecedented scale in post–World War II America, the Navajo uranium miners and their other plaintiffs had been needlessly and recklessly put in harm's way. High-level officials of the AEC knew of the dangers associated in working with uranium, Udall discovered, as scientists had completed ample reports on the possible and substantial effects of uranium on human beings. AEC officials, however, arrogantly disregarded them and covered them up. As the former interior secretary put it, "The AEC blocked creative thinking by impeding exchanges among scientists. It restricted critical review by denying citizens access to nuclear information. It fostered what David Lilienthal described as 'arrogant self-adulation by atomic experts.' And the Big Brother attitude that dictated the AEC's radiation safety policies ultimately engendered a poisonous mistrust between the nuclear establishment and ordinary citizens."[7]

Udall also uncovered evidence that the AEC as well as other government contractors and officials created no safety guidelines and took zero precautions prior to allowing the Navajo men to go to work in the mines. "Had it been so inclined, the AEC could have ordered installation of low-cost ventilation systems to protect U.S. uranium miners," Udall observed. "AEC safety experts could have designed such a program in a matter of weeks.... The AEC's decision to put the flow of ore ahead of human health was a reckless act that sacrificed the lives of hundreds of miners." Essentially, then, the AEC denied Navajo uranium miners their moral and legal rights.[8]

Udall filed suit against the federal government as well as several contractors, including Kerr-McGee, the Vanadium Corporation, and others, and then a long period of waiting ensued. The Navajo cases were heard by the Arizona District Court in 1984. Unfortunately, however, according to Udall, even after listening and agreeing himself with Udall's arguments and himself claiming that the treatment of Navajo uranium miners was a "tragedy of the nuclear age," the judge declared that the US government had engaged in no legal wrongdoing due to a "discretionary function exception," namely, "that all the actions of various governmental agencies complained of by plaintiffs were the result of conscious policy decisions made at high government levels based on considerations of political and national security feasibility factors."[9] Udall referred to the judge's verdict as one essentially stating that "the king can do no wrong"— if it involved matters of national security, then the federal government was immune to all charges.[10]

In a sickening sort of irony, Udall and his legal team even pleaded with the judge that the government officials involved in overseeing the uranium mine operations disobeyed the Nuremberg Code, the international set of research ethics established in 1949 in light of Nazi war crimes and wrongdoing, which stated that voluntary consent of the human subjects in scientific experiments is absolutely essential. The judge ruled, however, that in the case of the Navajo uranium miners, government physicians who completed studies on them "were not experimenting on human beings" but rather "gathering data" on them. Udall and his legal team were dumbfounded, as they didn't see a difference between "experimenting on" and "gathering data on."[11]

With the failure at the US District Court level, on behalf of his Navajo plaintiffs Udall then pleaded the case before the US Court of Appeals. Throughout both cases during this time period, according to the former interior secretary, government lawyers in court whom Udall faced argued three main points as to why the government was not at fault. First, secrecy and national security were Siamese twins—both were needed in the 1950s to protect the United States from the threat of communism, and one way to protect the country from "the Red Scare" was by creating atomic bombs and not sharing the dangers of doing so with the miners. A second argument claimed that the cancer that former uranium miners were getting and dying from was from smoking cigarettes, not from working in the uranium mines. However, Udall knew that very few of the Navajo men smoked. Third, and perhaps most shocking to Udall's ears, was the claim that uranium mine safety standards were supposed to be put into place *after* doctors and scientists observed what happened to the Navajo in the mine. Even in light of this, and even though Udall recalled that one judge officially stated that the Navajo had been used as "human guinea pigs," both cases were lost. In the case of the uranium miners, national security was placed above Navajo rights to justice.[12]

Because many of the Navajo families he worked with were so impoverished and could not really afford to pay him for his work, during the early and mid-1980s Udall was constantly having to raise funds to keep the cases from petering out. In one instance, he was able to pull together a benefit concert at the Santa Fe Indian School that included legendary folk singer Pete Seeger as well as award-winning author Edward Abbey. In other cases, nonprofit organizations helped Udall and the Navajo out, most notably a group known as the Youth Project.[13]

However, after the losses in court, and after a shot-in-the-dark attempt to have the US Supreme Court take the case, Udall reported that "I was so drained," both emotionally and financially. And he had the emotionally difficult task of writing a letter to his Navajo clients, explaining the failed results of the "long quest for justice in the white man's court of law.... I tried, but I could not write that letter," remembered Udall. Later, when he was asked to attend a meeting with his plaintiffs in order to explain the outcome of the lawsuits, Udall asked someone else to attend.

> I did not go because I was humiliated and sick at heart.
>
> I did not go because for so many years, and on so many occasions, I had urged the Navajos to be patient and to have faith in their country's system of justice.
>
> I did not go because I was ashamed of the outcome of their lawsuit and could not think of a convincing way to explain to them such concepts as "national security" and "government immunity."
>
> And I was ashamed to go because I didn't know how to explain to friends who had trusted me that the government in Washington that had betrayed them—and needlessly sacrificed the lives of their husbands in the name of national security—could, under the law I had urged them to respect, avoid responsibility for the tragedies that had engulfed their lives.[14]

Udall eventually gave up on the judicial branch and began lobbying Congress and the executive branch directly to help compensate the affected families and 'fess up to the wrongdoings of the past. Yet this became a major challenge as well. "The balanced budget–minded Reagan administration has shown it will not support legislation to compensate radiation victims," Udall lamented in the mid-1980s. "The administration is very economy-minded. From what they say you'd think if they did justice it would bankrupt the United States."[15] The former interior secretary was also probably discouraged by the fact that the Navajo uranium miners had begun organizing themselves in the 1960s and '70s, before he had discovered the cases, and that they had tried multiple times unsuccessfully to push a compensation bill through Congress.

Nevertheless, Udall lobbied for what became known as the Radiation Exposure Compensation Act for years. The Department of Justice (DOJ) firmly opposed the bill, but it helped that Udall had friends in politics, such as Representative Wayne Owens (D-UT). Udall also wrote a letter to key congressional committee members, tearing apart the department's opposing arguments. The bill was watered down but passed Congress in 1990, thanks to strong endorsements from Senators Orrin Hatch of Utah and Pete Domenici of New Mexico, both Republicans, as well as Ted Kennedy (D-MA). President George Herbert Walker Bush signed the act into law aboard Air Force One in 1992.[16]

As a result of the Radiation Exposure Compensation Act, beginning later that year hundreds of Navajo families were compensated up to one hundred thousand dollars for the government's and mining corporations' wrongdoing. The act also officially included a government apology for the hardships the Navajo had endured. Author and human rights activist Peter Eichstaedt notes that Udall personally lobbied to keep the apology in the act through all the various bill amendments because he believed it was very much needed morally and as part of the healing process for the Navajo.[17] And while monetary aid cannot heal a heart that has been broken due to the wrongful loss of a loved one, at least these families got something. They picked up their compensation checks from the home of the "white man" who had worked so hard on their behalf, Stewart Udall.[18]

Unfortunately, while many Navajo families did pick up their checks, the bill that was enacted called for the DOJ to administer the compensation program and ultimately decide who got the checks and who didn't—and several DOJ senior leaders were adamantly against the Radiation Exposure Compensation Act in the first place. As such, the Department of Justice made it very difficult and stressful for many Navajo to collect their compensation. Hundreds of Navajo claims got stuck in "the bowels of bureaucracy," according to Eichstaedt. Arguing that it didn't want the Navajo to commit fraud, DOJ officials decided they wouldn't approve payments until the widows of the miners could show them their official marriage licenses to prove that they were the rightful widows. Yet Navajo marriages of the mid-1900s took place during a "horse-and-buggy" phase for the American Indian group; most on the reservation did not have electricity and running water, and most were not able to obtain official marriage licenses, but rather married informally. The DOJ further asked for worker paperwork proving that the Navajo men had worked in the mines, even though in many instances, the mining corporations did not have the men sign paperwork but instead relied on a gentleman's agreement.[19]

Extremely frustrated that numerous uranium miners' widows were being denied compensation by the DOJ, Udall told the *New York Times* in the early 1990s, "They've put these people in a bureaucratic legal maze designed to prevent compensation to Navajo miners. There's no pity for what happened to these people. No understanding. You have a compassionate program administered in an utterly uncompassionate manner."[20] After researching, Udall also pointed out that non-Indian radiation victims were getting compensated twice as fast as Navajo victims.[21] Continuing with these sentiments, in the final months of the Bush administration, Udall wrote a scathing letter to high-level DOJ administrators. He sent copies of the letter to Hatch, Kennedy, and others. "You and your staff have turned a program Congress enacted to provide 'compassionate payments' to the victims of our nation's radiation tragedies into a nightmare of frustration and confusion," Udall wrote.

> Based on my own first hand encounters with you and your staff I have prepared a list of objectionable policies which have delayed the handling of meritorious claims and placed onerous, unnecessary burdens on many deserving claimants.
> 1. You have grossly neglected the applications of elderly uranium miner widows who should have been accorded places at the head of the line.
> 2. The pattern of your payments reveals an anti-Indian bias.

3. The regulations your staff devised concerning documentation of medical facts severely penalize Navajo applicants.

4. The staff has made it much more difficult for Navajo applicants to qualify by disregarding a key regulation approved by the attorney general.[22]

Perhaps no other letter that Udall ever wrote was as scathing and angry. After serving as a progressive government leader in the 1960s and helping to uncover some major government and uranium industry wrongdoing in the late 1970s and '80s, losing battles for his Navajo defendants time and time again must have been disheartening and demoralizing for Udall. After all this, adding DOJ discrimination to the mix really set him off. Fortunately, however, by 1994 the Department of Justice had picked up its pace in providing the Navajo their compensation, and the Radiation Exposure Compensation Act was improved in 2000.[23]

The uranium lawsuits were a major component of Udall's 1980s and early '90s life. The end result of his frustrating experiences and research into the history of US atomic energy culminated in his 1994 book, *The Myths of August: A Personal Exploration of Our Tragic Cold War Affair with the Atom.*

Notes

1. "Stewart L. Udall: Career Chronology," Udall Papers, library.arizona.edu /exhibits/sludall/career.htm.

2. "Toxic Chemicals and Radiation," *Mercer Law Review* 38 (1986–87): 515–16.

3. Ibid.

4. Ibid.; Stewart Udall, *The Myths of August: A Personal Exploration of Our Tragic Cold War Affair with the Atom*, 184.

5. For a sobering look at how the miners were affected by the uranium, see Doug Brugge, ed., *Memories Come to Us in the Rain and the Wind: Oral Histories and Photographs of Navajo Uranium Miners and Their Families*.

6. Udall, *Myths of August*, 20, 185; Peter H. Eichstaedt, *If You Poison Us: Uranium and Native Americans*, 103; Stewart Udall, "We Aimed for Russia and Hit the West," *High Country News*, August 22, 1994, hcn.org/issues/14/438.

7. Udall, *Myths of August*, 174–75.

8. Ibid., 174–76, 183–202. For more on governmental wrongdoing regarding Navajo uranium miners, see Doug Brugge and Rob Goble, "The History of Uranium Mining and the Navajo People," *American Journal of Public Health* 92, no. 9 (2002),

ajph.aphapublications.org/doi/full/10.2105/AJPH.92.9.1410; Judy Pasternak, *Yellow Dirt: A Poisoned Land and the Betrayal of the Navajos;* Doug Brugge, Timothy Benally, and Esther Yazzie-Lewis, eds., *The Navajo People and Uranium Mining* (Albuquerque: University of New Mexico Press, 2007); and Eichstaedt, *If You Poison Us.*

9. *John N. Begay, et al., Plaintiffs, v. United States of America,* 591 F. Supp. 991, District Court D, Arizona, 1984.

10. Udall, *Myths of August,* 199–202; Eichstaedt, *If You Poison Us,* 115, 120.

11. *Begay v. United States;* Udall, *Myths of August,* 199–202.

12. Udall, *Myths of August,* 199–202. Regarding the second argument's false claims, see L. S. Gottlieb and L. A. Husen, "Lung Cancer Among Uranium Miners," *Chest* 81, no. 4 (1982), journal.publications.chestnet.org/article.aspx?articleid =1053870; and Jonathan M. Samet et al., "Uranium Mining and Lung Cancer in Navajo Men," *New England Journal of Medicine* 310, no. 23 (1984), nejm.org/doi/pdf /10.1056/NEJM198406073102301.

13. Eichstaedt, *If You Poison Us,* 119.

14. Udall, *Myths of August,* 202; Eichstaedt, *If You Poison Us,* 124.

15. Ed Vogel, "Udall Sees No Help from Feds for Victims of A-Bomb Tests," *Las Vegas Review-Journal,* November 9, 1981, box 244, folder 6, Udall Papers. Udall became so disturbed by what he believed to be a hostile president and Congress in the 1980s that at mid-decade, he considered running for Congress again to try to change things and shed light on governmental wrongdoing. He eventually decided not to run, however.

16. Eichstaedt, *If You Poison Us,* 121–25.

17. Ibid., 126.

18. Udall, *Myths of August,* 185.

19. Eichstaedt, *If You Poison Us,* 153.

20. Keith Schneider, "A Valley of Death for the Navajo Uranium Miners," *New York Times,* May 3, 1993, nytimes.com/1993/05/03/us/a-valley-of-death-for-the -navajo-uranium-miners.html.

21. Eichstaedt, *If You Poison Us,* 169.

22. Stewart Udall to US Department of Justice Assistant Attorney General Stuart M. Gerso and Torts Branch director Helene Goldbergs, December 17, 1992, box 244, folder 8, Udall Papers.

23. Eichstaedt, *If You Poison Us,* 169. Many of the Navajo uranium miners and their widows were compensated in the 1990s and 2000s. However, dozens of sites within the Navajo Nation remain highly toxic, as the mining corporations left after the uranium craze was over without cleaning up the sites. Exposure to air, dust, groundwater, surface water, and rock piles contaminated with uranium is very threatening to human, animal, and overall environmental health.

Fortunately, after ample lawsuits, Kerr-McGee, one of the major companies involved in uranium mining on the Navajo Nation, settled with the Environmental Protection Agency in early 2015. The company is being forced to pay almost one billion dollars to clean up the contaminated lands and waters of the reservation.

For more on this, see US Environmental Protection Agency, "$2 Billion in Funds Headed for Cleanups in Nevada and on the Navajo Nation from Historic Anadarko Settlement with U.S. EPA, States," news release, January 23, 2015, yosemite.epa .gov/opa/admpress.nsf/0/2E47E97C62ACF44385257DD6007428C5; and US Department of Justice, Office of Public Affairs, "Historic $5.15 Billion Environmental and Tort Settlement with Anadarko Petroleum Corp. Goes into Effect," January 23, 2015, justice.gov/opa/pr/historic-515-billion-environmental-and-tort-settlement -anadarko-petroleum-corp-goes-effect-0.

16 | Climate Change Activist and Historian

It is clear that the world is waiting for the United States to step forward...and organize a bold agenda of technological cooperation that reverses global warming.

UDALL HAD A BROADER FOCUS in the 1960s than just national parks and more endeavors in the 1970s than just the energy crisis, and, similarly, he was involved in numerous adventures in addition to uranium lawsuits in the 1980s, 1990s, and 2000s. Graying hair and the addition of wrinkles did not necessarily slow Stewart Udall down.

Two things Udall continued to embrace in his sixties and seventies were his passions for environmental law and working with ambitious, progressive young people. This culminated in the former interior secretary teaching several environmental law seminars at the University of Denver. In one three-week toxic chemical law course, Udall based his students' grades on their "being the judge" and turning in a twenty-five-page written decision on pending court cases. "I hope they will get some understanding of the properties of harmful agents and new techniques used to prove them—the marriage of chemistry, physics, medicine, and the law," Udall noted at the time.[1]

Outside of teaching, Udall in the 1980s and continuing into the 1990s served on the boards of numerous environmental and natural resource-focused nonprofit groups. He sat on the Central Arizona Water Conservation Board as well as on the advisory council of the Electric Power Research Institute. In addition, Udall served as chairman of the board for the Santa Fe–based Archeological

Conservancy, a nonprofit that acquires and preserves archaeological sites throughout the country. Finally, he sat on the board of directors for the Washington, DC–based Minerals Policy Center, an organization seeking to change and update the antiquated General Mining Act of 1872.[2]

Udall also spent significant time in his later years speaking up about the need to combat global warming and in writing and researching, specifically regarding US history. He also continued to publish books. The primary events of Udall's last thirty years of life are spotlighted below.

1980s Climate-Change Activist with Robert Redford

In the mid-1980s, Udall served for several years as the director of Robert Redford's Institute for Resource Management (IRM), a nonprofit organization formed to promote balance between natural resource use and preservation. In a decade when Republicans and Democrats grew further apart on the environment, Udall organized conferences that brought extraction industry representatives, government officials, and environmental leaders together to collaborate and try to solve important resource problems. He also facilitated symposiums focusing on power-industry problems and prospects, including one on nuclear power development. While it is unclear how Redford and Udall first met, the famous actor came to be an admirer of Udall's writings, and the two men became somewhat close during the decade, with Redford once noting that Udall's face belonged on the back of a nickel.[3]

In 1989, the year the Soviet Union began dissolution, Redford, Udall, and others organized, through the IRM, a two-day conference seeking to bring US and Soviet political, environmental, scientific, industrial, and business leaders together to address a growing concern: the issue of global warming. Designed specifically to get the two countries speaking and planning jointly on ways to decrease carbon dioxide use, the meeting, dubbed the "Greenhouse Glasnost," took place at Redford's Sundance Resort in the high mountains of Utah, just east of Provo and Salt Lake City. Notable attendees included professors Carl Sagan and Paul Ehrlich, Jim Hanson of

In the 1980s, in addition to working to defend Navajo uranium
miners, Udall worked closely with actor-activist Robert Redford at
the Institute for Resource Management. The two are shown here
sitting together at an IRM conference. Redford is in the center,
wearing a vest, and Udall is seated to the actor's immediate left.
Courtesy of the Institute for Resource Management.

NASA, Senator John Heinz (R-PA), Idaho governor (and Carter administration interior secretary) Cecil Andrus, Soviet Academy
of Science member and Climate Institute of Atmospheric Physics
chief Georgi S. Golitsyn, USSR chairman of the Supreme Committee on Ecology and Rational Use of Natural Resources Kakimbek A.
Salykov, and more.[4]

Toward the end of the conference, attendees came to agree that
global warming was poised to flood coastal areas, create droughts
in some inland areas, disrupt agricultural systems, create vast populations of human refuges, and cause national security issues. They
made a list of technological and industrial barriers to combating
global warming, including "entrenched wisdom and power, a political process that often encourages parochial action, a short term
outlook, economies based on fossil fuels," and more. Furthermore,
Udall and the executive director of the Natural Resource Defense
Fund both agreed, and spoke about their conviction, that, with the
arms race and especially the buildup of military and associated

technology during the Reagan era, inadequate funding was being allocated to solving environmental and human problems. Therefore, "ending the cold war is the best way to help solve global warming," the former interior secretary noted.[5]

The result of the conference was a farsighted, progressive letter, written and signed by each of the attendees, to President George H. W. Bush and his USSR counterpart, Mikhail Gorbachev. The letter asked the world leaders to work together to significantly decrease carbon dioxide emissions from their countries. Udall, Redford, and others urged the two world leaders to push for extensive tree-planting programs on each continent. They also recommended a massive increase in the production and use of non-greenhouse-gas-emitting forms of alternative energy, population control programs, more-efficient energy use, the ultimate phaseout of chlorofluorocarbons, grassroots education programs, a decrease in military and defense budgets to allow for upticks in environmental protection budgets, and more.

Lambasting the Reagan Administration for Environmental Negligence

In addition to serving on various boards, working closely with Robert Redford, and teaching, Udall in the 1980s and 1990s continued to indulge his lifelong passions for writing and researching. In 1988 he completed and published an expanded new version of his first book, titling it *The Quiet Crisis and the Next Generation*. "What I did was bring it up to date. If you live long enough you can do that," Udall joked.[6]

The new chapters focused on the positive influences that private citizens and nonprofit organizations had had on the environmental movement beginning in the 1960s and ever since. Humbly not mentioning his own name and personal work and involvement with the subject even once, Udall lauded the hard work of David Brower in helping establish Redwood National Park as well as going against dam building in Dinosaur National Monument and the Grand Canyon. "If one believes, as I do, that the American people altered their thinking about their environment in the 1960s, in due

course there will be laurels aplenty for David Brower, for his lieu-
tenants, and for other leaders of the Sierra Club as well," wrote the
former interior secretary. Udall also sang the praises of Howard
Zahniser and his fight to save wilderness; Ralph Nader, who "was a
knight that needed no armor" in taking on General Motors; the uncommon Barry Commoner, who pushed for the widespread use of
solar power in the late 1970s; and the Environmental Defense Fund,
among other organizations and individuals.[7]

One man Udall did not praise in the new edition was Ronald
Reagan. "I am convinced historians will one day indict the Reagan
administration for its lack of vision concerning resources and its
abdication of the traditional U.S. role of leadership in global environmental matters," Udall stated. "History will confirm that Ronald
Reagan's legacy created a massive fiscal debt restricting the options
of his successors and of the American people for positive action on
behalf of their air, water, and land." Worst of all was the fortieth
president's reversal of energy conservation and renewable energy
measures, Udall believed.

> It was in the area of energy economics that Ronald Reagan's
> nonstewardship did the greatest harm to the nation's future.
> Leadership by presidents and by Congress in the 1970s made it
> possible for the country to pass rigorous energy conservation
> laws and conduct successful campaigns to reduce its depen-
> dence on imported oil. These efforts encouraged the Ameri-
> can people and U.S. industries to make decisions about homes,
> autos, public transportation, and industrial plants that saved
> hundreds of billions of dollars and put the nation on a path of
> energy efficiency.
>
> During the Reagan years the government abdicated leader-
> ship of this effort. Federal funding for energy research was
> drastically cut, the rules that compel Detroit to produce more
> efficient autos were relaxed, and the Reaganites not only
> sought to dismantle the energy conservation programs they
> had inherited, but to systematically oppose new legislation
> fostering energy efficiency. Reagan's decision that the open

market, not federal leadership expressed through energy conservation laws and programs, should determine the nation's
energy policy is a judgment that is now setting the stage for
an economic disaster in the 1990s as our commitment to end
energy waste slackens and our dependence on imported oil
increases each day.[8]

While certainly not all environmental and conservation measures pushed for in the 1970s were passed, as Udall suggests, the
advances made did diminish significantly in the 1980s. Reagan's
first secretary of the interior, James Watt, was openly hostile toward
conservationists and environmentalists and had a goal of reversing
what he saw as "twenty-five years of bad resource management" on
public lands, never mind that the past twenty-five years had encompassed administration of public lands by both Democrat and Republican interior secretaries. Udall had, of course, played a significant
role during those years, and Watt's commentary hit the former interior secretary "right between my eyes."[9]

Aside from lambasting Reagan and praising the environmental
work of others, in the ending pages of *The Quiet Crisis and the Next
Generation*, Udall revisited themes from his book on energy policy.
He called once again for the need for widespread recycling (not just
in the form of residential curbside programs but much broader in
scope) as well as replacing the automobile with more sustainable
forms of transportation. Finally, he noted that the struggle ahead,
in light of climate change, would be for "tomorrow's environmentalists…to reach across artificial barriers erected by nation states,
languages, and cultures and become earthkeepers [sic] who stead-
fastly use their talents to nourish all causes that promote life on
this planet."[10]

Promoting Spanish and
Pioneer Influence on US History

During the same time that Udall was speaking up on climate-change
mitigation, staying busy with Navajo uranium miner lawsuits, and
serving on boards of environmental nonprofits, the aging Arizonan

also spent time enjoying and exploring the landscapes and heritage of his native Southwest. Two of Udall's final book projects shed new light on the region's history.

Was an interest in history new to Udall? The answer is part yes, part no. The former interior secretary was well read; he knew a lot about conservation history in particular. The heritage of the US Southwest and West were not unknown to him, but he certainly grew to appreciate them more and learn more about them in his later years.

In the mid-1980s, Stewart worked on a project involving both Supreme Court justice Sandra Day O'Connor and former first lady Jacqueline Kennedy Onassis. The project involved the publication of an article and then a book analyzing Spain's colonial influence on the United States.

It began in 1981 when Udall wrote an "innocent memo" addressed to the president of the Phoenix-based Heard Museum, asking if the entity would like to sponsor him on a three-day trip retracing the 1500s expedition of Francisco Vásquez de Coronado through the present-day US Southwest. Coronado had traveled through the area where Udall had grown up, and the interior secretary particularly remembered a family friend's deep interest in the Spanish conquistador. At any rate, the museum president, whom Udall referred to as "a local judge named Sandra Day O'Connor," sent a quick, positive response, asking Udall to become an advisory member to the museum's board in addition to leading the expedition. *Arizona Highways* magazine then heard about the trip and asked Udall if he would be interested in writing an article about it. Udall was, and the magazine teamed the former interior secretary with photographer Jerry Jacka to complete the project.[11]

The article proved a success, and afterward Udall, though not close to Jackie Kennedy in the early 1960s, sent her a copy of it. The former first lady, now Jacqueline Kennedy Onassis, was serving as an editor at Doubleday and Company, a publishing firm, and Udall sent her the article and personal note "out of the blue," asking whether the two should team up and turn the article into a book. Like the Supreme Court justice's reply, Jacqueline's was positive.[12]

As a result, Stewart and Lee Udall met up with Onassis and ex-plored the Southwest by car, horseback, and foot for two weeks. Re-tracing the route of Coronado and his search for the fabled Seven Cities of Gold, the entourage visited archaeological and historical sites, including Canyon de Chelly, a picturesque canyon inhabited continuously for more than five thousand years and today jointly administered by the National Park Service and Navajo Nation. They also visited the ancient American Indian pueblos of Acoma and Taos, El Morro National Monument, and other natural and cultural lo-cales of Arizona and New Mexico. After the trip, touched by Udall's having reached out to her in the first place and enamored with the journey itself, Jackie sent Udall a handwritten letter, notifying him that "I have never spent such happy days nor been so absolutely knocked out by the beauty of all that we saw."[13]

With Jackie as his editor, Udall published *To the Inland Empire: Coronado and Our Spanish Legacy* in 1987. Later updated and retitled *Majestic Journey: Coronado's Inland Empire*, the book spotlighted what Udall called "the sunrise part of our national story" and a "lost cen-tury of our history."[14]

Decades before English settlers colonized Jamestown and Plym-outh Rock, Spanish conquistadors such as Coronado and others were already exploring, settling, mapping, and in some cases Chris-tianizing the present-day United States. Calling attention to these stories and the Spanish heritage of the United States in general, Udall's book was appreciated by Spain. As a token gesture, King Juan Carlos actually knighted the former interior secretary.[15]

Senior Citizen Stewart Udall

Since one of Udall's final writing projects highlighted the early influences of Spain on the United States, it is fitting that Lee and Stewart moved to Santa Fe in the late 1980s, a unique city with a rich cultural combination of Spanish, American Indian, and Cau-casian influences. They loved the New Mexico town's high eleva-tion, picturesque adobe architecture, and surrounding landscapes. "I like the natural ambiance, the cultural ambiance, just the beauty. I never tire of what Ansel Adams called the 'light and vistas' of the place," Udall said of Santa Fe. "I can stand on my own doorstep and see Mount Taylor, 100 miles away."[16]

While one can imagine Stewart and Lee sitting and enjoying the expansive southwestern views from inside their house and outside on their patio, Udall did not really quiet down and go into retirement until late in the first decade of the twenty-first century. As a resident of Santa Fe in his seventies and eighties (in the 1990s and 2000s), Udall continued to do the things he had been doing for many years. He continued fighting on behalf of the Navajo uranium miners, working for the protection of landscapes both near and far, enjoying Santa Fe's cultural offerings with Lee, and serving on boards of environmental organizations. "I spend most of my time these days trying to get off boards," Udall joked in a 1990s interview.[17]

Nevertheless, the former interior secretary enjoyed a successful stint, from 1993 to 2000, as a founding board member of the Santa Fe Conservation Trust, a land-preservation nonprofit organization. In particular, Udall was a key figure in the establishment of the Santa Fe Rail Trail, a fifteen-mile public-use trail that encouraged cyclists, walkers, and joggers to get and stay fit.[18]

Udall was also heavily involved in Think New Mexico, another Santa Fe–based nonprofit that he helped start in the late 1990s. Serving as chairman of the organization's board of directors until his death in 2010, Udall believed in Think New Mexico's nonpartisan mission of improving quality of life for the state's poorer inhabitants. Twenty percent of New Mexico's population lives in poverty, with only Mississippi ranking lower. Representing the organization, Udall regularly appeared before the state legislature, editorial boards, and other entities.[19]

Apart from his professional duties, Udall also continued to enjoy spending time outdoors in his later life. "This is good wilderness. Any time you have to struggle a bit to cross a stream you've got good wilderness," the former interior secretary told a reporter while hiking a popular seven-mile stream-side trail in the Santa Fe National Forest at eighty-five years of age.[20] Udall, with sons, daughters, and grandchildren, also hiked to the bottom and back to the top of the Grand Canyon on the Bright Angel Trail in his mideighties,

Revisiting Canyonlands National Park in 2006,
Udall made a special presentation on the park's establishment.
Courtesy of the National Park Service.

and enjoyed a trip back to Canyonlands National Park in 2006. In
his final decade, Udall also enjoyed toiling in his vegetable garden
in Santa Fe, conducting what he called "small-scale ecological experiments" of his own.[21]

Finally, the former interior secretary continued writing, and
also began being interviewed by local and national journalists. In
an age of partisan politics, when every bill seems to be "controversial" and difficult to pass, many wanted to learn from Udall about his
experiences in a seemingly bygone era of bipartisanship. "The 60s
were a wonderful period where the conservation cause was bipartisan," Udall said in a 1997 interview. And in 2009, only a year before
his passing, he wrote:

> I had the great fortune to come into office at a time when
> people wanted new policies.... The conservation movement
> was very powerful, and most of the people in this country
> thought that preserving land and creating parks were good
> for their communities. We felt we had a moral responsibility,
> a legacy, to leave the Earth, or that part of it where we lived,
> better. Recently, I went back and found the Congressional
> Record: the wilderness bill passed by a vote of seventy-eight

to twelve. Of the twelve, six were Democrats and six were Republicans. I use some of my time now trying to remind people of the wonderful, broad bipartisan support that we had then.[22]

In part due to watching the spread of partisan politics, in his final decade and a half of existence Udall began referring to himself as "a troubled optimist," knowing that the world he was slowly fading from needed to tackle the monumental interrelated problems of man-made climate change and oil addiction or it would face major problems.[23] In an earlier piece of writing, Udall had quoted Albert Schweitzer, a Nobel Prize–winning author, philosopher, theologian, and physician, in saying, "Man has lost the capacity to foresee and forestall. He will end by destroying the world." The former interior secretary hoped and believed that Schweitzer would be proven wrong, but Udall also knew that America would need to change drastically in order to disprove Schweitzer.

In Udall's personal life, his wife, Lee, developed breast cancer in the early 2000s. Things worsened, then improved, leading Stewart to pen a poem for her while she was in hospice care:

Would she last until Easter?
She would
Would she persevere to her next birthday?
She would.
Would she be there to see newborn Rachel?
She was.
Mystery has no domain here.
Where there is indomitable love
Death has no dominion![24]

However, Stewart's wife of fifty-four years, his rock of stability and support and love, did die on December 21, 2001. It was a tough loss for Stewart to take, and it's readily apparent how close Stewart and Lee were. As he had dedicated many others, Stewart Udall dedicated his final book, published in 2002, to her. "For Lee," the dedication read. "My companion and collaborator of 54 years, whose judgements about people, words, and human events were so fine."[25]

Udall's Last Writing Project:
The Forgotten Founders

Throughout Udall's adult years, he attempted to deconstruct myths through his writings. In *The Quiet Crisis*, published way back in 1963, he had criticized Americans subscribing to the Myth of Superabundance in their raid on natural resources in the 1800s. Udall then wrote about the Myth of Scientific Supremacy, and in the 1970s and afterward what one might call the Myth of Oil Longevity. In his last book, the historian in Udall came out again, as he had in his book on Coronado, and the former interior secretary focused on disproving what he saw as the Myths of Western History.

With experiences gained from a lifetime of living and traveling throughout the West as well as through his lifelong hunger for knowledge, Udall wrote and published *The Forgotten Founders: Rethinking the History of the Old West*, in 2002. In the book, one of the central myths Udall attempted to deconstruct was the widespread belief, thanks in part to John Wayne films and Louis L'Amour novels, that the West was mostly characterized by lawlessness and violence in the form of gunfights, corrupt sheriffs, and legendary outlaws. Udall criticized historians who promoted this myth and called for its correction. "We all know the standard images—the six-gun-toting sheriff, the gunfight at the corral or watering hole…fisticuffs in the saloon. In this whirl, as we see it in film or read it in popular accounts of the West's history," Udall said, "remarkably little attention is given to the pioneering work of the early settlers, who did so much to establish permanent communities in a wild, inhospitable land." Udall believed that the true founders of the West, namely, American Indians, Spanish missionaries, Mormon pioneers, and others, had not been given their true and important place in history. The book was an attempt by the lifelong environmental advocate and historian to correct this.[26]

In a sense, the book also brought Udall full circle, back to his Mormon upbringing and heritage. While the former interior secretary considered himself, in his grown years, "his own type of Mormon," it's clear that he had a profound respect for his religion, specifically its heritage.²⁷ "I'm Mormon born and bred, and it's inside me, and I still have elements of faith in some things. I prize my Mormon heritage and status," Udall said in a 1999 interview.²⁸ In the book, regarding Mormonism, Udall spent many pages tracing his family's history, as well as Lee's. He also shed light on the close-knit communities and hardworking, conservation-minded ethics of Mormon pioneers.

End of the Trail

A few years after his last book was published, Udall began to slow down physically. His eyesight deteriorated, but he continued to enjoy time with close family and friends and was even interviewed on several occasions. As things must, however, his health eventually failed, and on March 20, 2010, Stewart Udall passed away at the age of ninety. "I have had a long, rich life," he had said a few years earlier.²⁹

Notes

1. "Stewart Udall 'Pioneering' Toxic Chemical Litigation," *Denver Post*, January 8, 1984, box 244, unknown folder, Udall Papers.

2. Daniel Gibson, "Vignette: Stewart Udall," *Santa Fean Magazine*, November 1992, Udall Papers, library.arizona.edu/exhibits/sludall/articlepages/article19 .html. See also Ralph Whitaker, "Stewart Udall: Conservationist by Heritage," EPRI *Journal* (October 1987), Udall Papers, library.arizona.edu/exhibits/sludall/article retrievals/stewartx.html.

3. Whitaker, "Stewart Udall"; Tom Miller, "The West's Defender of Wild Places," *Los Angeles Times*, July 12, 2005, latimes.com/science/la-os-udall12jul12 -story.html; Michael Morris, "Udall Pushes Use of Nuclear Power," *Deseret News*, October 22, 1989, deseretnews.com/article/69069/UDALL-PUSHES-USE-OF -NUCLEAR-POWER.html?pg=all.

4. Michael Feeney Callan, *Robert Redford: The Biography* (New York: Alfred A. Knopf, 2011), 316–18; "The IRM Greenhouse Glasnost," *Overnight*, August 25, 1989, digitalcollections.library.cmu.edu/awweb/awarchive?type=file&item=686509; "Greenhouse Glasnost: U.S.-Soviet Symposium on Warming Underway," *Park City (UT) Daily News*, August 24, 1989, news.google.com/newspapers?nid=1696&dat =19890825&id=7rQaAAAAIBAJ&sjid=HEgEAAAAIBAJ&pg=5654,5450719&hl=en. Glasnost was a policy introduced by Soviet premier Mikhail Gorbachev, calling for increased public access, openness, and transparency within the government of the USSR. The goal of the policy was to decrease corruption. Redford's "Greenhouse Glasnost" was a play on the term.

5. "The IRM Greenhouse Glasnost."

6. Gibson, "Vignette: Stewart Udall."

7. Stewart L. Udall, *The Quiet Crisis and the Next Generation*, 211, 202–42.

8. Ibid., 257–62.

9. Ibid.; Stewart Udall interview, Center for the American West, Boulder, September 24, 2003, centerwest.org/wp-content/uploads/2011/01/udall.pdf.

10. Udall, *The Quiet Crisis and the Next Generation*, 265–70.

11. Stewart L. Udall, *Majestic Journey: Coronado's Inland Empire*, 2.

12. Ibid.

13. Ibid., 1–2.

14. Ibid.

15. Ministerio de Asuntos Exteriores (de España), Documento, Su Majestad el Rey: Gran Maestre de la Orden de Isabel de la Católica, a Stewart L. Udall, 24 de Junio de 1988, box 246, folder 3, Udall Papers. See also Walter Howerton Jr., "Living Between the Lines," *Santa Fe Reporter*, 1996, Udall Papers, library.arizona.edu/exhibits/sludall/articleretrievals/living.html; and Stewart L. Udall, *In Coronado's Footsteps*.

16. Howerton, "Living Between the Lines."

17. Gibson, "Vignette: Stewart Udall."

18. Charlie O'Leary, "Stewart Udall and Trusting in the Future," *Santa Fe New Mexican*, May 15, 2010 santafenewmexican.com/opinion/my-view-stewart-udall-and-trusting-in-the-future/.

19. "Board," Think New Mexico, thinknewmexico.org/board/; "Board Profile: Stewart Udall, thinknewmexico.org/wp-content/uploads/pdfs/3rdAnnualReport.pdf.

20. Quoted in Miller, "West's Defender of Wild Places."

21. Gibson, "Vignette: Stewart Udall."

22. Tulane University, "Stewart Udall Speaks at Tulane University," video, December 19, 2007, youtube.com/watch?v=ppDel8JoxJ4.

23. Gary Jahrig, "Wilderness and Wisdom: Environmental Movement's Future Lies with Young People, Udall Says," *Missoulian*, July 19, 1997, Udall Papers, library.arizona.edu/exhibits/sludall/articleretrievals/wilderness.html.

24. Quoted in Finch, *Legacies of Camelot*, 153.

25. Udall, *Forgotten Founders*.

26. Ibid., 1.

27. Marc Bohn, "Remembering Stewart Udall," *Times and Seasons*, March 22, 2010, timesandseasons.org/index.php/2010/03/remembering-stewart-udall/.

28. Udall interview in Ure, *Candid Conversations*, 72.

29. Ibid., 74.

Conclusion

THE LIST OF STEWART UDALL'S lifetime achievements is vast. In eight years as US secretary of the interior, he helped establish four new national parks, six national monuments, nine national recreation areas, eight national seashores and lakeshores, and fifty-seven national wildlife refuges. He was a major contributor to the passing of the Wilderness Act, the Land and Water Conservation Fund Act, the National Wild and Scenic Rivers System Act, and the Endangered Species Preservation Act. His actions pushed for cleaner water and air and the preservation of wild places and wild animals. After leaving the Department of the Interior, he pushed for widespread energy conservation measures as well as for the switch from fossil fuels to the large-scale use of solar power. These facts and more have been well documented in the previous pages.

More important than facts, though, are what can we learn from them. Stewart Udall was not a perfect individual, but three themes that repeated throughout his life suggest three lessons for us today. First, Udall's accomplishments in the realm of working successfully with people of differing opinions and beliefs for the common good serve as a model for "working together" and bipartisanship. Udall was a Democrat who worked well with and fleshed out conservation compromises with many Republicans, including, perhaps most notably, John Saylor and Thomas Kuchel. The significance of this cannot be overstated in a day and age when partisan politics seem to rule supreme, particularly in the areas of environmental and climate-change mitigation laws. LBJ referred to bipartisanship as "reasoning together." This reasoning together was in good supply in the 1960s and '70s in the United States, and those on both sides of the political aisle today would do well to remember this and do more of it.

Second, Udall's proposals and recommendations, specifically in regard to energy conservation and oil-addiction solutions, are still relevant and deserve more than just thought and consideration today. Increases in high-speed passenger trains, bicycle paths in cities, and solar panels on rooftops nationwide, to list just three of Udall's recommendations, could all lead to major decreases in our use of dirty fossil fuels. While headway has been made and continues to be made on these necessary transitions, a good question to ponder is, why have the recommendations of Udall and others gone largely unheeded for more than forty years?

Third, and perhaps most important, Stewart Udall's writings, sayings, and doings teach us to take the long view of things. In his *1976: Agenda for Tomorrow*, Udall provided blueprints for how the country could create both a life-giving and life-sustaining environment during its third century of existence. In the book, he wrote about the threats posed by global warming twenty-five years *before* it became a common household term. In his 1974 book, *The Energy Balloon*, cowritten with two colleagues, the former interior secretary called for major energy-saving measures *before* widespread catastrophes caused by oil shortages occurred. In the 1960s, Udall declared several wildlife species as officially endangered *before* they went extinct, thus leading to their increased protection. Udall recommended being proactive in solving problems rather than letting things get to the brink of catastrophe. He also believed in making decisions based not on what is best for today but what is best for tomorrow, next week, next year, the next generation, and the generation after that.

At the beginning of his tenure as interior secretary, Udall wrote an article discussing the importance of taking a long-view approach to resolving the country's conservation and environmental problems. In the article, Udall noted that "as a tribute to Teddy Roosevelt's conservation credo, someone once called him a man with 'distance in his eyes.'" Udall continued, "At their best the American conservationist has always looked to the horizon, seeking through works of restoration and preservation to make visible their love for the land and his respect for the rights of the unborn."[1] Stewart Udall was someone who looked to the horizon; he had distance in his eyes himself.

~

Due to all of Udall's lifetime accomplishments and messages, shortly after he died, on Earth Day in 2010, New Mexico's congressional delegation, including Udall's son, Senator Tom Udall, introduced legislation to change the name of the US Department of the Interior Building in downtown Washington, DC, to the Stewart Lee Udall Department of the Interior Building. In a seemingly unprecedented age of partisan politics, the US House of Representatives voted 409 to 1 in favor of the bill. In the US Senate, the bill achieved unanimous support. President Barack Obama signed the bill into law on June 8, 2010.[2]

"Without question, our nation would not be the same without Secretary Udall's vision, leadership, or writings," said then secretary of the interior Ken Salazar during the name-change ceremony a few months later. "Stewart Udall's name on the Department of the Interior building will not only honor a great man, but will serve as a challenge to all who enter to uphold his legacy and commitment to protecting America's natural treasures and resources."[3]

At the same event, Tom Udall proclaimed, "My father was honored to lead the Department of Interior during a banner era for conservation, and would have been greatly humbled by this recognition." The US senator continued, "My family and I are so proud of his legacy as a visionary conservationist and fierce protector of America's people and special places."

When new employees and visitors enter "Main Interior"—the colloquial name bestowed on the building by current capital-area Department of the Interior employees—they will see an official plaque designating the naming of the building after Stewart Udall. If they ask who this person was, there will be much to tell them.

Notes

1. "We Need 'Distance in Our Eyes,'" *Life*, December 22, 1961, online copy, Udall Papers.

2. "H.R. 5128 (111th): To Designate the United States Department of the Interior Building in Washington, District of Columbia, as the Stewart Lee Udall Department of the Interior Building," gpo.gov/fdsys/pkg/CRPT-111hrpt485/html/CRPT-111 hrpt485.htm. The lone dissenter in the House was Representative Don Young of Alaska, a longtime congressman of the state who is known for his pro-business, anti–National Park System, anti-environmental stances.

3. US Department of the Interior, press release, "Secretary Salazar Honors Stewart Lee Udall at Interior Building Dedication Ceremony," September 21, 2010, doi.gov/news/pressreleases/Secretary-Salazar-Honors-Stewart-Lee-Udall-at -Interior-Building-Dedication-Ceremony.

Selected Bibliography

Significant research for the book took place in the University of Arizona's Special Collections Department in Tucson, where the extensive Stewart L. Udall Papers (AZ 372) are held. Major research was also conducted using my personal book collection, which includes many of the books that Udall wrote. Other significant research was conducted at the Library of Congress in Washington, DC; among the online papers and oral history interviews of both the John F. Kennedy and Lyndon Baines Johnson Presidential Libraries; and, to a lesser extent, in the *Washington Post* online archives. Below is a listing of the main primary and secondary sources referenced in the book.

Amos, Wayne. "Inside Interior's Udall: A Long Affair with the Out-of-Doors." *Arizona Magazine* (June 4, 1967). library.arizona.edu/exhibits/sludall/article retrievals/insidex.html.

Bailey, James Michael. "The Politics of Dunes, Redwoods, and Dams: Arizona's 'Brothers Udall' and America's National Parklands, 1961–1969." PhD diss., Arizona State University, 1999.

Bracy, Terry, and Ellen Wheeler. "Stewart Udall: Renaissance Man." *Arizona Journal of Environmental Law and Policy*, no. 1 (2010).

Brower, Kenneth. *American Legacy: Our National Forests*. Washington, DC: National Geographic Society, 1997.

Brugge, Doug, ed. *Memories Come to Us in the Rain and the Wind: Oral Histories and Photographs of Navajo Uranium Miners and Their Families*. Jamaica Plain, MA: Red Sun Press, 1997.

Carson, Donald W., and James W. Johnson. *Mo: The Life & Times of Morris K. Udall*. Tucson: University of Arizona Press, 2001.

Coate, Charles. "'The Biggest Water Fight in American History': Stewart Udall and the Central Arizona Project." *Journal of the Southwest* 37, no. 1 (1995).

Cockrell, Ron. *A Signature of Time and Eternity: The Administrative History of Indiana Dunes National Lakeshore, Indiana*. Washington, DC: National Park Service, 1988.

Day, Joe, and Grant Taylor. *Stewart Udall: Advocate for the Earth*. Documentary film. Santa Fe, NM: New Mexico in Focus, KNME-TV, 2010.

Duncan, Patricia D. *Tallgrass Prairie: The Inland Sea*. Kansas City, KS: Lowell Press, 1978.

Eichstaedt, Peter H. *If You Poison Us: Uranium and Native Americans*. Santa Fe, NM: Red Crane Books, 1994.

Everhart, William C. *The National Park Service*. New York: Praeger, 1972.

Fiege, Mark. *The Republic of Nature: An Environmental History of the United States*. Seattle: University of Washington Press, 2012.

Finch, L. Boyd. *Legacies of Camelot: Stewart and Lee Udall, American Culture, and the Arts*. Norman: University of Oklahoma Press, 2007.

Fitch, Edwin M., and John F. Shanklin. *The Bureau of Outdoor Recreation*. Washington, DC: Praeger, 1970.

Frome, Michael. *Regreening the National Parks*. Tucson: University of Arizona Press, 1992.

Gahan, Andrew H., and William D. Rowley. *The Bureau of Reclamation: From Developing to Managing Water, 1945-2000*. Vol. 2. Washington, DC: US Bureau of Reclamation, 2012.

Gould, Lewis L. *Lady Bird Johnson: Our Environmental First Lady*. Lawrence: University Press of Kansas, 1999.

———. "Lady Bird Johnson and Beautification." In *The Johnson Years*. Vol. 2, *Vietnam, the Environment, and Science*, edited by Robert A. Divine, 150-80. Lawrence: University Press of Kansas, 1987.

Graham, Otis L., Jr. *Presidents and the American Environment*. Lawrence: University Press of Kansas, 2015.

Hartzog, George B., Jr. *Battling for the National Parks*. Mt. Kisco, NY: Moyer Bell, 1988.

Hays, Samuel P. *Beauty, Health, and Permanence: Environmental Politics in the United States, 1955-1985*. Cambridge: Cambridge University Press, 1987.

Heacox, Kim. *Visions of a Wild America: Pioneers of Conservation*. Washington, DC: National Geographic Society, 1996.

John, Andrew A. *Lyndon Johnson and the Great Society*. Chicago: Ivan R. Dee, 1998.

Johnson, Lady Bird. *A White House Diary*. Austin: University of Texas Press, 2007.

Kaufman, G. Robert. *Henry M. Jackson: A Life in Politics*. Seattle: University of Washington Press, 2000.

Leunes, Barbara Laverne Blythe. "The Conservation Philosophy of Stewart L. Udall, 1961-1968." PhD diss., Texas A&M University, 1977.

Lifset, Robert, ed. *American Energy Policy in the 1970s*. Norman: University of Oklahoma Press, 2014.

"Lyndon B. Johnson: Remarks upon Signing Four Bills Relating to Conservation and Outdoor Recreation." 1968. University of California at Santa Barbara, American Presidency Project. presidency.ucsb.edu/ws/?pid=29150.

Melosi, Martin V. "Lyndon Johnson and Environmental Policy." In *The Johnson Years*. Vol. 2, *Vietnam, the Environment, and Science*, edited by Robert A. Divine, 113-49. Lawrence: University Press of Kansas, 1987.

Miles, John C. *Guardian of the Parks: A History of the National Parks and Conservation Association*. Washington, DC: Taylor & Francis, 1995.

Montrie, Chad. *To Save the Land and People: A History of Opposition to Surface Coal Mining in Appalachia*. Chapel Hill: University of North Carolina Press, 2003.

Muhn, James, and Hanson R. Stuart. *Opportunity and Challenge: The Story of BLM*. Washington, DC: US Department of the Interior, Bureau of Land Management, 1988.

Murphy, Robert. *A Heritage Restored: America's Wildlife Refuges*. New York: E. P. Dutton, 1969.

Negri, Sam. *Movers and Shakers: The Creation of Tucson Mountain Park*. Tucson: Pima County Natural Resources, Parks and Recreation Department, 2010.

Outdoor Recreation Resources Review Commission. "Outdoor Recreation for America: A Report to the President and to the Congress by the Outdoor Recreation Resources Review Commission." January 1962. nps.gov/parkhistory /online_books/anps/anps_5d.htm.

Pasternak, Judy. *Yellow Dirt: A Poisoned Land and the Betrayal of the Navajos*. New York: Free Press, 2010.

Platt, Corrinne, and Meredith Ogilby. *Voices of the American West*. Golden, CO: Fulcrum, 2009.

Popkin, Roy. *Desalination: Water for the World's Future*. New York: Frederick A. Praeger, 1968.

"President Kennedy's Message on Conservation to the Congress of the United States." February 28, 1962. Papers of John F. Kennedy, JFK Presidential Library and Museum. jfklibrary.org/Asset-Viewer/Archives/JFKPOF-098-005.aspx.

Richardson, Elmo. *Dams, Parks, and Politics: Resource Development and Preservation in the Truman-Eisenhower Era*. Lexington: University Press of Kentucky, 1973.

Ridenour, James M. *The National Parks Compromised: Pork Barrel Politics and America's Treasures*. Merrillville, IN: ICS Books, 1994.

Roman, Joe. *Listed: Dispatches from America's Endangered Species Act*. Cambridge, MA: Harvard University Press, 2011.

Runte, Alfred. *National Parks: The American Experience*. Lincoln: University of Nebraska Press, 1979.

Sabin, Paul. "Crisis and Continuity in U.S. Oil Politics, 1965–1980." *Journal of American History* 99, no. 1 (2012).

Schulte, Steven C. *Wayne Aspinall and the Shaping of the American West*. Boulder: University of Colorado Press, 2002.

Sellars, Richard West. *Preserving Nature in the National Parks: A History*. New Haven, CT: Yale University Press, 1997.

Sirgo, Henry B. *Establishment of Environmentalism on the U.S. Political Agenda in the Second Half of the Twentieth Century: The Brothers Udall*. Lewiston, NY: Edwin Mellen Press, 2004.

———. "The Moral Work of Stewart L. Udall to Extend Ethics to Encompass Ecological Thinking." *Global Virtue Ethics Review* 4, no. 1 (2003).

Skillen, James R. *The Nation's Largest Landlord: The Bureau of Land Management in the American West*. Lawrence: University Press of Kansas, 2009.

Smith, Thomas G. *Green Republican: John Saylor and the Preservation of America's Wilderness*. Pittsburgh: University of Pittsburgh Press, 2006.

———. "John Kennedy, Stewart Udall, and New Frontier Conservation." *Pacific Historical Review* 64, no. 3 (1995). markstoll.net/HIST4323/2008/John_Kennedy _Stewart_Udall_and_New_Frontier_Conservation_-_Thomas_G_Smith.pdf.

———. *Showdown: JFK and the Integration of the Washington Redskins*. Boston: Beacon Press, 2012.

Sorenson, Theodore C. *Kennedy*. New York: Harper & Row, 1965.

Stegner, Wallace. *Marking the Sparrow's Fall: The Making of the American West*. New York: Henry Holt, 1998.

Strong, Douglas H. *Dreamers and Defenders: American Conservationists*. Lincoln: University of Nebraska Press, 1971.

———. Introduction to *Nature and the American: Three Centuries of Changing Attitudes*, by Hans Huth. Lincoln: University of Nebraska Press, 1990.

Sturgeon, Stephen C. *The Politics of Western Water: The Congressional Career of Wayne Aspinall*. Tucson: University of Arizona Press, 2002.

Udall, Morris K., Bob Neuman, and Randy Udall. *Too Funny to Be President*. Tucson: University of Arizona Press, 1988.

Udall, Stewart L. *1976: Agenda for Tomorrow*. New York: Harcourt, Brace & World, 1968.

———. *American Natural Treasures: National Nature Monuments and Seashores*. Waukesha, WI: Country Beautiful, 1971.

———. "Encounters with the Reagan Revolution." In *Crossroads: Environmental Priorities for the Future*, edited by Peter Borrelli. Washington, DC: Island Press, 1988.

———. "The Energy Crisis: A Radical Solution." *World Magazine* (1973).

———. Foreword to *The Whooping Crane: The Bird That Defies Extinction*, by Faith McNulty. New York: E. P. Dutton, 1966.

———. Foreword to *The Wilderness from Chamberlain Farm: A Story of Hope for the American Wild*, by Dean B. Bennett. Washington, DC: Island Press, 2001.

———. *The Forgotten Founders: Rethinking the History of the Old West*. Washington, DC: Island Press, 2002.

———. "Human Values and Hometown Snapshots: Early Days in St. Johns." *American West* (1982). library.arizona.edu/exhibits/sludall/articlepages/article1.html.

———. *In Coronado's Footsteps*. Tucson: Southwest Parks and Monuments Association, 1991.

———. Introduction to *Wild Peninsula: The Story of Point Reyes National Seashore*, by Laura Nelson Baker. New York: Atheneum, 1969.

———. "Is Our Country Running Out of Water?" *Coronet* (1964).

———. *Majestic Journey: Coronado's Inland Empire*. Santa Fe: Museum of New Mexico Press, 1995.

———. *The Myths of August: A Personal Exploration of Our Tragic Cold War Affair with the Atom*. New York: Random House, 1994.

———. "New Adventures: Wild Rivers—Shooting the Wild Colorado." *Venture* (February 1968).

———. "Paradise in Peril: An American Epilogue." In *Wildlife Crisis*, by HRH Prince Philip, Duke of Edinburgh, and James Fisher. New York: Cowles, 1970.

———. *The Quiet Crisis*. New York: Holt, Rinehart, and Winston, 1963.

———. *The Quiet Crisis and the Next Generation*. Layton, UT: Gibbs Smith, 1988.

———. "Restoration and Conservation: The Importance of Perspective." *Arizona Law Review* 42 (2000).

———. "Some Second Thoughts on Stockholm." *American University Law Review* 22 (1973).

———. "Supertechnology: Another God That Failed." *New Mexican Alumnus* 49, no. 8 (1977).

———. "Toxic Chemicals and Radiation." *Mercer Law Review* 38 (1986–87).

———. "The West and Its Public Lands: Aid or Obstacle to Progress?" *Natural Resource Journal* (University of New Mexico School of Law) 4, no. 1 (1964). heinonline.org/HOL/LandingPage?handle=hein.journals/narj4&div=9&id =&page=.

Udall, Stewart Lee, Charles Conconi, and David Osterhout. *The Energy Balloon.* New York: McGraw-Hill, 1974.

Ure, James R. *Candid Conversations with Inactive Mormons.* Salt Lake City: Signature Books, 1999.

US Department of the Interior. *Final Report of the Task Force on the Availability of Federally Owned Mineral Lands.* Washington, DC: US Department of the Interior, 1977.

———. *The Nation's River: A Report on the Potomac from the U.S. Department of the Interior with Recommendations for Action by the Federal Interdepartmental Task Force on the Potomac.* Washington, DC: US Department of the Interior, 1968.

———. "Remarks by Secretary of the Interior Stewart L. Udall Before the 66th Annual Convention of the American National Cattlemen's Association." US Department of the Interior, Washington, DC, January 30, 1963.

———. *Surface Mining and Our Environment: A Special Report to the Nation.* Washington, DC: US Department of the Interior, 1966.

US Department of the Interior, Bureau of Outdoor Recreation. *Trails for America: Report on the Nationwide Trails Study.* Washington, DC: US Department of the Interior, 1966.

US Department of the Interior, Bureau of Reclamation. *Pacific Southwest Water Plan Report.* Washington, DC: US Department of the Interior, 1964.

US Department of the Interior, National Park Service. *Parks for America: A Survey of Park and Related Resources in the Fifty States, and a Preliminary Plan.* Washington, DC: US Department of the Interior, 1964.

Warren, Louis S., ed. *American Environmental History.* Malden, MA: Blackwell, 2003.

Welsh, Frank. *How to Create a Water Crisis.* Boulder, CO: Johnson, 1985.

Winks, Robin W. *Laurance S. Rockefeller: Catalyst for Conservation.* Washington, DC: Island Press, 1997.

Wirth, Conrad. *Parks, Politics, and the People.* Tucson: University of Arizona Press, 1980.

Wyckoff, William, and Lary M. Dilsaver, eds. *The Mountainous West: Explorations in Historical Geography.* Lincoln: University of Nebraska Press, 1995.

Zaslowsky, Dyan, and T. H. Watkins. *These American Lands: Parks, Wilderness, and the Public Lands.* Washington, DC: Island Press, 1994.

About the Author

A Napa, California, native with a BA in history from California State University-Chico, Scott Einberger is an environmental historian and public lands enthusiast. Einberger served as superintendent of Georgia's Cloudland Canyon State Park for a year and a half and also served as an interpretive park ranger for the US National Park Service for eight years in locations including Lassen Volcanic National Park, Craters of the Moon National Monument, Chamizal National Memorial, Gila Cliff Dwellings National Monument, Denali National Park, and Rock Creek Park. Einberger lives in the nation's capital with his family and is the author of *A History of Rock Creek Park: Wilderness and Washington, D.C.* Einberger welcomes comments at scott_einberger@yahoo.com. See more of Einberger's writings and work at publiclandslover.weebly.com.

Index

Italicized page numbers indicate photographs.

Interstate Highways Act. *See* Federal Aid Highway Act of 1956

Iran, 154

Jacka, Jerry, 262

Jackson, Henry "Scoop," 211, 219, 237; as chair of the Senate Committee on Interior and Insular Affairs, 171; as a champion of conservation and environmental protection, 53; and the Columbia River Treaty, 150; Udall's letter to, 225; and the Youth Conservation Corps, 194

Javits, Jacob, 53, 96, 111n10

Johnson, Harold "Bizz," 85

Johnson, John, 162n38

Johnson, Lady Bird, 52, 196; Udall's relationship and work with, 7, 51, 158, 196–202, 200, 217

Johnson, Lyndon Baines, 152, 181, 188, 194, 199, 214; assumption of presidency by, after Kennedy assassination, 185–86; and dam building, 147; failure of, to sign Udall's proposal for additions to National Park System at the end of his presidency, 215, 217–21, 224n34, 227; and land added to the national park system, 69, 77, 94, 102, 104, 106, 117, 145; and the politics of oil, 165, 167; and promotion of democracy and capitalism, 154; Udall's relationship with, 4, 37–38, 158, 186, 215, 217–21, 224n34, 226–27; and water conservation, 153–54; and the Wilderness Act, 181, 181

Johnston, Velma, 132

Jordan, 110, 154

Juan Carlos (king of Spain), 263

Keating, Kenneth, 96

Kelly, John, 55

Kempthorne, Dirke, 38n2

Kennedy, Jacqueline. *See* Onassis, Jacqueline Kennedy

Kennedy, John F., 7, 40n33, 55, 73, 119, 153, 155, 206n38; appointment of James Carr by, 55; assassination of, 184–85, 187, 196; on conservation, 50, 51, 65n13, 84, 85, 86, 132; conservation trips of, 51, 147–49, 148, 149, 161n20, 206n31; Frost reading at inauguration of, 44–45, 64n3; and land added to the national park system, 69, 77, 78, 79, 216; leadership style of, 50; and the President's Advisory Council on Pennsylvania Avenue, 197; and promotion of democracy and capitalism, 154; Udall's affinity for, 24, 26, 36–38, 186; and the Wilderness Act, 180

Kennedy, Robert F., 185; assassination of, 196; meeting on pesticides at home of, 114; offers interior secretary job to Udall, 37–38; Udall's friendship with, 185, 187

Kennedy, Ted, 158, 251, 252

Kennedy family, 20

Kentucky Civil Liberties Union, 169

Kentucky Coal Association, 172

Kenya, 154, 162n38

Kenyatta, Jomo, 162n38

Kerr-McGee, 248, 254–55n23

Key deer, 49, 120, 123

Key Deer National Wildlife Refuge, 61, 123

Khrushchev, Nikita, 7, 85; meeting of, with Udall, 155–57

King, David, 71

King, Martin Luther, Jr., 3, 202, 204

Kuchel, Thomas, 53, 179, 225, 270

Kuwait, 154

Labor-Management Reform Act of 1959, 36

Lady Bird Johnson Park, 199

Lake Erie, 141, 157

Land and Water Conservation Fund, 3, 63, 66n19, 81, 167, 181; acquisitions of land funded by, 82, 97, 105, 195; Udall's push for, 29, 59–61, 270

Landstrom, Karl, 128

Lasker, Mary, 198

life of, 18, 19, 43, 192, 227, 243, 245,
247, 262, 263, 272; meeting of, with
Khrushchev, 156–57; Mormon faith
of, 3, 6, 16, 17–18, 36, 267–69; and the
presidential election of 1960, 36–38;
primary reasons for success of, as
interior secretary, 51–64; protection
of wildlife and expansion of the
National Wildlife Refuge System by,
114–23; on the Reagan administration and environmental negligence,
259–61; transitioning the Bureau of
Land Management to multiple use
by, 126–38; war experiences of, 18;
work of, on the urban environment,
184–204; and the Wilderness Act,
178–82; writings of, 7, 61–64, 108,
186, 188, 189, 193, 236, 241, 253, 259,
261–63, 267–68, 271–72
Udall, Tom, 247, 272
Uganda, 154
urban environmental decline and re-
newal, 49, 187–204
U.S. Army Corps of Engineers, 137, 140,
155, 161n21
U.S. Fish and Wildlife Service, 49, 108,
114, 117, 180; and endangered species,
120–21, 122; LWCF grants for, 60;
organization and responsibilities of,
24, 45, 67n38, 123–24n2; and pesticide research, 119
U.S. Forest Service, 45, 85, 104; clashes
of, and cooperation with, the National Park Service, 58–59, 84; and
grazing fees, 133; LWCF grants for,
60; and the Multiple Use Sustained
Yield Act of 1960, 29, 127, 129; and
a national trails system, 104, 106;
organization and responsibilities of,
24, 27, 127, 130, 136, 180; and outdoor
recreation, 29; Pinchot as chief forester of, 9, 26, 27
U.S. Geological Survey, 46, 83, 158, 164,
175, 232
U.S. Grazing Service, 127

Vanadium Corporation, 248
Venezuela, 166, 176n6
Virgin Islands National Park, 29

Washington, Walter, 198
Washington Redskins, 202–3,
206nn38–39
Water Quality Act of 1965, 157–59
Water Resources Council, 140
Watt, James, 261
Watt's Branch Park, 198
Western Region of the National Associ-
ation of Counties, 129
West Virginia Surface Mining Associa-
tion, 169–70
Whiskeytown Dam, 149, *149*
Whiskeytown National Recreation
Area, 84–86
White, Lee, 58
Whole Earth Catalog, 232
Wilderness Act, 7, 30, 66n19, 87n18,
178–82
Wild Horse Annie. *See* Johnston, Velma
Wildlife Society, 123
Wilson, Bates, 73, 87n9
wind energy, 1970s proposal by Udall,
240–41
Wirth, Conrad, 72, 87n6, 99, 109
Wolf River, 145
Woody Guthrie Substation, 161–62n29
World Conference on National Parks,
110
World War II, 22n8, 47–48; Udall's expe-
riences in, 6, 17, 18

Yarborough, Ralph, 82
Yellowtail Dam, 149
Young, Brigham, 13
Youth Conservation Corps, 193–94

Zahniser, Alice, 181
Zahniser, Howard, 178, 179, 181, 182n2,
260
Zinke, Ryan, 38n2
Zipf, Henry, 20–21